ENGLISH LANGUAGE SERIES

TITLE NO 7

An Introduction to
Modern English Word-formation

ENGLISH LANGUAGE SERIES
General Editor : Randolph Quirk
Title no:

An Introduction to
Modern English
Word-formation

VALERIE ADAMS

Lecturer in English
University College London

LONGMAN

LONGMAN GROUP LIMITED *LONDON*
Associated companies, branches and representatives throughout the world

© Longman Group Ltd 1973

First published 1973
ISBN 0 582 52194 7

Made and printed in Great Britain by
William Clowes & Sons, Limited, London, Beccles and Colchester

Foreword

English is the text-book example of a language that expands its vocabulary by unashamedly raiding other languages. For a thousand years new words have, like dockside imports, often borne an easily readable stamp of their country of origin: *outlaw* from medieval Scandinavia, *gentle* from medieval France, *madrigal* from Renaissance Italy, *chutney* from nineteenth-century India and *karate* from twentieth-century Japan, to name a few examples that indicate the chronological and geographical range. Such words clearly and interestingly reflect the contact that English-speaking peoples have had with other countries and other cultures, and so fascinated have scholars been for several generations by the patterns of word adoption that we have tended to regard this process as virtually the sole means by which changes in our vocabulary take place.

It is not, of course. We sometimes translate the foreign word we need, as Bernard Shaw did with Nietzsche's *Übermensch* to produce *superman*; or we achieve a new means of designation by using an existing word in a different sense, as with the homosexual meaning of *gay*. Or – to come to the concern of the present book – we can permute existing words and parts of words to make new combinations such as the nouns *boathouse*, *houseboat*, or the adjective *ungovernable*.

With all of these devices, we see vocabulary change triggered off by cultural change even where no transparently 'exotic' word appears as a result: the homely *corn* becomes the American word for the exotic maize when and because Americans start encountering maize in their daily life. But changes in vocabulary by the processes of word-formation have, in addition to their cultural and historical interest, a purely linguistic interest. That is to say, there are abstractly describable patterns which explain the regularities in the new words we coin and which explain also why certain formations would be unlikely or impossible (such as a negative adjective **ableungovern*). By contrast, there are few generalizations that one could make in predicting the shape or internal structure of foreign words that we might adopt. Thus, although foreign words are normally given a 'domesticated' pronunciation, we cannot even say that an adopted word will be repronounced with only English sounds and sound sequences (*raison d'être*).

This is not to say that there are rules of word-formation as freely available to the native speaker as his rules of sentence-formation. Where almost every sentence we use is composed *ad hoc* to suit the occasion and is thus a 'new sentence', it is relatively rare for us to form a 'new word' and when we do our hearers or readers are more or less conscious both of its newness and of the rarity with which they encounter the phenomenon of newness. Even so, they would be generally able to distinguish a new word that seemed well-formed ('This wretched cupboard is *ungetinable*') from one that is not (**getunablein*). To this extent, word-formation is interestingly rule-bound and Valerie Adams gives careful consideration to the many complex kinds of regularity that are to be observed. She deserves especial praise, however, for resisting the temptation to sweep under an exquisitely patterned carpet the irregularities and striking idiosyncrasies which are – to say the least – no less characteristic of the creative side of lexical usage.

The volume makes a welcome contribution in a difficult and controversial field. As English has increasingly come into world-wide use, there has arisen an acute need for more information on the language and the ways in which it is used. The English Language Series seeks to meet this need and to play a part in further stimulating the study and teaching of English by providing up-to-date and scholarly treatments of topics most relevant to present-day English – including its history and traditions, its sound patterns, its grammar, its lexicology, its rich variety in speech and writing, and its standards in Britain, the USA and the other principal areas where the language is used.

University College London   RANDOLPH QUIRK
March 1973

Preface

The study of word-formation offers a great many puzzles to the present-day student of language; as Esko Pennanen (1972) observes in a discussion of some of the difficulties, not the least of these is its status as a branch of linguistic study. I have not tried in this book to grapple with major issues, such as the possibility of devising rules to account for just those compounds and affixed words which exist and are acceptable, and those which could exist and would be acceptable if they were to be formed; or the possibility of giving convincing reasons why some words are unacceptable while others of similar make-up are not. In the final pages I suggest – as others have recently suggested – that if we are to make much progress in understanding such matters, the topic of 'word-formation' as it is here defined may have to be recognized as after all rather superficially conceived: our real business should be with meanings and how they are expressed and combined. Questions like these, however, await a better understanding of many syntactic and semantic matters; they are for the future, and for works far more ambitious than this one.

The chapters which follow are chiefly concerned with data, and with classifications of data. As an introduction to the subject, they cannot claim to be complete, since a comprehensive treatment of the prefixes and suffixes is lacking. But I have tried to indicate to some extent, though in no very systematic way, how the various traditionally-recognized patterns of word-formation are interrelated; how, for instance, the make-up of noun compounds, verb compounds and compounds containing particles may be considered along with the patterns of zero derivation; how blends and compounds may be compared; how compound-elements and blend-elements may be more, or less, like prefixes and suffixes; and how certain concepts, such as 'instrumentality', 'location', 'resemblance', appear and re-appear in words of various types.

Throughout, I have included illustrative examples gathered from the most recent sources, chiefly from newspapers and magazines. I believe that such transient coinages are valuable in helping us – and occasionally surprising us – when the dictionary lets us down. I have used them to show, for instance, how we are capable of making new compound verbs, such as *to chauffeur-drift*, or *to consumer-test;* and how patterns which we might have thought were played out are still alive. Thus we are able to form adjective compounds like *browfurrowed* and *yawning dull* on the patterns of the cliché-like *heart-broken* and *scalding hot;* and the little group of 'animal' verbs such as *to ape, to wolf*, gets a new member with the coining of *to squirrel*. Examples from these sources also provide interesting evidence of how word-elements of all kinds may be taken up and used in new formations. It was as natural for the Victorian journalist of the 1880s to coin the word *camelcade* for a procession or cavalcade of camels as it was for the reporter of the 1960s; and Sir Thomas More might have been surprised to learn that his invention, *utopia,* was to serve as a precedent for such twentieth-century creations as *pornotopia*.

I am very grateful to many friends and colleagues for their help and advice; in particular to Wolf-Dietrich Bald, Michael Black, Derek Davy, Geoffrey Leech and Eugene Winter for their valuable comments on portions of earlier drafts; and to John Wells for his help with the section on Esperanto. I am especially indebted to Ruth Kempson, who was a most helpful critic of most of the final draft. Lastly, I record my gratitude to Randolph Quirk for his encouragement throughout; for his patient and stimulating criticism of the whole book; and for his generously-given attention to every aspect of my work, from the most general issues down to the contribution of examples, and practical advice on the setting-out of the material. Having acknowledged such debts, I can only conclude by emphasizing that all the shortcomings which remain are mine alone.

University College London   V A
March 1973

Contents

Acknowledgments

Our thanks are due to all the copyright owners whose material is quoted in the text, where full acknowledgment to source is made; and for readers outside the United Kingdom we would point out that every reference to the *Daily Express* and to the *Evening Standard* should be understood to mean the *London Daily Express* and *London Evening Standard* respectively.

Chapter 1

The word

1.1 Introductory

The ways in which new words are formed, and the factors which govern their acceptance into the language, are generally taken very much for granted by the average speaker. To understand a word, it is not necessary to be aware of how it is constructed, or of whether it is simple or complex, that is, whether or not it can be broken down into two or more constituents. We are able to use a word which is new to us when we find out what object or concept it denotes. Some words, of course, are more 'transparent' than others. We need only have met the separate elements of the adjectives *unfathomable*, *indescribable*, to be able to recognize the familiar pattern of negative prefix + transitive verb + adjective-forming suffix on which many words of similar form, like *uneatable*, are constructed. Knowing the pattern, we can guess their meanings: 'cannot be fathomed', 'cannot be described' – although we are not surprised to find other, similar-looking words, for example *unfashionable*, *unfavourable*, for which this analysis will not work. We recognize as 'transparent' the adjectives *unassuming*, *unheard-of*, while taking for granted the fact that we cannot use *assuming* or *heard-of*. We accept as quite natural the fact that although we can use the verbs *to drum*, *to pipe*, *to trumpet*, we cannot use the verbs *to piano*, *to violin*; and we cope effortlessly with the apparent paradox of *to dust*, meaning either 'to remove dust from something' or 'to apply a dust-like substance to something'.

But when we meet new coinages, like *tape-code*, *freak-out*, *shutup-ness*, *beautician*, *talkathon*, we may not readily be able to explain our reactions to them. We may find them acceptable and in accordance with our feelings about how words should be built up; or they may seem to us offensive, and in some way contrary to the rules. Innovations in vocabulary are capable of arousing quite strong feelings in people who may otherwise not be in the habit of thinking very much about language. Quirk (1968) quotes some letters to the press of a familiar kind, written to protest about 'horrible jargon', such as *break-down* (of figures), 'vile' words like *transportation*, and the 'atrocity' *lay-by* (127–8). The apologist who wrote the following in *The Times* of 3 September 1943 showed an unusually liberal attitude:

> On August 27 this journal reported a speech in which Mr Herbert Morrison used the word 'triphibious'. . . . On [August 31] a public school man, a master of English, fitted Mr Morrison's new adjective with its corresponding noun. . . . A new word that catches on, or can be forced on, is no monster; it is a happy invention. 'Triphibian' therefore may now join 'happidrome', 'sportsdrome', and 'normalcy' . . .

Perhaps the status of the master of English mentioned – Winston Churchill – had something to do with *triphibian*'s favourable reception. But to protest against lexical innovations is very often to appear ridiculous to later generations: who today would wince at *aviation* (now that we are thoroughly used to it), about which *The Daily Chronicle* commented in 1909: 'You could hardly think of a worse word.'

It is clear that various factors are involved in our attitudes to words. *Lay-by* was objected to because it appears to be formed from the non-standard verb *to lay* (= 'to lie'), and *triphibian* is the result of the splitting up of an element *amphi-*, in *amphibian*, which anyone with a knowledge of Greek knows means 'both' and should not be split. Our knowledge of the classical languages causes us to object to 'hybrid' words, composed of a Latin and a Greek element, like *television*, or a classical and a native element, like *speedometer*. The objectionableness of *break-down* and *transportation* is not a matter of the breaking of rules, and is less easy to pinpoint. Unfamiliarity alone may be enough to cause prejudice against a word. *Patrial* (1629, = 'of or belonging to one's native country') was recently re-introduced for legal purposes connected with the Immigration Act of 1971. Although obviously useful and of wholly respectable Latin ancestry (from a presumed form *patrialis*, from *patria*, 'fatherland'), it was at once denounced (by a professor of law) as 'barbarous'. *Manual*, on the other hand, a word of similar make-up (from Latin *manualis*, 'pertaining to the hand'), causes no such reaction – indeed its secure establishment in the language was probably responsible for the prejudice against its synonym of Teutonic origin, *handbook*, which appeared in Old English, fell into disuse after the Middle Ages, and was denounced in 1838 as a 'tasteless innovation' (see Jespersen 1905, §47). Speakers of English appear to be conservative in matters of vocabulary, or at least to think that they are; but it may be that British speakers are more conservative than Americans: during the present century, attention-catching neologisms like *aquacade, sexploitation, swelegant,* have appeared more frequently in American newspapers and magazines than in British ones.[1]

In the chapters that follow, I shall be concerned with some unconventional patterns of word-making, seen against a background of those established and productive patterns on which most generally-acceptable new words are formed. The reader will come across a number of ephemeral formations, illustrated to a large extent by quotations from newspapers. And in Chapter 13, we shall look at some developments that have been taking place over the last four hundred years or so, and it will be clear that it is not only modern word-coiners who break the 'rules' (*cf* the characteristic remark of a correspondent to the press quoted by Quirk (1968, 127): 'In these days of scientific as opposed to cultural education we need specially to be on our guard against debasement of language'). From an inspection of a range of established and transient coinages, we may gain some idea of the various forces at work in English word-formation and, incidentally, come to appreciate the irrelevance of Fowler's indignant protest: 'word-making, like other manufactures, should be done by those who know how to do it. Others should neither attempt it for themselves, nor assist the deplorable activities of amateurs by giving currency to fresh coinages before there has been time to test them' (1965, 253).[2]

1.2 Word-formation and linguistics

The subject of word-formation has not until recently received very much attention from descriptive grammarians of English, or from scholars working in the field of general linguistics. As a collection of different processes – compounding, affixation, 'conversion', 'backformation' and so on, about which, as a group, it is difficult to make general statements, word-formation usually makes a brief appearance in one or two chapters of a grammar. And the subject has not been attractive to linguists for two reasons – its connections with the non-linguistic world of things and ideas, for which words provide the names, and its equivocal position as between descriptive and historical studies. A few brief remarks, which necessarily present a much over-simplified picture, on the course which linguistics has taken in the last hundred years will make this clearer.

The nineteenth century, the period of great advances in historical and comparative language study, saw the first claims of linguistics to be a science, comparable in its methods with the natural sciences which were also enjoying a period of exciting discovery. These claims rested on the detailed study, by comparative linguists, of formal correspondences in the Indo-European languages, and their realization that such study depended on the assumption of certain natural 'laws' of sound change. As Robins observes in his discussion of the linguistics of the latter part of the nineteenth century:

> The history of a language is traced through recorded variations in the forms and meanings of its words, and languages are proved to be related by reason of their possession of words bearing formal and semantic correspondences to each other such as cannot be attributed to mere chance or to recent borrowing. If sound change were not regular, if word-forms were subject to random, inexplicable, and unmotivated variation in the course of time, such arguments would lose their validity and linguistic relations could only be established historically by extra-linguistic evidence such as is provided in the Romance field of languages descended from Latin. (1967, 183)

The rise and development in the twentieth century of synchronic descriptive linguistics meant a shift of emphasis from historical studies, but not from the idea of linguistics as a science based on detailed observation and the rigorous exclusion of all explanations dependent on extra-linguistic factors. As early as 1876, Henry Sweet had written:

> before history must come a knowledge of what exists. We must learn to observe things as they are, without regard to their origin, just as a zoologist must learn to describe accurately a horse or any other animal. Nor would the mere statement that the modern horse is a descendant of a three-toed marsh quadruped be accepted as an exhaustive description ... Such however is the course being pursued by most antiquarian philologists. (1875–6, 471)

The most influential scholar concerned with the new linguistics was Ferdinand de Saussure, who emphasized the distinction between external linguistics – the study of the effects on a language of the history and culture of its speakers, and internal linguistics – the study of its system and rules. Language, studied synchronically, as a system of elements definable in relation to one another, must be seen as a fixed state of affairs at a particular point in time. It was internal linguistics, stimulated by de Saussure's work

(1916), that was to be the main concern of twentieth-century scholars, and within it there could be no place for the study of the formation of words, with its close connections with the external world and its implications of constant change. Any discussion of new formations as such means the abandonment of the strict distinction between history and the present moment. As Harris expressed it in his influential *Structural Linguistics* (1951, 255): 'The methods of descriptive linguistics cannot treat of the productivity of elements since that is a measure of the difference between our corpus and some future corpus of the language.' Leonard Bloomfield, whose book, *Language* (1933), was the next work of major influence after that of de Saussure, re-emphasized the necessity of a scientific approach, and the consequent difficulties in the way of studying 'meaning', and until the middle of the nineteen-fifties, interest was centred on the isolating of minimal segments of speech, the description of their distribution relative to one another, and their organization into larger units. The fundamental unit of grammar was not the word but a smaller unit, the morpheme, about which Chapter 11 will have more to say.

The next major change of emphasis in linguistics was marked by the publication in 1957 of Noam Chomsky's *Syntactic Structures*. As Chomsky stated it, the aim of linguistics was now seen to be 'to make grammatical explanations parallel in achievement to the behavior of the speaker who, on the basis of a finite and accidental experience with language can produce and understand an indefinite number of new sentences' (15). The idea of productivity, or creativity, previously excluded from linguistics, or discussed in terms of probabilities in the effort to maintain the view of language as existing in a static state,[3] was seen to be of central importance. But still word-formation remained a topic neglected by linguists, and for several good reasons. Chomsky (1965, Chapter 1) made explicit the distinction, fundamental to linguistics today (and comparable to that made by de Saussure between *langue*, the system of a language, and *parole*, the set of utterances of the language), between linguistic competence, 'the speaker-hearer's knowledge of his language' and performance, 'the actual use of language in concrete situations' (Chomsky 1965, 4). Linked with this distinction are the notions of 'grammaticalness' and 'acceptability'; in Chomsky's words, 'Acceptability is a concept that belongs to the study of performance, whereas grammaticalness belongs to the study of competence' (1965, 11). A 'grammatical' utterance is one which may be generated and interpreted by the rules of the grammar; an 'acceptable' utterance is one which is 'perfectly natural and immediately comprehensible . . . and in no way bizarre or outlandish' (1965, 10). It is easy to show, as Chomsky does, that a grammatical sentence may not be acceptable. For instance, *this is the cheese the rat the cat caught stole* appears 'bizarre' and unacceptable because we have difficulty in working it out, not because it breaks any grammatical rules. Generally, however, it is to be expected that grammaticalness and acceptability will go hand in hand where sentences are concerned.

The ability to make and understand new words is obviously as much a part of our linguistic competence as the ability to make and understand new sentences, and so, as Pennanen (1972, 293) points out, 'it is an obvious gap in transformational grammars not to have made provision for treating word-formation'. But, as we noticed in the first section of this chapter, we may readily think of words, like *to piano, to violin*, against which we can invoke no rule, but which are definitely 'unacceptable' for no obvious reason. The incongruence of grammaticality and acceptability, that is, is far greater where words are concerned than where sentences are concerned. It is so great, in fact, that the exercise of setting out the 'rules' for forming words has so far seemed to many linguists to be of questionable usefulness. The occasions on which we would have to describe the output of such rules as 'grammatical but non-occurring' (*cf* Zimmer 1964, 18) are just too numerous. And there are further difficulties in treating new words like new sentences. A novel word (like *handbook* or *patrial*) may attract unwelcome attention to itself and appear to be the result of the breaking of rules rather than of their application. And, as we saw with *aviation*, the more accustomed to a word we become, the more likely we are to find it acceptable, whether it is 'grammatical' or not – or perhaps we should say, whether or not it was 'grammatical' *at the time it was first formed*, since a new word once formed, often becomes merely a member of an inventory; its formation is a historical event, and the 'rule' behind it may then appear irrelevant.

I shall largely ignore these problems and issues, since I am concerned in this book mainly to describe and exemplify the results of some present-day processes of word-formation. I shall return briefly in Chapter 14 to the matter of word-formation and general rules; meanwhile it will be convenient to employ two useful terms suggested by Jespersen, who was grappling with related topics in the nineteen-twenties. The following passage, taken out of context, appears to present a gross over-simplification, but it provides us with a useful rough distinction: 'While in handling formulas memory, or the repetition of what one has once learned, is everything, free expressions involve another kind of mental activity; they have to be created in each case anew by the speaker, who inserts the words that fit the particular situation' (Jespersen 1924, 19). We may say, for the time being, that it is with formulas, or fixed expressions, that word-formation is mainly concerned, while syntax deals with the patterns on which free expressions are constructed, though we should remember that the distinction between free expressions and fixed ones is not by any means clear-cut. I shall be concerned in the rest of this chapter, and in Chapter 2, with the boundary which I shall set between 'word-formation' and 'syntax', and with the areas in which this boundary is blurred, before beginning to describe the main products of 'word-formation'. But in Chapter 14 I shall look again at the distinction between syntax and word-formation, and try to present the matter in a rather different light.

1.3 Defining the word

What exactly is a word? This is a term which is usually taken for granted, and never offers any difficulty until we try to state precisely what we mean by it. The failure of general linguists to provide a consistent definition of the word across languages has shown that it can only be defined with respect to a particular language; but it is also evident that a word-like unit is equally central and unmistakable for speakers of very diverse languages. Edward Sapir relates in support of the word's 'psychological validity' his experience in teaching two American Indians to write their own languages:

> Both had some difficulty in learning to break up a word into its con-
> stituent sounds, but none whatever in determining the words . . . the
> words, whether abstract relational entities like English *that* or *but* or
> complex sentence-words . . . are . . . isolated precisely as I or any other
> student would have isolated them. (1921, 34 n.)

The word in English may be simple, composed of one constituent only, like *bat*, *hammer* or *sycamore*; or it may be complex, containing more than one constituent, such as *blackbird*, *fourth*. The elements of a complex word may be free forms: elements which in other contexts are independent, as those in *blackbird*, *devil-may-care*; or they may be bound forms: prefixes and suffixes, which never appear independently, like the first and last constituents of *uneatable* or the *-th* of *fourth*. Simple and complex words alike are distinguished from other constructions, it is generally agreed, by the fixed order of their constituents and by the impossibility of interrupting them by a pause, or of inserting other elements. Exceptions to this rule look very odd indeed (and are effective because they are exceptions), *cf abso-bloominlutely* [Alan Jay Lerner, *My Fair Lady*, 1956, Penguin 1959, 23] and *fanfuckingtastick* [*sic*]: ' "Well, how are you? Have you had a good time?" "Fanfuckingtastick! Never stopped laughing, have we?" ' [John Osborne, *The Hotel in Amsterdam*, 1968, 130].[4] However, complex words composed entirely of free forms exhibit among their elements the same kinds of relationships that are found in sentences – for instance attributive adjective–noun, as in *blackbird*, verb–object, as in *forget-me-not* – and for this reason they are sometimes considered to be on the borderline between syntax and word-formation. As will appear later in this book, complex words of many different kinds contain relationships which are also found in free expressions. But there are structures, word-like in their semantic unity, whose elements are only partially fixed in their order, or which to a limited extent permit interruption, and it is these which can more properly be regarded as on the borderline. Some examples of such structures are given in the next section.

1.4 Words and phrases

Sometimes phrase-like characteristics of a sequence are betrayed by the way in which the plural is formed. This is not always so, and some complex nouns which form their plurals in an unorthodox manner must be seen simply as exceptions to the rule of the uninterruptibility of the word. Among such exceptions are certain compounds with *man-*, *woman-* as first element, which generally pluralize both elements, as in *men-servants*, *women-folk*. Other similar compounds, like *maid-servant*, *boy friend*, have normal plurals. Another exceptional group of compounds in which usage is divided over the placing of the plural marker is exemplified by *lord lieutenant*, *court martial*, which are made up of a head noun and a following modifying adjective on the Romance pattern. (The OED gives the plural of *court martial* as '*courts martial*, sometimes incorr. *court martials*'.)

The interruptibility of words like *man-servant*, *court martial* is due to accidents of historical development, and does not indicate that the constituents of such words are less firmly attached to one another than those of compounds which form their plurals normally. Noun compounds with *-ful(l)* as second element are rather different. These vary as to the placing of the plural marker: for such words as *handful*, *bagful*, *sackful*, *spoonful*, Webster (1961) gives two plural forms, *handfuls*, *handsful*, and so on. Here, interruptibility by *s* shows doubtful word-status. There is a progression from phrase to word (along with a semantic change from 'container' to 'contents') which can be seen in the series (*three*) *bags full* – *bagsful(l)* – *bagfuls*. A less familiar combination with *-ful(l)* is more likely to have its first element pluralized than a very common one which has had time to become fixed, like *mouthful*, which admits *s* only finally. Certain noun–preposition–noun phrases also show their incomplete unification by the possibility of pluralizing the first noun: *dogs in the manger, men of war, sons in law, tugs of war.*

Phrasal verbs, combinations of verb and adverb, like *to build up, to take over*, and prepositional verbs, combinations of verb and preposition, like *to laugh at* are both word-like and phrase-like, and are in fact sometimes called 'semi-compounds', for instance by Kruisinga (1932). Though they often form a semantic unit, and may be equivalent to a single-item verb (*to build up: to erect, amass; to take away: to remove; to laugh at: to deride, ridicule*), their constituents are interruptible by the inflections of the verb, and in the case of transitive phrasal verbs, by an object as well. But unlike some other 'semi-compounds' (see below), these verbs are uniform in their syntactic behaviour, and are not subject to closer unification of their elements with the passage of time. Nominal structures derived from verb–particle collocations, however, may be more, or less, word-like. (For more about particles, see 3.3 below.) In noun–particle compounds like *looker on, passer by, summing up*, from the verb–particle collocations *look on, pass by, sum up*, the two elements retain some independence. The *-er* and *-ing* endings are attached to the first elements (though colloquially both elements may take an *-er*, *cf* 'Girls . . . might be keen to invest £1·25 in a boot taker-offer' [*Evening Standard* 19 February 1971, 23/1]). The plural *s* is also added to the first constituents. This is not true of the much larger non-suffixed group of nouns exemplified by *build-up, take-over*, which form their plurals in the normal way. Other features contribute to the feeling that words like *looker on* are less firmly 'solidified' than those like *build-up*: they are less frequently hyphenated than compounds of non-suffixed noun and particle; and their accentual pattern is similar to that of the verb–particle collocations on which they are based (see 8.2.1 below). While *looker ón* has its primary accent on the same element as the phrasal verb *to look ón*, the noun *táke-over* is accentually distinguished from the verb *to take óver*. (For a note on 'accent', see 3.5 below.) This accentual noun–verb distinction however is not entirely clear-cut, as Bolinger (1961a) shows with such examples as *a frantic wriggle loose, with a dart up and a scurry off*, which, as new and probably non-permanent formations, are likely to retain the accentual pattern of the verb phrases on which they are based. And Fairclough (1965, 82) cites an example: 'no great leaps forward are planned', in which the placing of the *s*, as well as the likelihood of an accent on *forward*, shows that noun and particle are incompletely unified, and cannot be regarded as forming a complex word.

Marchand (1969, 202) notes that adjectives in *-able* from verb–particle collocations may drop the particle, as in *accountable, reliable*, from *account (for), rely (on)*, or they may retain it as a kind of infix, as in *(un)get-at-able, (un)putdownable*. But notice also *fallable-in-love-with*, in which the suffix intervenes between verb and preposition: 'Nobody could *ever* meet *anyone* remotely fallable-in-love-with on the Irish Mail' [*Evening Standard* 30 July 1968, 8/5].

Phrases consisting of verb + complement + preposition, such as *give rise to, take advantage of*, are also called 'semi-compounds' by Kruisinga. These are fixed in varying degrees. *Give rise to* (= 'cause') for instance, may not be interrupted by modification of the noun, as in **give immediate rise to*; its elements are not separated in the passive: . . . *was given rise to* is possible, but not *rise was given to* . . . *Take advantage of*, however, is not subject to these restrictions: *he took full advantage of* . . . and *advantage was taken of* . . . are both grammatical sequences.[5] Another kind of 'semi-compound', similar in many respects to these verbal phrases, consists of preposition–noun–preposition sequences like *in view of, by dint of*. At the 'most fixed' end of the scale are examples like these two, in which the prepositions are invariable and the noun is isolated. *Dint* appears only in this context, and *view*, like *rise* in *give rise to*, lacks much of the meaning which it has in free phrases. *For want of, in process of*, show more freedom: the first preposition may be varied, the noun is not semantically isolated, and it may be modified by *the*. *At the request of* has more flexibility still, with the potentiality for premodification of the noun by an adjective, and replacement in a sentence by *at (his) request*.[6]

'Binomials' – sequences of two words, usually nouns or adjectives, linked usually by a conjunction – vary in their fixity. *Fun and games, wild and woolly*, for example, are not reversible, whereas *gold and silver, knife and fork* are, though this order is more frequent than the reversed one. At the 'most free' end of the scale are expressions like *shoes and socks*, for which there is no generally preferred order.[7] And, finally, we may notice that idiomatic phrases generally may acquire a certain fixity, usually as regards their nominal elements. The plural of *still life* (= 'picture of inanimate objects'), for some speakers is *still lives*, but for others *still lifes*. It is possible to admonish one person: *use your loaf!*, and we may put the verb into the past tense: *he used his loaf;* but a group of people could hardly be told: *use your loaves!*

These few examples give some indication of the distinction I am making between free expressions and fixed expressions. I shall say no more about phrasal verbs and other partially fixed structures, like *give rise to*, *in view of*, *fun and games*. There is an important difference between the ways in which these take on the identifying characteristics of words, and the central processes of word-formation which are described and exemplified in later chapters. The fixing of, for instance, a preposition–noun–preposition phrase takes place gradually, sometimes over centuries. For example, the OED records a first instance of *ine stude of* in 1225 (when the noun (='place') could be used freely in other contexts), and notes: 'the two words *in stead* = "in place", rarely written as one word before 1620, but seldom separately after *c* 1640 exc. when separated by a possessive pronoun . . . as *in my stead*. . . . formerly also *in the stead of*, which is still used dialectally, *eg* in the southern counties of Scotland' [OED, s.v. *instead*]. The first recorded appearance of *instead* used alone, adverbially, is dated 1667. The formation of a compound word, like *chicken-coop* or *cold cream*, on the other hand, though this too may be the result of the frequent collocation of items, can be seen as taking place in a single step, with no intermediate stages. It is true that an expression like *cold cream* can be either fixed or free; but in using it we make a choice. Either it is free (= 'cream which is cold') or fixed (= 'a particular kind of cream for the face'). It is true, however, that the boundary between compound and phrase may be uncertain in individual cases: this is discussed in 5.1, 6.1, 8.1.1, 8.1.2, and 8.1.4 below.

1.5 Derivation and inflection

Derivation by affix resembles inflection in some respects, and in Chapter 2 it will be seen that, from the historical point of view at any rate, they are not always distinct. Their differences, however, are important for an understanding of the distinction between word-formation and syntax with which I am concerned in these first two chapters.

The chief inflectional affixes of English are the plural marker, spelt *s* in *cats*, *dogs*, *es* in *glasses*, *en* in *oxen*, expressed by a change of vowel in *geese*, and by zero in *sheep;* the genitive *'s;* the verbal endings, *s* for the singular present tense forms, *ing* for the present participle, *ed* and the various 'strong' verb forms as in *hit*, *hidden*, *caught*, *sold*, for the past tense and past participle; and the adjectival *er* and *est* of the comparative and superlative forms. Derivational and inflectional processes alike involve a relation between the members of a pair, consisting of the 'unmarked' base form and the 'marked' affixed form. In the case of inflectional pairs this is a two-way relation: the existence of a singular (countable) noun necessarily implies that of its plural form, and (usually) *vice versa;* and almost every verb has a present and a past participle. With derived words, on the other hand, though the affixed form presupposes a base from which it was constructed, the reverse is not necessarily the case. The fact that we have formed *unclean* on the familiar pattern of negative *un-+* adjective base does not mean that we can do the same with *dirty.*

Affixes operating as inflections are stable in function and meaning. Plural *s* and past tense *ed* (or their variants) have the same significance whatever their context. This is often not the case with derivational affixes, though semantic predictability, and productiveness – the potential ability to appear in a great many words – tend to go together. Affixes like *-ness,* forming abstract nouns from adjectives, or *-er,* forming agent nouns from verbs, which are very productive, are also markedly stable in meaning. Many derivational affixes, however, have more than one meaning and can be added to more than one category of base words. Notice the difference between *-able* added to a verbal base: *allowable* = 'can be allowed', and to a nominal one: *knowledgeable* = 'having knowledge', *companionable* = 'fitted to be, behaving like, a companion'.

Both inflectional and derivational affixes are 'grammatical' rather than 'lexical' elements. The 'grammatical' elements of the language, which may be words or affixes, form groups which are relatively small, and stable in membership, compared with the 'lexical' classes of nouns, adjectives, verbs and adverbs, which are large and much more subject to the addition of new members and the loss through obsolescence of old ones. Grammatical items may be members of a system, like the personal pronouns, or the determiners, *a, the, this, that, these, some, every* and so on. The members of a system have complementary functions and are inter-dependent, so that any change – the addition or subtraction of one member – would have an effect on the group as a whole. It is usual to think of 'lexical' elements as characterized by specific meanings, while 'grammatical' elements have rather general significations, but this somewhat vague distinction is only useful as a rough generalization. It is helpful to think of 'lexical' and 'grammatical' as opposite poles: inflections, pronouns, determiners are nearest to the 'grammatical' pole; prepositions are less 'grammatical', and not so distant from the 'lexical' pole. They form a much larger, less tightly organized class, whose members may have over-lapping functions and are not so closely dependent on one another; and their number may be increased from time to time – notably by the formation of the complex prepositions referred to in 1.4.

Similarly, the class of derivational affixes is much larger than that of the inflectional affixes, its members are less interdependent, and new ones emerge now and then. Derivational affixes tend to be much less generalized in meaning than inflectional affixes, though there is considerable variation in this respect. -er and -ness are rather general in meaning: this characteristic too is associated with productiveness, since a more specialized suffix would not be suited to a very wide range of contexts. Contrast the rather more 'lexical' and much more restricted suffixes -iana, as in *Johnsoniana*, meaning something like 'a collection of the notable sayings of, or objects associated with . . .', -ese, as in *computerese, officialese*, meaning 'jargon, language peculiar to . . .' and -esque, as in *Romanesque, Rembrandtesque*, meaning 'in the (artistic) style of . . .'.

Finally, the function of inflections is to indicate relationships between words: the addition of an inflection to a word in a sentence is not a matter relevant to that word alone. Contrast *a cow eats grass* with *cows eat grass*: we choose the verbal forms *eats* or *eat* according to whether the subject noun is singular or plural, and we should not want to say that *eats* and *eat* are different words: they are different forms of the verb *to eat*. Derivational affixes, on the other hand, are not dependent in this way on the form of other words in the sentence: their function is to signal the formation of new words. The addition of -er to the verbal stem *eat*, for example, produces the noun *eater*, taking nominal inflections and behaving just like other nouns.

The behaviour of genitive 's needs special notice. When it refers to a word which is part of a noun phrase, it is usually attached, not to that word, but to the last one in the group. When plural s, or any other affix, behaves like this, it shows that the group has become unified into a single lexical item, for example in *jack-in-the-boxes, a devil-may-care-ish attitude, do-nothingism, he extract-of-beefed his bread.*[8] This is not so with the genitive. In *the man in the brown coat's newspaper*, the free phrase *the man in the brown coat* has a word-like role in this context only. The function of 's here is not relevant to the word to which it is attached; it links the following head word, *newspaper*, with the structure premodifying it, in a certain relationship. From this point of view, the 's is rather more like a preposition than an inflection. Jespersen in fact suggests that we call it an 'interposition' and drop the apostrophe, writing for example, *the man in the brown coat s newspaper*, to show that the s belongs equally to its preceding and following structures (1918, §§144–5).

1.6 The relevance of word classes to word-formation

The suffix -er, added to the verbal stem *eat* to make the noun *eater*, is an example of a class-changing derivational affix. Many prefixes are non-class-changing: *do* and *undo* are both verbs, *room* and *anteroom* are both nouns. Some suffixes too may be non-class-changing, like the ending -ery added to nouns to make collective nouns: *machine, machinery*; or -hood, which makes abstract nouns from concrete ones: *child, childhood*. But these derived nouns behave differently in certain respects from their corresponding bases: *machinery* has no plural, *childhood* is inanimate. The majority of suffixes in English are class-changing, and so form words which behave syntactically very differently from their bases. Word-formation in its derivational aspect therefore, acting as a 'bridge' between the different classes or between differently-behaving members of the same class, can be seen as the link between syntax and lexicon. The distinction of word classes is the province of syntax, since nouns, verbs, adjectives and adverbs are identified, not primarily by anything characteristic in their formal make-up, but by the way they behave in sentences. The various classes are, however, by no means rigidly compartmentalized, but shade into one another to varying extents. This means that in order to get a clearer idea of the limits of word-formation, it is necessary to have a look at the nature of the word classes, and at the features which differentiate them from one another.

Notes

1 Pennanen (1966, 144) suggests, with a reference to Bladin (1911), that American verbal inventiveness is connected with 'a certain freedom from conventionalism', and with the nature of the United States as 'the melting-pot of nations', combined with the survival of Elizabethan habits of inventiveness in vocabulary. This last suggestion in particular seems rather implausible.

2 I refer here to the revised edition of Fowler's work of 1926 by Sir Ernest Gowers. Throughout this book, references to Fowler should be understood to mean 'Fowler as revised by Gowers'.

3 Harris discusses it in these terms:

A question of some interest is that of productivity of elements: *ie* given an extremely large sample, with elements of classes A, B, C, etc, occurring with various members X_1, X_2, etc of class X, which elements out of A, B, C have a high probability of occurring with any new member X_n of X, and which elements out of A, B, C, etc do not? Those elements which have a high probability of occurring with any new X_n are called productive in respect to X. (1951, 374–5)

4 Notice that the flouting of rules here has its limits: the interruption is inserted before the most prominent syllable (*absolútely, fantástic*), thus contributing to the

emphatic effect, but it could hardly appear in any other position. *Abbloomin-solutely* has not at all the same impact as *absobloominlutely*. (I owe this observation to Professor R. Quirk.)

5 Fairclough (1965, 134*ff*) examines the extent to which some expressions of this kind are fixed.

6 These examples are taken from a detailed examination of preposition–noun–preposition sequences in Quirk and Mulholland (1964).

7 See Malkiel (1959) for numerous similar examples.

8 This last example, quoted from *Punch*, is from Robins (1959, 141).

Chapter 2

Word classes

2.1 Total and partial conversion

When a word which has hitherto functioned as a member of one class undergoes a shift which enables it to function as a member of another, we have what is traditionally called 'conversion'. Is the result of such a shift two words, one derived from the other, or one word with extended functions? 'Conversion' is usually subdivided into 'total conversion' and 'partial conversion'. The former is a derivational process and plays an important part in several word-formative patterns; the latter is a syntactic matter, and it is important to establish the difference between the two. In the following sections I shall discuss conversion generally, as well as the aspects of it which are relevant to word-formation.

To begin with, 'conversion' is a rather unsatisfactory term. A better name for 'total conversion' is that suggested by Jespersen (MEG VI, 6.1$_2$): derivation by a zero suffix, since 'conversion' implies that one word has somehow been turned into another, thereby losing its former identity. This can only be said to happen in cases where, over a long period of time, the antecedent use is no longer found. For example, the adjective *stimulant*, which gave rise to the noun of the same form, is now used only rarely, if at all. However, in order not to add to the confusion which has often accompanied discussions of conversion, both partial and total, I shall continue in this chapter to use the traditional terms, and without quotation marks.

Instances of total conversion are the noun *chemical*, derived from the adjective, the verb *bottle* from the noun *bottle*, the noun *find* from the homonymous verb. An example of partial conversion is the word *poor* in *the poor are always with us*. Is this a noun, an adjective acting as a noun, or must we say that 'it really belongs to two parts of speech at once' (Zandvoort 1969, §773)? To answer this question, and to make explicit

the essential difference between *poor* here and the examples of total conversion just given, we must examine and compare the various characteristics of nouns and adjectives.

2.2 Nouns

Among the features that we expect of nouns are: the ability to take the
plural and genitive inflections, to take certain characteristic suffixes like
-er, -ance, -ness, -ism, to be preceded by determiners, like *a, the, this, my,
another,* to follow prepositions, to act as the subject or the object of a
sentence. Adjectives are identified by such characteristics as the ability to
assume comparative and superlative forms, to be preceded by adverbs of
degree, like *very,* to appear in both positions in the frame *the* noun *is/
are.* . . . Some of these criteria concern the forms of nouns and adjectives;
others concern their positions in sentences, and for this reason some
linguists have set up partially parallel classes: nouns, adjectives, verbs
and adverbs, defined on the basis of the first, formal, kind of criterion and
nominals, adjectivals, verbals and adverbials, defined on the basis of the
second, positional, or functional kind. James Sledd for instance (1959, 81)
solves the problem of *the poor* in this way: ' *poor* is always and everywhere an
adjective since it fits into the series *poor, poorer, poorest,* but . . . in this sentence
[*the poor are always with us*] it is a nominal, since it fills a position which
nouns usually occupy.' However, the various criteria are not independent
of one another, they are not of equal weight, and different combinations
of them can be fulfilled by words in different contexts. In the following
paragraphs I shall consider all of them together and exemplify some of the
combinations that can occur.

The partial correspondence of the two sets of classes, noun:nominal
etc, shows that for each (traditional) word class there are positions in the
sentence which its members most typically occupy. But criteria of position alone are not very helpful in the distinguishing of nouns and adjectives,[1] since neither class has exclusive rights to any of the positions
involved. Any noun, for instance, can appear as an attributive between a
determiner and a head noun (like *milk* in a *milk pudding*), a position typical
of adjectives, so that it is reasonable to say that this position is characteristic
of nouns as well. It may also be occupied by almost any phrase-like or
sentence-like combination of words, for example *a yes-or-no answer, an
up-to-the-minute fashion, a four-thousand-a-year job, a never-to-be-forgotten
occasion, an I-turn-the-crank-of-the-Universe air.*[2]

Nouns in the other position in the frame '*the* noun *is/are* . . .', following the verb, sometimes show adjective-like features: they may appear without a determiner and drop the singular–plural distinction, as in *he was heir to a fortune;* '*The Comedians* is box-office' [*Listener* 18 January 1968, 94/3]; 'In one of his less self-congratulatory moments Mr Durrell confessed that writing was 'pure dentist's chair' [*Listener* 23 May 1968, 678/2]. When this happens, they may be modified by a degree adverb, as in 'hats too small and too cardboard to be anything but party decorations' [*New Statesman* 26 April 1968, 544/2]; 'it's quite science-fiction really' [*Evening Standard* 3 May 1968, 10/3]; 'Her symptoms were almost textbook' [*Evening Standard* 17 January 1969, 20/3]. Examples of nouns in attributive position so modified are 'a somewhat bird's-eye view' (quoted by Jespersen MEG II, 13.51); 'the heady, almost nutmeg scent' [*Evening Standard* 27 April 1968, 10/1].[3]

2.3 Adjectives

Adjectives may behave in various noun-like ways. In general, any adjective may take the definite article and function like a plural noun, as *poor* does in *the poor are always with us*, to denote a class of persons having the quality of the adjective, or like a singular noun denoting that quality itself, as in *the sublime, the ridiculous*. This is an identifying feature of the class. Adjectives when used in this way do not take nominal inflections, but they occasionally take premodifiers other than *the*: *our poor, the Soviet young, the idle rich*. Or they may combine this nominal function with the adjectival features of comparative and superlative form, and premodification by an adverb. Examples are *the poorer than oneself, the greatest of pities, the most corrupt of them all; the clearly inevitable, the comparatively rich*.

2.4 Conversion between noun and adjective

Adjectives, then, like nouns, appear as subjects and objects of sentences, and, also like nouns, they may appear with determiners; but we may say that a new noun has been derived from an adjective when the word in question appears with nominal inflections, since this important nominal criterion implies also the possibility of premodification by the indefinite article and the full range of nominal modifiers, and the impossibility of modification by an adverb. Adjectives which have been the starting-point for new nouns are numerous; examples are *imbecile, intellectual, juvenile, moderate, progressive, rustic*. Many such words have typically adjectival endings, but this feature does not seem to hinder the process.

Some grammarians make a distinction between conversion of an adjective to a noun, and shortening of an adjective–noun phrase by the dropping of the noun, which produces the same result.[4] Examples like *weekly* (newspaper), *final* (examination), *empty* (bottle) have arisen in this way. But probably a great many nouns whose derivation from adjectives is ascribed to conversion have been formed in the same way: this distinction is a difficult one to make consistently. The more established and frequent such a word becomes, the less it is felt to be representative of a truncated longer phrase. Where the head noun that can be supplied is fairly specific in meaning, like *newspaper*, *examination*, the process is most often labelled 'shortening'; where the head noun is fairly general in meaning, like *one*, *man*, *people*, *thing*, the process is likely to be called 'conversion'.

An adjective derived from a noun may be identified by those adjectival features which cannot accompany the nominal inflections. These features are: the potentiality for assuming comparative and superlative forms, and for forming an adverb in -*ly* or an abstract noun in -*ness*; the ability to take an adverbial modifier, and the ability to appear in both positions in the frame *the* noun *is/are*. . . . The editor of Webster (1961), however, points out that these conditions may be too strict for a realistic account of the facts. There are many words in English which are very commonly used attributively, in senses distinct from those associated with their nominal use, but which are resistant to some or all of the identifying adjectival features. These are labelled 'adjective' in Webster (1961). Examples are *bottom* (drawer), *head* (cook), *animal*, *brute*, *model*, *slave*, *capsule*, *mammoth*, *dwarf*. (See Gove 1964, 166*ff*.)

Noun-derived adjectives are far less numerous than adjective-derived nouns. Such long-established examples as *level*, *dainty*, *shoddy*, *bridal*, were probably, as Jespersen suggests (MEG II, 13.82), helped in the direction of adjective-hood by the accidental similarity of their endings to those typical of adjectives. Some other examples are *game*, *commonplace*, *partisan*, *matter-of-fact*, *average*.

Partial and total conversion between nouns and adjectives may be understood in terms of the two sets of typical characteristics, nominal and adjectival. In spite of the extensive sharing of features by the two classes, it is usually possible to fix a fairly clear boundary between them, and to decide when it has been crossed and total conversion has taken place. Partial conversion is a term descriptive of certain kinds of syntactic behaviour, the limited overlapping of the classes. It is, strictly speaking, not a stage on the way to total conversion, the derivation of new lexical items – although when a noun is commonly used as an attributive modifier, like the Webster examples given above, it is perhaps reasonable to say that the way is being prepared for the derivation of a new adjective by total conversion.

2.5 Adjective and adverb/preposition

The noun and adjective classes are not the only ones which encroach on one another: the distinguishing of adjectives from adverbs also offers problems. Adverbs may appear as attributive modifiers, as in *the down line, an off day, a today image, after events*, occasionally with a difference of form: *outdoor games*, but *games outdoors*. Such attributives, however, rarely show the more positive adjectival features of comparison or modification by an adverb. Adjectives may take on an adverb-like function: there is a tendency for a word which precedes an adjective in premodification to function as an intensifying adverb. Jespersen (MEG II, 15.21*ff*) discusses this in connection with adjectives, and in Chapter 6 below, which deals with adjective compounds, it will be seen that nouns too are susceptible to this development. Jespersen sketches the development of the adverbial *very* from the adjective (= 'true') via combinations with adjectives of similar or related meaning. In Chaucer's *a verray parfit gentil knight* it was perhaps on the way to adverbial status; in his *a verray trewe wyf* it looks more like the present-day *very*.[5] In the fifteenth century *very* began to appear before a wider range of adjectives as it became more firmly established as an intensifier. *Pretty* seems to have had a similar career: in the OED its first appearance as an intensifier is dated 1565, though the adjective was in use by about 1400.

Turning to more recent times, it is easy to think of sequences which look like two adjectives but which are understood rather as intensifier + adjective: *precious little, bitter cold, dirty great, shocking bad, bloody awful*. Mitchell (1966, 350) suggests that the more or less fixed order of some familiar sequences of adjectives, like *a fine sunny day, a cold frosty morning*, may be related to this tendency. *Cf* also phrases with *nice and*, such as *nice and warm*. Adjectives used as intensifiers, however, seem to be very susceptible to changes in fashion; or perhaps this use of them is less common than it has been. Jespersen gives a long list of examples, such as *uncommon, monstrous, beastly, devilish, confounded, infernal*, which now have a very dated air.

The conversion of adverbs to nouns is not very important for word-formation (see 4.7 below). Temporal adverbs may adopt nominal sentence positions or functions, as in *now is the time, yesterday was wet*, but we may take inflectional features as indicating when a new noun has been derived, as in *one today is worth two tomorrows*. Examples like *the here and now, the long ago* are like partially converted adjectives such as *the poor, the unspeakable*: their noun-like behaviour is usually limited to their function in the sentence and accompaniment by the definite article.

2.6 Verb (participle) and adjective

Present and past participles may be attributive modifiers of nouns, and in this function they are to varying degrees adjective-like. The class of 'participial adjectives' is a rather mixed one, resistant to generalizations and to tidy description. As a start, we may say that verbs are typically associated with reference to time, with activity and changing conditions, and adjectives with qualities and characteristics; but this is a very rough distinction. Jespersen (MEG IV, 7.6) distinguishes two kinds of verbs, 'conclusive verbs', which denote the action of a moment, or one that is begun in order to be finished, and 'inconclusive verbs', denoting feelings or states of mind – activities not begun in order to be finished. Participles of the 'conclusive' kind of verb retain in attributive position the verbal feature of reference to time: *playing children* (= 'children who are playing (now)'); *appointed time* (= 'time which has been appointed'). Attributively-used participles of 'inconclusive' verbs are more like adjectives in their characterizing significance: *a pleasing prospect, an admired colleague*. However, participles may not always premodify nouns. We may speak of *a damaging remark*, for instance, corresponding to a sentence like *the remark damaged his reputation*, but not of *a damaging accident*, corresponding to *the accident damaged his car*. Bolinger (1967) discusses possible reasons why some participles may not be used attributively, for instance *a distressing remark* but not *an angering remark*, *departed guests* but not *arrived guests*, and illustrates the point that attributive position is more natural for adjectives and participles with a marked descriptive, 'permanent' meaning. Non-participial adjectives, it should be noted, may have a predominantly verbal, 'action' sense, as in *suppressive drug* (= 'drug which suppresses'), *depressant effect, attractive power* (*eg* of a magnet), *resistant strain* (of bacteria).

Huddleston (1971, 3.6.3), following Curme (1931), makes a somewhat similar distinction between 'actional' and 'statal' passives.[6] Statal passives are like predicative adjectives in that they have no active counterpart and they may be coordinated with adjectives; they may sometimes take the negative prefix *un-*, and the accompanying auxiliary verb may commute with *become, remain, seem*. Such participial adjectives, like other adjectives, have the potentiality of being converted to nominal function: *the living, the wounded*. Occasionally they may be totally converted: *the accused* (singular), *the last-named, coloureds, knitteds, frustrateds:* 'two suicides, one depressive and various frustrateds' [*Observer* 10 September 1967, 22/4]. Participles of verbs in 'conclusive' senses – 'actional' participles – unlike adjectives, take the verbal intensifier *much*. Compare *a much disappointed man* (= 'often': conclusive sense) with *a very disappointed man* (= 'extremely': inconclusive sense, describing a state of mind).

The use of the *un-* prefixes, negative as in *unhappy* (= 'not happy'), and reversative or privative as in *undo* (*ie* 'reverse the action of'), *unclothe* (= 'remove clothes from'), with participles further reflects the dual nature of the latter. The negative *un-* is normally attached only to adjectives, the reversative *un-* only to verbs. With participles and other derived adjectival forms, there may be ambiguity between the two prefixes: the prefix may be seen as attached to the whole word, that is, as negative, or to the verbal base only, as reversative. Compare *an unlockable door*, which can be negative: *un-* + *lockable*, 'a door which cannot be locked', or reversative: *unlock* + *-able*, 'a door which can be unlocked'; *an unlocked door*, which can be negative: *un-* + *locked*, 'a door which is not locked', or reversative: *unlock* + *-ed*, 'a door which has been unlocked'. In the latter pair the distinction is to some extent neutralized, since here the result of a 'reversing' action is a 'negative' state. The whole phrase may indicate which *un-* is meant: contrast *an undone task* with *an undone plait*, where misunderstanding is unlikely. And compare Gerard Manley Hopkins's unambiguous 'the widow-making unchilding unfathering deeps' ['The Wreck of the Deutschland', 13], in which we understand the participles as having the structure (*un-* + verb) + *-ing*.

On the whole, however, *un-* prefixed to a participle in attributive function is understood as having negative import, and the participles of established reversative verbs, like *undo, untie, unpack*, show a resistance to attributive position. Negative *un-*, however, may appear attached to participles in non-attributive, verbal, function, as in passive sentences like *he was unimpressed by the evidence*, in which *unimpressed* behaves verbally in having an agent-phrase, but there is no corresponding infinitive *to un-impress*.[7]

We may distinguish two *-ed* suffixes, the past participle ending, and the adjective-forming suffix added to nouns as in *talented* (= 'having talent'), *honeyed*. In adjectives ending in *-ed* whose base forms may be either nominal or verbal, we may of course be uncertain which *-ed* is involved.

Crowned, for instance, can be interpreted as having a verbal base (= 'having been crowned'), or a nominal one (= 'having a crown'). Similar examples are *shaped, clothed*. Because of this ambiguity of the *-ed* ending, adjective compounds in *-ed* may have either an adjective or an adverb as first constituent. In *strangely-shaped*, for instance, the adverbial first element shows the verbal nature of the second (= 'shaped in a strange manner'); *strange-shaped*, on the other hand, is formed from the adjective – noun phrase *strange shape* and the adjective-forming suffix. And we have *internationally-minded* beside *single-minded*, even though *minded* has no verbal use other than in the idiomatic *I am minded to.* ... *Well-intentioned* is an interesting example in that the second element can only be interpreted as a noun with an adjective-suffix, as there is no verb *to intention*, but the adverbial first element is appropriate to a verbal form (*cf: he intends well*).[8] Some ambiguous examples of adjective compounds in *-ed* are given below in Chapter 6.

Examples like *scathing, grasping, calculating, charming, demanding, agitated, detached, elated*, which behave in all respects like orthodox adjectives, and in which senses markedly distinct from those of the underlying verbs have developed, are most obviously contributions from the class of verbs to that of adjectives. Participles play an important part in word-formation in connection with compounds, particularly adjective compounds, as we shall see in Chapter 6. And participles, both present and past, sometimes act as 'intermediaries' in the derivational processes by which verbs are formed from nouns and adjectives. *To terrace*, for example, may have been suggested by the form *terraced* (from the noun *terrace* and the adjective-suffix *-ed*, = 'having terraces'), which was subsequently taken to be a past participle. And some noun-derived verbs like *to honeycomb, to telescope*, are most naturally used in past participle form (see p. 45, 4.3, IC 3 below). Some, in fact, are only found as past participles, for example *fated, rumoured* (... *is fated/rumoured to be* ...). Many compound verbs too occur only or chiefly as participles: *he is henpecked* (*by his wife*) is perhaps a more probable utterance than *his wife henpecks him*. Examples of derived verbs which appear only in present participle form are *to coast* (as in *a coasting vessel*), and *to bald* (as in *a balding pate*).

2.7 Verb (gerund) and noun

Conversion between the noun and verb classes is of great importance in word-formation. Examples like those mentioned in 2.1, *to bottle*, from the noun, and *a find*, from the verb, which are representative of quite productive processes, present no problems of class membership: the base form and the derived form are always clearly members of different classes. For some more examples of this kind, see Chapter 4. It is in the gerund that the two classes have a meeting-point, and I shall now glance at the ways in which this happens, and at the relationship of the nominal -*ing* form to derived abstract nouns.

Non-finite clauses containing gerunds and infinitives may have nominal functions in sentences. The non-finite verbs in such clauses may take objects or adverbial modifiers, *cf: eating people is wrong, to do that would be a mistake, his fault is working too hard, I asked you to do it quickly.* About the infinitive no more need be said here. It may appear alone in nominal function, as in *to err is human*, but it cannot take on any further nominal features. The gerund is more interesting in this respect, and we need to examine it briefly in order to be clear about the distinction between the -*ing* inflection and the -*ing* that we may regard as a derivational suffix.

In some combinations the gerund seems to be equally nominal and verbal, as in *sailing is over for this year, I like swimming*, in which it appears with neither nominal nor verbal modifiers; or in *his secretly appointing John to the post*, in which it appears with a nominal premodifier, and a direct object and an adverb. However, in constructions like this one, the gerund indicates merely the fact of an action, and cannot show any further nominal characteristics. Aside from expressions like *there is no persuading them*, it may be premodified only by possessive pronouns: such sequences as *This sudden sending him away must seem Deliberate pause* [*Hamlet* IV iii, quoted by Jespersen (MEG V, 8.3$_5$)] have an archaic flavour today. But a gerund which is followed by a prepositional phrase can be freely premodified: *his/the secret appointing of John*, and for the gerund here, which refers to the action itself, we can substitute a form with another (derivational) suffix, if there is one available: *the secret appointment of John.*[9] Both *appointing* and *appointment* here may still mean 'the action of appointing', but the latter word may also have the meaning of a completed activity, and, too, the meaning of 'post', as in *John's appointment was a lucrative one.*

Verbs which collocate with particles and which can enter into noun–particle compounds appear, in -*ing* form, in stages intermediate between verb and noun. Contrast the more verbal *they object to their tearing up their flag* (Fairclough 1965, 89), in which the particle is movable: . . . *their tearing their flag up*, with the more nominal 'The cruel gunning-down of another Kennedy' [*Evening Standard* 10 June 1968, 7/1], where the -*ing* form and the particle are more closely bound together. We could not write *the gunning of another Kennedy down*: the more nominal *-ing* form of the *of* construction requires a closer link with the particle, which in fully nominalized forms is of course the second element of a compound.

The relationships of *-ing* forms to abstract nouns formed with other suffixes are rather idiosyncratic. We can say

$$ his\ speedy \left.{sale \atop selling}\right\} of\ the\ goods, $$

$$ her\ careful \left.{arrangement \atop arranging}\right\} of\ the\ flowers, $$

$$ his\ skilful \left.{development \atop developing}\right\} of\ the\ argument $$

referring in each case to the action, even though *sale, arrangement, development* are commonly used in more concrete senses; but *confidence* will not substitute for the *-ing* form in *his confiding of the secret*: its senses of 'trust', 'communication made in confidence' have now become too firmly associated with it for the verbal, 'action', sense to be possible.

It is easy to see that the *-ing* form, from denoting simply the action of the verb, may become fully nominal and develop an associated concrete sense such as 'the result of the action' or 'something associated with the action'. (For a note on the use of the term 'concrete', see 4.6 below.) As we might expect, in many cases the concrete sense of an *-ing* form is attested rather later than its first appearance in the 'action' sense. The following, denoting the action of the verb, are all dated by the OED in the fourteenth century: *drawing, failing, finding, meeting*. The related senses of 'picture', 'defect', 'discovery', 'assembly' are recorded as occurring two or three hundred years later. The role of the *-ing* ending in these words in their later senses is just like that of noun-forming suffixes such as *-ation* and *-ment*, and we may say that it is a derivational suffix here. Nouns with the derivational *-ing* fall into various semantic groups; the possibilities are illustrated in 4.6 below, where examples of nouns derived from verbs by zero affix are given. Like the latter, *-ing* nouns may denote the object or result of an action, for example *building, drawing, dripping;* the (collective) agent of an action, for example *following;* the instrument of an action, for example *covering*, and so on. All these senses are dependent on the underlying verbal 'action' sense, so that it is misleading to say, as the OED does, that nominals like *ballooning* (1821), *blackberrying* (1885) and *nutting* (1824) are 'formed directly from sbs' [OED, *-ing*[1] 1c]. They could not have been formed without assumed underlying verbs. (In fact, *to balloon* appeared at the same time as *ballooning; to go blackberrying*, where the *-ing* form is half gerund, half participle, appeared earlier (1861) than Miss Yonge's 'We never had such a blackberrying', and *to nut* dates from 1604.) But it is true that, like the participles mentioned in the previous section – *balding, honeycombed, henpecked* and so on, nominal forms in *-ing* may be 'intermediaries' in the process of forming verbs, appearing at an earlier stage than the infinitive and the finite forms. And there are nouns in *-ing* which have no underlying 'action' sense, and which presuppose no corresponding verb; these may be said to be derived directly from base nouns. As the OED points out [s.v. *-ing*[1] 1g], where a noun of the same form as its corresponding verb exists (for example, *ship*, noun; *ship*, verb), the noun in *-ing* (from the verb), *shipping*, may come to be more closely associated with the non-suffixed noun (and so thought of as derived from it), and this paves the way for the derivation of *-ing* nouns from nouns without corresponding verbs. In *carpeting, clothing, shipping*, the suffix has a 'collective' sense comparable with *-age* in *tankage, yardage*, or *-(e)ry* in *machinery, rocketry*, and words with this 'collective' *-ing* seem to have nominal rather than verbal bases. *Scaffolding, shirting, tubing* are certainly derived from nouns.

The Old English derivational suffix *-ing*, or *-ung*, was originally added, restrictedly, to nouns to form abstract nouns; but the nominal stems to which it was attached were subsequently taken to be those of weak verbs corresponding in form to them.[10] Old English *weddung*, 'wedding', for example, corresponds to the noun *wedd*, 'pledge' and the verb *weddian*. Jespersen (1905, §206) notes that by the beginning of the fifteenth century the noun in *-ing* had acquired the verbal characteristics illustrated in the examples at the beginning of this section, and the *-ing* ending could be added to every verb to form the gerund. It had now become an inflection. However, as we have seen, it remained productive as a derivational suffix (directly, or via the gerund), and as with the nouns derived from adjectives mentioned in 2.4, we can recognize a fully nominal *-ing* form by its potentiality for taking the nominal inflections and the indefinite article.

2.8 Syntactic and lexical derivation

In the preceding sections I have looked at some ways in which words belonging to one word class can behave, to limited extents, like those of another (partial conversion), or can actually give rise to new words of different class-membership (total conversion), and I have tried to show that this distinction cannot always be very neatly made. Like other processes of word-formation, total conversion tends to be sporadic and unpredictable, contrasting with the freer and more regular partial conversion; and it characteristically involves marked changes of meaning between base and derived forms. This last feature is sometimes thought to be more important than the syntactic and inflectional ones which have been discussed above, and it is responsible for a somewhat different placing of the boundary between inflection and derivation, syntax and word-formation. The distinction which is sometimes made between 'syntactic derivation' and 'lexical derivation' does not wholly correspond to that between partial and total conversion; it rests on the difference between processes (inflectional and some derivational) which do not involve marked difference of meaning between base and derived forms, and those (derivational) which do. It was most explicitly made in an article by J. Kuryłowicz (1936), 'Dérivation lexicale et dérivation syntaxique'.[11] Kuryłowicz defines a syntactic derivative as a form which has the same lexical content as its base; for example *amans*, present participle of *amo*, *franchement*, adverbial derivative of the adjective *franc*, the nominals *das Hier und Jetzt*, from the homonymous adverbs. Lexical derivation is a second stage in the derivational process, and takes place when the syntactic derivative acquires some additional component of meaning. For instance, *height*, 'vertical dimension' is a lexical derivative, from the syntactic derivative *height*, 'quality of being high', from the base adjective *high*.

Sweet, too, makes essentially this distinction when he remarks that some derivative elements are 'very similar to inflections': 'Thus the change of *white* into *whiteness*, *good* into *goodness*, etc, can hardly be said to form a new word, for it comes to the same thing whether we say *snow is white* or *snow has the attribute of whiteness*' (1891, §80). And there is sometimes disagreement as to whether the suffix *-ly*, forming adverbs from adjectives, is inflectional or derivational. In view of such regular pairs as *move rapidly*:*rapid movement*, *utterly dark*:*utter darkness*, adverbs have been seen as merely 'positional variants' of adjectives.

-ly and *-ness* are two suffixes which show much of the stability, predictability and generality of meaning that, as we saw in 1.5, tend to go together and are characteristic of inflections; and with them it is possible to form an adverb and a noun respectively, from almost any adjective. But we may distinguish between high productivity and the *obligatory* relation between pairs of marked and unmarked forms, accompanied by a regular semantic relation, which characterizes inflection. And there is no satisfactory way of deciding when a derivatively marked form con-

tains 'the same meaning' as its base, and when some new component of meaning has been added, allowing us to say that lexical derivation has taken place. It seems more practical therefore, to distinguish word-formation from syntax by making use of formal evidence such as the ability to take inflections, as I have done, and only then to examine the changes in content which frequently follow, if they do not accompany, the transference of forms from one class to another.

In the following chapters I shall abandon the unsatisfactory term 'total conversion' and refer instead to 'derivation by a zero suffix'. This is examined in detail in Chapter 4.

Notes

1 The reverse, however, is often assumed, *cf* Robins (1964, 227): 'words are assigned to word classes on the formal basis of syntactic behaviour, supplemented and re-inforced by differences of morphological paradigms.' 'Syntactic' is commonly used to refer to order and position; it is in contrast with 'morphological', or inflectional and derivational. 'Formal', rather confusingly, may be used for either, or both. *Cf* also Fries (1952, 144): 'In general, "position" markers in any particular sentence supersede morphological or form markers.'

Taking positional criteria to be all-important may lead to confusing explanations. *Cf* Vechtman-Veth (1962, 69), who states that examples such as *the poor laws*, *abnormal psychology*, *delinquent specialist*, *wireless enthusiast* are 'interesting instances of *double conversion*. The first element is originally an adjective; after having established itself as a noun with the meaning it has acquired *as a noun* . . . it enters into compound [*sic*] as an attributive word, *ie: as an adjective.*'

2 This last example is from J. R. Lowell, quoted by Jespersen (MEG II, 14.82). In that chapter, Jespersen discusses in detail the various structures that can premodify nouns.

3 See Jespersen (MEG II, 13.51) and Poutsma (1914, Chapter 23, §16) for a number of examples of these constructions.

4 Kruisinga (1932) has a rather confusing set of terms. Apart from 'complete' and 'partial' conversion, he refers to 'real' and 'apparent' conversion – the latter descriptive of the shortening of an adjective–noun or attributive noun–noun phrase (§1848).

5 F. N. Robinson, however, in his second edition of Chaucer's works (1957, 652) says: 'Manly notes that Chaucer apparently never uses "very" (*verray*) as an intensive adverb.'

6 This distinction of Huddleston's is related to the one which he makes between dynamic verbs, expressing actions or processes, and non-dynamic verbs, expressing states or relations. He shows why he prefers this to Jespersen's conclusive/inconclusive division.

7 On this, see Svartvik (1966, especially 24, 137).

8 Jespersen (MEG II, 15.34*ff*) gives a number of contrasting examples. See, however,

5.1 below on the characteristic 'neutrality' of first elements of compounds. A recent article on the -ed suffixes is Hirtle (1970).

9 See Lees (1960, Chapter 3, especially 64–7), where constructions of this kind are examined in detail; and also Fraser (1970).

10 Something similar happened with the agentive -er, which resembles an inflection in that it can be added to any verb stem. This suffix has a history complicated by Old French and Latin borrowings, but its Teutonic ancestor was added to noun stems to form words like Old English bocere (= 'booker', 'scribe'). Cottager, hatter, villager contain -er in its pre-Old English function. Some nouns which could take this suffix had weak verbs derived from them (like Old English bocian = 'to supply with books'); the derived nouns in -ere then appeared to be the 'agents' of these verbs, and the pattern was extended. See OED, s.v. -er[1].

11 Cf Rensky (1964), where the verb-to-noun pattern exemplified by to look→to have a look is described as syntactic derivation.

Chapter 3

Some terms and definitions

3.1 Compounding and derivation

A 'compound word' is usually understood to be the result of the (fixed) combination of two free forms, or words that have an otherwise independent existence, as in *frostbite*, *tape-measure*, *grass-green*. These items, though clearly composed of two elements, have the identifying characteristics of single words: their constituents may not be separated by other forms, and their order is fixed. In a 'derived word', at least one element, the affix, is a bound form, with no independent existence and, characteristically, the more general meaning that one would expect a 'grammatical' element to have. Thus, compounding may be distinguished from derivation both formally, in terms of the presence or absence of a bound form, and semantically, according to whether both elements are 'lexical' or not. But we shall see that this distinction is not so simple: 'lexical' elements are not always free, and 'grammatical' ones not always bound.

Some second elements of compounds appear to have a status somewhere between 'lexical' and 'grammatical'. The second elements of *ironmonger*, *playwright*, *clockwise*, for instance, are now not used independently; those of *godlike* and *seaworthy* are so used, but *worthy* at least has not quite the same meaning in the compound as it has in isolation. In *chairman*, *dustman*, *policeman*, *postman*, the second element, /mən/, is pronounced in a way distinct from *man* in *man-made*, *remittance man*; it is perhaps more like an agentive suffix, such as -*er* than the word *man*. -*ful*(*l*) in many words is weakened to /fl/ or /fəl/, as in *dreadful*, *pitiful*; but in *brimful*(*l*) (= 'full to the brim') its 'lexical' status is supported by the pronunciation /fʊl/. -*dom* and -*hood* are elements which have gone all the way from 'lexical' to 'grammatical' status: the former, as the Old English noun *dōm* (our *doom*), meant 'judgment', 'authority', and appeared as first element in such compounds as *dōm-bōc*, 'doom-book, book of decrees or laws', *dōm-dæg*, 'doomsday, judgment day'; but it was frequent as second element, as in *cynedōm*, 'kingdom', *freodōm*, 'freedom', *wīsdōm*, 'wisdom', with the meanings of 'domain', 'status', 'condition'; in time, it came to be seen as a suffix, which is productive in these senses today. The suffix *-hood*, from Old English *hād*, 'rank', 'condition', has had a similar history.

3.2 Neo-classical compounds

Complex words like *bibliophile, microscope, telegraph* contain no free forms, and yet they seem best considered as compounds. Very many classical elements, such as *micro-, -scope, tele-, -graph*, occur frequently in new words: although they may look 'foreign', and appear only in combination with other like elements, they are nonetheless productive. As Jespersen points out, 'one needs only a smattering of science to be acquainted with technical words from Latin and Greek that would have struck Demosthenes and Cicero as bold, many of them even as indefensible or incomprehensible innovations' (1905, §121). These neo-classical words are not always understood in terms of their parts, but we nevertheless have no difficulty in recognizing them as complex.[1] Some words of this kind are more 'transparent' than others; many people for whom *aquaplane* is instantly comprehensible as meaning an object (noun) or activity (verb) associated with water, might be less likely to perceive *aqueduct* as a complex word, or to realize that aquamarines were so named because of the likeness of their colour to that of sea-water. Without analysing *autograph, democracy, philology*, we may easily abstract the 'self', 'rule' and 'study' components to coin words like *auto-suggestion, mobocracy, kremlinology*. The coinage in the following passage depends on an understanding of *anthropomorphic* as a complex word, and of how it is constructed: 'Behaviourism started by rejecting the pathetic fallacy; it ended up by replacing the anthropomorphic view of the rat with the ratomorphic view of man' [*Observer* 18 September 1966, 26/7]. And in the following quotation, notice that a neo-classical element is regarded as an English word: 'Next Friday Jeyes . . . starts a £100,000 advertising campaign to launch its re-formulated "bio-active" Brobat bleach. Unlike the washing powders which use the word "bio" to indicate their enzyme content, Brobat is being boosted as an enzyme killer. "The word 'bio' simply means 'doing a job more thoroughly'"' claims Maurice Wiseman, chairman . . .' [*Sunday Times* 1 March 1970, 25/1].

In Greek and Latin, the stem, the lexical form which underlies all the members of an inflectional paradigm, is an incomplete form, since it is never used without an ending. In a complex word, as first element, the ending takes the form of a 'combining vowel', unless the second element begins with a vowel, in which case the combining vowel is omitted. In classical times each declension and conjugation had its own combining vowel, but through analogy, and factors involving ease of pronunciation, *o* and *i* became the most common ones. As second element, the stem always appeared with a suffix. Compare the two stems *anthrop-*, from *anthropos*, 'man' and *phil-* from *philein*, 'to love', *philos*, 'dear', 'friend', as first and second elements in *anthropology, philanthropy, bibliophile*.[2] Many neo-classical elements, like 'native' compound-elements, can appear in both initial and final position in complex words, for example *anthrop-* in *anthropology, misanthrope, chrom-* in *chromometer, monochrome, morph-* in *morphology, anthropomorph*. They may appear with prefixes and suffixes: *a-morph-ous* is comparable in structure with *un-adventur-ous*. And they tend to have specific, 'lexical' meanings comparable with those of 'native' compound elements. The elements mentioned above can be translated as 'man', 'colour', 'measure', 'form'. It is clear, therefore, that we should treat them as 'lexical' elements, even though they are not free forms, rather than as affixes.

Some neo-classical elements, however, are restricted to initial position in words, like *bio-, crypto-, pseudo-*, or to final position, such as *-cracy, -nym, -scope*, and here we must rely only on the imprecise criterion of 'lexical' meaning if we want to support the decision that these are compound elements, not affixes. How unsatisfactory this may be can be seen from a comparison between the words *pseudo-patriot* and *patrioteer*, both of which mean 'falsely patriotic', 'not genuinely a patriot'. In the first word the notion of falseness is conveyed by what I shall define as a compound-element, and in the second it is carried by a suffix. (For further remarks on *pseudo-* and *-eer*, see 13.1 below.) However, the distinction between affix and neo-classical compound-element is a useful one to make, in spite of such difficulties, and I shall go on to talk about two kinds of compounding, native and neo-classical, and two kinds of 'lexical' element, free and bound.

3.3 Particle compounds

The label 'particle' here is used for a 'core' of words which may function both as adverbs and as prepositions, and which have locative ('place at which' or 'direction to or from') meanings. Examples are *down, out, over, under.* Such words, of course, are frequently used with non-locative meanings, *cf: we talked it over* (adverbial); *they sat over their drinks* (prepositional). It is convenient to include in this group some 'peripheral' particles which do not meet both of these conditions. Among these are *with,* which may be used only as a preposition, and *back* and *forth,* which are used only as adverbs. And a few items that I shall mention among the particles meet neither condition and are quite unlike the examples just mentioned except in certain uses. Bolinger (1971, Chapter 6) points out the similarity between sentences like *he knocked the man out* and *he knocked the man cold,* or *he got away* and *he got free.* It is however the verb+adverb/ preposition combination which takes part in a productive pattern of word-formation, and not the verb+adverb/adjective one. Thus, we can speak of a *knock-out* and a *get-away,* but hardly of a *knock-cold* or a *get-free.* But it is convenient to put a few words with non-locative, adverb/ adjective second elements such as *die-hard, standstill,* with the particle compounds (see 8.2, VC below).

I shall call complex words containing particles 'compounds', although many particles are similar in meaning to prefixes, for example, *over, out, under, cf: super-, ex-, sub-.* But bound particles behave in English no differently from other prefixed elements, that is, they appear in initial position only; whereas independent ones, like 'lexical' compound-elements, may occur either initially or finally in a complex word. Compare *overstep* (verb), *walk-over* (noun); *infighting* (noun), *teach-in* (noun); *outdo* (verb), *blackout* (noun).

3.4 The constituent structure of complex words

If we 'take apart' a complex word, we must usually subtract its elements one by one in a certain order. Thus *unadventurousness* may be first broken down into the adjective *unadventurous* and the nominalizing suffix *-ness;* from the former the negative prefix may then be subtracted, leaving the adjective *adventurous,* composed of the noun *adventure* and the adjective-suffix *-ous:*

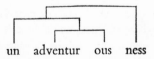

Formations which do not have this one-by-one order of elements are called parasynthetic. Examples are *extraterritorial* and *intramuscular:* in these cases, if we subtract the suffix we find that there is no word *extraterritory* or *intramuscle*; and the prefix is clearly not the outermost element, since in both words it can be seen to modify the stem only (*territory*, *muscle*). We may here think of the prefix and the suffix as being added 'simultaneously' to the stem. Sometimes a prefix and a suffix appear to form a 'partnership' and operate together as a productive pattern. Examples of such pairs are *de-* and *-ize/-ization* or *-ify/-ification*, and *un-* and *-able*. Words with these elements are not really parasynthetic, though they are sometimes so called because words containing the suffix only, such as *nazify*, *eatable*, are often less familiar than those with both prefix and suffix: *denazify*, *uneatable*.

Milk *shake* is an example of a parasynthetic compound. Its second element is a deverbal noun, but we do not use the noun *shake* in this sense outside the compound, so that the two processes, of compounding with *milk* and deriving the noun from the verb by zero suffix, may be seen as operating 'simultaneously' on the verb *shake*. Other parasynthetic compounds, of which the head elements have no independent existence are *leg-pull*, *nosebleed*, *sunset*, *break-down*, *input*. Compounds like *blockhead* and *highbrow* may also be seen as parasynthetic: *head* and *brow* exist independently, but the compounds mean 'person having (characteristics associated with) a head like a block, a high brow', so we could say that their head elements have a 'humanizing' zero suffix.

Some of these parasynthetic compounds may be described as 'exocentric'. Bloomfield (1933, 235*ff*) explains that an endocentric compound is one which functions as a whole in the same way as its head element, for example *blackbird*, which is a kind of bird. An exocentric compound is one whose function is not the same as that of its head element, for example *blockhead*, *highbrow*, *pickpocket*. An example like *break-down* is exocentric if we regard the first element as really a verb, but endocentric if we see it as a zero-derived noun. Such parasynthetic compounds, containing a zero suffix, can be called 'derivational compounds', since the processes of derivation and composition are both involved in their formation. In Chapter 5 I shall refer to them as 'derivational compounds with a zero suffix'.

Derivational compounds which are not parasynthetic are exemplified by *first-nighter*, *broken-hearted*, made up of the compound stems *first night*, *broken heart*, and the suffixes *-er*, *-ed*. In *eye-opener*, *book-binding*, on the other hand, the suffixes *-er* and *-ing* belong only to the second elements: these are therefore not derivational compounds. Complex words may sometimes allow of two different analyses: is *water-skiing*, for example, made up of *water ski+-ing*, or *water+skiing*? *Non-acceptability* may be split up into *non-* and *acceptability*, or *non-acceptable* and the noun-suffix. *Bespectacled* and *beturbaned* may be analysed as prefix+(noun-stem+adjective-suffix) or as prefixed verb+the participial *-ed*.

3.5 'Native' and 'foreign' complex words, and accentuation

A consequence of the mingling of classical and native means of word-formation in English is that the accentuation of words in English is a complicated matter. I shall deal only briefly with this topic in connection with neo-classical words, but in the case of the native compounds of Chapters 5, 6 and 8, the accent, or nucleus is indicated. A note is needed therefore about the use of the terms 'accent' and 'nucleus'.

Most writers on the sound-patterns of words use the term 'stress', but there is often confusion as to whether 'stress' means 'loudness' or, more generally, 'prominence', from whatever cause, of a syllable. Since it is by now well established that change of pitch has more power to make a syllable stand out from its neighbours than increase of loudness, the term 'stress' seems best avoided. The most prominent syllable of a word, for example the first syllable of *phótograph*, bears the nucleus, or primary accent; the third syllable has secondary accent. The second syllable, we may say, is unaccented. There are perceivable differences in prominence among secondarily accented syllables: the first syllable of *lead péncil* is more prominent than the second syllable of *bláckboard*, and this is why compounds like the former, with the nucleus on the second element, are often referred to as 'double-stressed', and those like the latter, with the nucleus on the first element, as 'single-stressed'. In the following pages the nucleus is marked with (′) over the syllable; other syllables are left unmarked. And a reference to 'accent' will always mean 'primary accent'.

The addition of a suffix to a word of classical provenance may have an effect on the placing of the accent: compare *ínstrument, instruméntal; phótograph, photógraphy, photográphic*.[3] But the tendency in English is to place the accent near the beginning of the word, or at any rate on a 'lexical' syllable, so that in our use of neo-classical words a certain amount of inconsistency has arisen. Compare the 'learned' *multíparous* (='producing many or more than one at a birth'), *multípotent* (='having power to do many things') with the more naturalized *múlticoloured, multirácial*. *Multiválent* (='having many values'), on the other hand, according to Webster (1961), is accented like *multirácial*, in contrast with the relatively familiar word *ambívalent*, in which the 'learned' accentuation has become established.

Notes

1 Words of this kind are not discussed by Jespersen in his *Modern English Grammar*, nor by Marchand (1969), who says (217) that since they are not understood as complex by the average speaker, they are of no relevance to word-formation.

2 Note that in some 'hybrid' examples the -*o*- appears to be part of the second constituent rather than the first. This has happened with a few frequently-used neoclassical elements, *cf* 'the *bureau-ocracy, shop-ocracy, trade-ocracy,* and other -*ocracies*', 'a professor of all the -*ologies*', 'galvanometers, lactometers, and other -*ometers*' [OED, s.v. -*o*, 3].

3 For accounts of these matters, see Gimson (1970, especially Chapter 9), Arnold (1957) and Kingdon (1958).

Chapter 4

Derivation by zero suffix

4.1 The concept of 'zero suffix'

We set up the 'zero suffix' because of the comparability of words like *to victimize* (noun stem + verb-suffix, = 'to make someone, treat someone like, a victim'), and *to beggar* (noun stem + no suffix, = 'to make someone a beggar'); or *to stabilize* (adjective stem + verb-suffix, = 'to make something stable'), and *to firm* (adjective stem + no suffix, = 'to make something firm'); or *driver* (verb stem + noun-suffix, = 'one who drives'), and *spy* (verb stem + no suffix, = 'one who spies'). The verb *to cage* (= 'to put someone or something into a cage') could be said to have a zero prefix, since we also have the verb *to encage*. It will be clear from the groups of examples in the following sections of this chapter that we have not one zero affix, but many, or to put it another way, one zero affix with many functions. However, since we shall be concerned with the relationship between a base word of one class and a corresponding derived word of another, and since in all but a few cases, it is the suffix rather than the prefix that indicates class membership, it is most natural to use the term 'zero suffix' where the derived word is not formally characterized as such.

There are only a few verb-forming affixes in English – *be-*, *en-*, *-ate*, *-ify*, *-ize*, so, as we might expect, the zero element plays a large role in forming verbs from both nouns and adjectives. But there are many more noun-forming affixes, some of them very productive with verb stems, such as *-ation*, *-er*, *-ment*, and we find nevertheless that zero has an important part to play in forming nouns as well. We have already noticed the derivation of nouns from adjectives by zero suffix (2.4); the derived noun in this case always has the meaning 'person or thing having the quality denoted by the adjective'. There are not many suffixes forming nouns from adjectives; they tend to be non-productive, like those in *hardship*, *merriment*, *warmth*. A notable exception is *-ness*, forming nouns meaning 'the quality denoted by the adjective', as in *wickedness*. Adjectives, as we saw also in 2.4, are only rarely formed from nouns by zero suffix, although there are various much-used suffixes that perform this function, such as *-ic*, as in *angelic* (= 'like an angel'), *cyclic* (= 'occurring in cycles'), or *-ous*, as in *poisonous* (= 'containing, having the properties of poison'), *villainous* (= 'like a villain').

The most common, and interesting, functions of the zero suffix are to make new verbs from nouns and adjectives, and new nouns from verbs. Verbs may also be formed, rarely, from words of other classes in this manner, and there are a few zero-derived nouns from particles and verb phrases. Besides being of interest in its own right, the process of zero derivation may be seen at work in a great many of the compound words of Chapters 5, 7 and 8, so that, before going on to these, it will be convenient to examine the ways in which the zero suffix may function.[1]

4.2 Historical and other considerations

A difficulty which we have to face in examining the workings of the zero suffix is that of deciding which of two derivationally related words is to be considered the base, and which the derived word. In many cases the native speaker can consult his intuition and arrive at a fairly certain decision. Everybody would agree, for instance, without needing to consult a historical dictionary, that the verbs *to carpet* (someone), *to landscape* (a garden), *to tower* (over something), *to wolf* (one's food) are derived from the nouns of the same form. Our conclusions are due partly to our perception of certain typical, and to some extent productive, patterns, to be examined below. For instance, there is a group of verbs derived from the names of animals, which mean 'behave like that animal', to which *wolf* belongs. We may also feel that a word is derived if it seems less common than its homonym. This is true of the verbs *carpet* and *landscape*.

Sometimes there is some indication in the form of a word which tells us that it is derived. *To requisition* has a characteristic nominal ending, and therefore seems to be (as historically it is) derived from the noun. Some nouns in *-ure*, such as *gesture, lecture, puncture* were borrowed from Latin nouns of action and so seem to be nominalizations of verbs; but we also have the verbs *gesture, lecture, puncture* and these must be the derived members of the pairs, since they have the characteristic nominal shape. *To blacklist* is a compound: as we shall see in Chapter 7, verb compounds are far less common than noun compounds, and verb compounds which are formed directly, by the addition of a first word to a verbal second element, are extremely rare; the great majority are formed from nominal, or adjectival compounds. *To blacklist* therefore seems, and is, undoubtedly derived from the noun *black-list*. In this example, the second element, *list*, happens to be one which is also a base noun and a derived verb. But *to whitewash* is clearly derived from the noun of the same form, although *to wash* is not derived from the noun *wash*. Other examples of verb compounds derived from noun compounds having second elements which are nouns derived from verbs, are *to foxtrot, to nosedive*. The fact that we know the second elements of the noun compounds as verb-to-noun words does not affect our judgment with regard to the compound-pairs, since the verb-compound pattern is a strong indicator of 'derivedness'.

Two-syllabled verb and noun pairs of Romance origin often differ in accentuation. The verb preserves the French accentual pattern, with the nucleus on the second syllable, while the noun has a 'shifted' nucleus on the first syllable. Examples are *to combíne, a cómbine; to invíte, an ínvite; to prodúce, próduce*. Accentuation on the first syllable in such nouns may therefore contribute to a feeling that they are derived. (We need not of course consider those cases where difference of meaning makes the question of derivation irrelevant, as with *to incénse, íncense; to objéct, óbject*.) But the noun is not always the derived member of the pair: the verb *to segmént*, for instance, is derived from the noun *ségment*. And many pairs are not differentiated by accent: *cómbat, cómment, cóntact, prócess* are accented on the first syllable whether they are nouns or verbs; *debáte, concérn, rebúke, regrét, retúrn* are always accented on the second syllable. We may feel that the verbs of the first group are derived, since they have the typical accentual pattern of nouns, but in the case of the second group it is hard to decide one way or the other.

If both intuition and formal indications fail us, we may appeal to historical evidence. Historical records, however, may not be complete enough to be reliable. The noun *worship*, for instance, existed in Old English and the verb is first recorded in about 1200, but the latter may have been in the language from a much earlier date. The noun and verb *chase* were borrowed almost simultaneously from Old French (*chace, chasser*). Words like *sting* and *support* present a problem: *sting*, verb and noun, dates from Old English, *support*, verb and noun, from the fourteenth century. The oldest sense of the noun in both these pairs is that of 'the action denoted by the verb'; the 'object' senses developed later. Should we then consider *sting* (1398, = 'sharp-pointed organ') and *support* (1594, = 'prop', 'stay') to be derived from the verbs, or are they really derivatives of the action noun, and so irrelevant to a discussion of verb-to-noun patterns?

Cases where a number of senses have developed may also present difficulty. The noun *libel* (1297) clearly preceded the verb (1570). But the noun changed in meaning from 'formal document' (1297) through its use in law for 'document of a plaintiff' (1340), to 'pamphlet publicly circulated, especially one defaming the character of someone' (1521), and hence to 'any false or defamatory statement' (1618). The evidence in the OED suggests that the corresponding verb = 'to spread defamation' (1570), hence, 'to accuse falsely or maliciously' should be considered the base and the noun, in the sense in which we now use it, the derivative. The case of *shadow* is clearer: noun and verb both existed in Old English, the verb meaning 'to cover with shadow'. The sense 'to follow (a person) like a shadow' is clearly derived from the noun since it did not appear until 1602. The OED's evidence for *whistle* is puzzling: the noun (= 'instrument') existed in Old English, the corresponding verb dates from the sixteenth century; on the other hand, the verb (= 'to make a sound with the lips') is Old English and the corresponding noun appeared in the fifteenth century. *Level* is complicated by the fact that a noun, an adjective, and a verb of this form exist. According to the OED, the noun appeared first, in the fourteenth century, the verb next in the fifteenth century, and the adjective finally, in the sixteenth. The verb and the adjective therefore are probably derivatives of the noun; but the sense of the verb *to level*: 'to make (a surface) level' fits very well into the adjective-to-verb group (4.4 below), and it seems very likely that its use was quite early encouraged by the existence of the adjective.

Where a noun and verb are recorded as first occurring rather close to one another in time, we often cannot regard historical evidence as carrying much weight. It is likely in such cases that the accident of one word appearing in a manuscript or book before the other, or of the lexicographer happening to notice one word before the other, has obscured the true state of affairs. Clearly, *to bicycle* (1869) can be regarded as derived from *bicycle* (1868); *to guillotine* (1794) from *guillotine* (1793); *to ski* (1893) from *ski* (1885); but with earlier pairs the dates of first occurrence may be misleading. The OED indeed occasionally disregards them, as with *clown*: the verb is first attested in 1599, the noun in 1600, but the verb is stated to be the derivative. This seems reasonable, since it fits in well with the group of derived verbs meaning 'to behave like the person denoted by the noun' (IC 2 below).

Our intuitions in these matters are not easy to account for, but when historical evidence and intuition are in conflict with one another, we are led to ask whether history is really relevant to a discussion of productive patterns, since it may cause us to set up groups based on patterns which we might feel do not represent the way in which derivation works. Thus, some of the noun-to-verb examples in I A iii – *campaign, crusade, duel, journey, queue* – might fit more comfortably into the verb-to-noun section, under the heading of 'object/result of the action denoted by the verb'. It may happen on the other hand that a word has been derived according to a still productive pattern, but that the base word has come to be used less frequently than the derived one. We may then perceive the process as having operated in the other direction. The verb *to crowd*, for instance (= 'of persons, to gather closely so as to press upon one another'), looks similar to the noun-to-verb examples just mentioned. It appeared in 1400 (in Old English, its ancestor, *crūdan*, meant 'to press, push, thrust'). The corresponding noun dates from 1567. But without this historical knowledge, we might assume that the verb is the derived word, just as *to queue* is derived from *queue*. The noun *goad* may look like an example of an 'instrumental' nominalization of the verb, similar to examples under III B 2 below, such as *hoist, catch* (of a door), and this is how Marchand (1969, 376) sees it. The noun in fact existed in Old English, and the verb appeared in 1619; it fits into the Instrumental derived verb pattern, like *brake, bomb, screw* (ID 1 below). The noun *cook* looks like an agentive nominalization of the verb, *cf: cheat, spy* (III A below), and Marchand so classifies it. Again, it is Old English, and the verb did not appear until 1380. *To cook* is like the derived verbs of I C 1 below, such as *captain, father, ie* 'to take on the role denoted by the noun'.

In cases like *crowd, cook* and *goad*, the historical evidence is clear enough, and we may choose to regard it as settling the issue; but with many other related pairs it seems arbitrary to decide either way. Which of the following, for example, should be considered the base: *to stitch, a stitch; to wound, a wound; to chain, a chain*? Historical evidence indicates that the verbs in the *stitch* and *chain* pairs are probably derived: *to stitch* appears in Early Middle English, the noun is attested in Old English; *to chain* appears in the late fourteenth century, the noun at the beginning of that century (but both verbal and nominal forms existed in Old French). *Wund* and *wundian* existed in Old English, the verb having presumably been, at some stage, derived from the noun. All three may be considered as deverbal nouns on the ground that the noun is the 'object or result of the action'; in the case of *chain* it is 'instrumental' (*cf* III B 2 ii). And all three may be accommodated in noun-to-verb groups: *to stitch* = 'to produce the object/entity denoted by the noun' (I A ii), *cf: knot, pattern; to wound* = 'to give, provide with, inflict, what the noun denotes' (ID 2), *cf: hole, puncture, scar; to chain* = 'to perform an action by means of what the noun denotes' (ID 1), *cf: padlock, rope, strap.* In cases of this kind we have to accept the fact that the historical development of English has left us with loose ends that cannot always be tied into neat schemes.[2]

For a number of the following examples, conclusive historical evidence cannot be given, but I have not included any for which the historical evidence is clearly contradictory. The important question for us is of course not what happened historically, but what are the patterns on which new nouns and verbs may *now* be formed by zero suffix. Thus, *to man* is considered to be derived from the noun, though both noun and verb are Old English; *to people* is treated as derived (it actually did appear later than the noun in English), though both noun and verb existed in Old French and the verb may be a borrowing of Old French *peupler.* But *to police*, a clear case historically of noun-to-verb derivation, is a nineteenth-century coinage, and supports the existence of an intuitively-perceived pattern: noun ('entity, group of persons')→verb ('to provide with, furnish with, what the noun denotes'), which has come into being through the accumulation over a few hundred years of a sufficient number of pairs like *man* and *people.*

It will be obvious that many examples given below have metaphorical senses. In some cases, for example *to catapult,* ID 1, I have made a comment; in others I have not, for example *to axe,* ID 1, = 'to sack' as well as 'to use an axe on', *cf* 'Mr Heath is expected to axe some [ministers]' [*Evening Standard* 15 October 1971, 1/1–2].

The examples for whose derived nature there is clear support, historical or formal, are in roman type; the others are in italics.[3]

4.3 Noun to verb

I A *The noun is the object in a paraphrase sentence*
Examples of this kind fall into small groups according to the kind of verb which would be appropriate in such a sentence.

I A i Intransitive verbs meaning 'to hunt, catch, pick, collect'

fish (*cf: John catches, or seeks to catch, fish,*   blackberry
compliments, etc)[a]
fowl
whale

[a] In the extended (transitive) sense, *cf: John fished an old boot out of the river,* this verb belongs under I C 3 below.

IAii Intransitive verbs meaning 'to produce, make, give birth to, the entity denoted by the noun'

bloom	foal	echo	*coin*
bud	lamb	*foam*	knot
flower	litter	*lather*	pattern
seed	whelp	*smoke*	tunnel
		steam	
gesture	*joke*	*thunder*	
grimace	scheme		
	wisecrack		

IAiii Intransitive verbs meaning 'to perform the action implied in the noun'

campaign	*journey*	queue
crusade	motion	race
duel	orbit	view
file	*parade*	

IAiv Intransitive verbs meaning 'to play the instrument denoted by the noun (or to make a noise as if playing it)'

bugle	*harp*
drum	*pipe*
fiddle	trumpet
flute	whistle

IAv Verbs meaning 'to feel, experience, suffer, what the noun denotes'

[*a*] transitive

experience	pity

[*b*] intransitive

hunger	panic
lust	*thirst*

IAvi Transitive verbs meaning 'to copy', 'to produce a representation or simulacrum of someone or something'

caricature	parody
copy	picture
echo	*photograph*
mimic	silhouette[a]
model (*eg* in clay)	

[a] As the OED observes, this verb is chiefly used in the *-ed* form, followed by a preposition, *cf: silhouetted against the sky.*

IB *The noun is the indirect object in a paraphrase sentence*
Verbs in this group are transitive.

beggar (*cf: John makes Bill a beggar*)	cash
	chronicle
cripple	feature
fool	*heap*
knight	parcel
martyr	*phrase*
orphan	*pile*
outlaw	structure
widow	wreck

IC *The noun is the complement in a paraphrase sentence*

IC1 Transitive verbs meaning 'to take on the role denoted by the noun'

captain (*cf: John is the captain . . .*)	tailor
chaperon	tutor
father	umpire
pilot	witness
rival	

IC2 Verbs meaning 'to behave in the manner of, to act as, to resemble, the person, animal or object denoted by the noun'. This group is closely related to IC1; some examples represent extensions of IC1 senses, others have been formed without this mediation. Note the difference between *to father a child* (= 'to be, become, the father') and *to mother a child* (= 'to act in the manner of a mother').

[*a*] transitive

(i) verbs from human nouns

boss	lord (it)	shepherd
butcher	master	usher
doctor	mother	
dwarf	queen (it)	

(ii) verbs from animal nouns

ape	pig (it)
dog	squirrel (= 'to hoard')[b]
ferret (out)[a]	wolf
hog	worm (one's way), (something out of
parrot	someone)

[a] This verb was originally 'instrumental', from 'to hunt with ferrets', *cf* ID.[4]
[b] *Cf* 'I have not . . . squirrelled away all the precious data of these seventy vols' [*Sunday Times* 10 October 1971, 35/1–2].

(iii) verbs from inanimate nouns

bridge	head[a] (as in *he headed the*
cushion	*expedition*)
flood	shadow
ghost (= 'to write for and in the	*shield*
name of another')	snow[b]
	spirit (something away)

[a] *Head* might be considered to be from a human noun (*head (man)*), and placed under (i) above.

[b] This verb is usually used in the passive, *cf: snowed under by . . .*

[*b*] intransitive

(i) verbs from human nouns

bum (around)	slave
clown	soldier (on)
fool (around)	star[a]

[a] This verb is from the transferred, 'human' sense, = 'performer of the chief role'.

(ii) verbs from animal nouns

chicken (out of)	monkey (with)
clam (up)	snake
horse (around)	

(iii) verbs from inanimate nouns

balloon	rocket
cannonball (into someone)	snowball (= 'to grow as fast as a
cave (in)	snowball')
fork	spiral
jack-knife	sponge (on someone) (= 'to live in
mushroom (= 'to grow as fast	a parasitic manner')
as a mushroom')	tail (off)
ooze	tower (up), (over something)

IC3 Transitive verbs meaning 'to cause something to be, resemble, the object denoted by the noun' or 'to treat something like the noun'

badger[a]	riddle
honeycomb	sandwich
landscape	telescope
purse (one's lips)	treasure

[a] This verb once meant 'to bait someone or something as one baits a badger'.

Verbs in this group frequently appear in participial forms, *cf* 'the lime-stone country hereabouts is honeycombed with caves and grottoes'; 'leisure is not something sandwiched into the wee hours'; 'the front and end cars that took the shock were telescoped' [illustrations from Webster (1961)].

ID *Instrumental*

ID1 Verbs meaning 'to perform an action by means of what the noun denotes'

[*a*] transitive

axe (*cf: John fells the tree with an axe*)

brake	blue-pencil
cart	*bomb*
hammer	catapult (= 'to shoot something with a
ink	catapult')
mirror	gas
nail	guillotine
sandpaper	knife
screw	plague
soft-soap	shell
x-ray	stone

blanket	elbow	*ransom*
fence	eye	signal
handcuff	face	subpoena
padlock	finger	veto
ring	paw	
rope	voice	
strap		

[*b*] intransitive

bicycle
catapult (in the metaphorical sense: 'to move as if impelled by a catapult')
labour
ski
steam (as in *the boat steamed into the harbour, ie: was propelled by steam*)
toboggan

ID2 It is difficult to differentiate this group clearly from the preceding one. A verb like *to salt* (below) is classed as 'instrumental', since it is derived from the noun *salt*, which we can put into a sentence like *John seasons the food with salt*. We can also say however *John puts salt on the food*. The verbs in the group which follows all have the meaning 'to give, provide with, apply, the substance or entity denoted by the noun', but most of them could also be placed in ID 1. Similarly, *to handcuff* (above) means 'to put handcuffs on someone' as well as 'to shackle someone with handcuffs'.

[*a*] transitive

dust	*arm*	*man*
grease	finance	*people*
plaster	fuel	police
powder	*house*	
roughcast	label	
salt	mask	hole
shower	*name*	puncture
sugar	*saddle*	scar
tar and feather	shelter	terrace[a]
wax		*wound*
benefit	inconvenience	
discipline	safeguard	
ease	service	

[a] *Terrace* is possibly derived via *terraced*, noun + adjective-suffix, = 'having terraces', re-interpreted as a past participle (*cf* 2.6 above).[5]

[*b*] intransitive

age	coal
cloud	silt (up)

We may notice with some of these Instrumental examples, and also with some examples in the following, Locative, section, that a 'purpose' element is involved. *To arm* someone is not simply 'to supply with arms'; it implies 'for the purpose of attack or defence'; *to cage* something (below) is 'to put it into a cage for the purpose of confining it'. However, I have not set up a 'purpose' group of derived verbs, since this element of meaning seems to have a rather accidental or contingent nature. *To mask*, for instance, has various uses: it may mean simply 'to cover', 'to conceal from view by means of a "mask"', as in *trees masked the house*, or it may mean 'to conceal for the purpose of deception', as in *the thieves masked their faces*, or 'for the purpose of protection', as in *gas-mask*. All these uses are 'instrumental', but the first, unlike the second and third, has no 'purpose' component. *Cf* the remarks on 'purpose' in 5.2 below.

IE *Locative*

IE1 Verbs meaning 'to put someone or something, or to be in, go (in)to, the place, container, denoted by the noun'

[*a*] transitive

air	carpet	ground
bed	cloister	land
book	cocoon	list
bottle	corner	pocket
cage	cradle	table
can	floor	

[*b*] intransitive

centre (on)
coast (= 'to sail by or along the coast')[a]

hole (up in)
land
surface (= 'rise to the surface')

[a] This verb is usually in participial form, as in *coasting vessel*.

IE2 Verbs meaning 'to perform some activity in, and appropriate to, the place, container, denoted by the noun'

[*a*] transitive
bath
chair
field (= 'to stop and return a ball', as in a cricket match)
market[a]
school[a] (as in *he schooled himself to control his temper*)
stage

[a] *Market* and *school* have, strictly speaking, lost their locative meanings and may be defined respectively as 'sell' and 'control, teach'.

[*b*] intransitive
field (= 'to play the fielding role', as in cricket; *cf: Lancashire fielded first*)
garden
shop
yacht (= 'to sail in a yacht')[a]

[a] This verb is usually found in non-finite form, *eg: to go yachting, yachting-cap*.

IE3 Intransitive verbs meaning 'to spend, pass, the period of time denoted by the noun'

holiday	weekend
honeymoon	winter
vacation	

IF *Transitive verbs meaning 'to remove the object denoted by the noun from someone or something'*

bone	*milk*
brain	scalp
dust	skin
fleece (='to remove the fleece from', hence 'to strip of money or property by fraud or extortion')	top and tail
	weed
gut	

IG *Other*

A few examples are hard to classify. The verb *to moon* means 'to wander aimlessly'; it is clearly derived from the noun *moon*, and the OED indicates that *moonstruck* (1674), descriptive of the dazed condition supposed to be caused by the moon, may have had something to do with its coining. *To inch* means 'to proceed gradually (by inches)'. A small group is formed by verbs of 'measuring': *to fathom* (='to reckon the number of fathoms', hence metaphorically 'to get to the bottom of'); *to number* (='to reckon the number of', as well as 'to give numbers to', *cf* ID 2 [*a*]); *to price* (='to ask, calculate the price of', *cf* 'When I pass Northwest Orient Airlines, I always mean to price a ticket to Tokyo' [Saul Bellow, *Herzog* 1964, Penguin 1965, 180], as well as 'to set a price on'); *to sum* (='to calculate the sum of'); *to time* (='to calculate the time which something takes', as well as 'to do something at an appropriate time', *cf: John timed his arrival nicely*); *to total* (='to reckon the total number of').

In other cases, semantic change has made the question of derivational relationship irrelevant. The senses of the noun and verb *fashion* have drifted so far apart that they have now no real connection with one another. The verb *to fashion* (='to form, shape, something') was derived from a sense of the noun no longer in use, 'the form, shape of a thing'. The noun *fashion* (='vogue') must be considered merely a homonym of the verb.

4.4 Adjective to verb

Verbs derived from adjectives fall into three groups; they are few in number compared with verbs from nouns.

As Marchand observes (1969, 371), the only verbs from compound adjectives appear to be those ending in *-proof*: *to waterproof*, etc. It is noticeable that not one of the examples of compound adjectives in Chapter 6 seems at all acceptable or even possible as a verb.

II A *Intransitive verbs meaning 'to be, become, the quality denoted by the adjective'*

bald[a]	*pale*
dim	*slim*
idle	*sour*
mellow	*tense*

[a] *Bald* is usually found only in non-finite forms, as in *a balding pate.*

II B *Transitive verbs meaning 'to cause someone or something to be, become, the quality denoted by the adjective'*

bare	dirty	*right*
better (oneself)	*dry*	smooth
blind	*free*	*still*
blunt	humble	tame
busy (oneself)	ready	*warm*

Many verbs may belong to both these groups, for example

clear	*slow*
cool	sober (up)
empty	*weary*
narrow	

II C *Verbs expressing the manner in which an action is performed*

[a] transitive

brave	rough (it), (out a plan)
brazen (something out)	savage
gentle	*shrill*[a]
jolly (someone along)	

[a] *Cf* 'headlines have shrilled disquieting news' [illustration from Webster (1961)].

[b] intransitive

level (with someone) (= 'to be honest with . . .')
shy

Verbs in this group may be compared with the Instrumental examples under ID1[*a*]; *to labour* (='to move or work laboriously, by means of labour, 'strenuous effort') is placed in that group, since the noun is homonymous with it, not the adjective; whereas *to savage* (='to act savagely, by means of savagery') is placed here because in this case the adjective, not the noun, has the same form as the verb.

4.5 Verbs from other sources

A few verbs come from interjections, such as *encore, hurrah, shoo. To near* and *to further* are from adverbs, and the following are from particles: *to down* (tools), *to round* (on someone), (the corner), *to out, to up.* For the last two of these, Jespersen (MEG VI, 6.9₂) gives various illustrations, among them the following: 'I could not out with the truth'; 'I outs into the street'; 'I up and ran'; 'Why don't you up and run?'; 'I upped and said . . .'. The first illustration for *out* and the first two for *up* look more like ellipted forms of 'come out with', 'got (get) up'. *Out* and *up* seem to be genuine verbs only in the 'I outs' and 'I upped' examples. They may be used transitively in phrases such as *to up prices, to out someone* (*eg* from office).

Jespersen (MEG VI, 6.8₆) gives numerous examples of nonce 'quotation' verbs, for example 'but me no buts'; 'She neither sir'd nor my-lorded him'. *Cf* also ' "Ross said you were an impertinent ——. You'll impertinent your way right out of here before long" ' [Len Deighton, *The Ipcress File* 1962, Panther 1964, 49].

4.6 Verb to noun

Three main groups of zero-derived nouns from verbs may be distinguished, within which are various subgroups. They are those in which the noun denotes the agent of the action expressed by the verb, the concrete object or result of the action, and the abstract result of the action.

A note is needed here about the terms 'abstract' and 'concrete'. Some writers interpret the latter as 'tangible', and use the term 'abstract object' for such nouns as *upset* (III B 2 ii below). I have used 'concrete' in the sense in which Webster (1961) defines it: 'characterized by immediate experience of realities, whether physical things, sensations or emotions: belonging to or standing for actual things or events.' 'Concrete' therefore includes all count nouns. But *John's attack on Fred was unexpected* permits of an 'abstract' interpretation of *attack, ie: we didn't expect John to attack Fred; cf: he returned to the attack, ie: to attacking. . . . John's attack was a vicious one* may be 'concretely' interpreted to refer to an event: here *attack* is a count noun. Similarly, *John's surprise was obvious, ie: it was obvious that John was surprised*, is 'abstract', *cf: to John's surprise; but he had a surprise*, where *surprise* is a count noun, is 'concrete'.

III A *Agent of action*

[*a*] from transitive verbs

bootblack[a]   hunt (= 'persons engaged in
cheat   hunting')
home help[a]   *spy*
                                chimney sweep[a]

[a] *Black* in *bootblack* is of course from a verb which is derived from an adjective. These compound examples are included for the sake of their second elements: it is not suggested that they are derived from compound verbs.

[*b*] from intransitive verbs

drop-out   look-out
flirt   *rebel*
go-between   sneak
lay-about   *stray*

III B *Concrete object/result of action*

III B 1 Object of action: from transitive verbs

command (= 'ship', 'that which   eats[b]
   one commands')[a]   jigsaw puzzle
drink

[a] *Cf* 'I asked myself what I was to do there, now my boat was lost. As a matter of fact, I had plenty to do in fishing my command out of the river' [Joseph Conrad, *Heart of Darkness*, 1902, Dent 1946, 73].
[b] A noun *eat* (*æt*, = 'food', 'that which is eaten') existed in Old English.

III B 2 Concrete object/result of action

(i)[*a*] from transitive verbs

catch (of fish, etc)   reject
find   spit
hand-out   spread (= 'feast', 'that which is
import   spread')
kill   *suspect*
meet (= 'meeting of hounds   write-up
   and men in preparation
   for a hunt')

[b] from intransitive verbs

cough	smile
limp	whine
sigh	whisper

The verbs of 'saying' involved here may of course be used transitively, but I have regarded them as primarily intransitive.

(ii) instrumental: from transitive verbs

catch (*cf: John fastens the door by means of the catch*)	permit
	polish
cure (= 'medicine')	make-up
cover	bell-pull
hoist	refill
invite	*sting*
lift	*upset*

(iii) locative

[a] from transitive verbs

dump (= 'place where refuse, etc is dumped')	haunt

[b] from intransitive verbs

hide-out	*retreat*
lounge	bus stop
pass (= 'break in a mountain-range')	

III B 3 Concrete result of action: single instance or occasion
Examples of this kind typically, though not necessarily, occur following verbs like *give, have, make, take*, and are preceded by the indefinite article.[6]

give a	*cry*	shudder
	grunt	start
	howl	tug
	laugh	wriggle
have a	look	prowl
	think	ride
		swim
		try

make a *dash*
      dive
      move

take a look   stroll
        peep   turn

The examples have been chosen to illustrate the frequency with which verbs of perceiving, of sound and of movement occur in these frames. Verbs with other meanings are also found:

have a rest   make a guess
       smoke   an offer
       wash

Some nonce examples of deverbal nouns in this group appear only as complement to a verb like *have, give, make, take, cf: may I have a borrow of your pen, come and have a listen to this.*

III C *Abstract result of action*

Many of the following examples also have 'concrete result' or 'object' senses, which should be carefully distinguished from the intended abstract ones. In the main, only true abstracts have the property of being either 'subjective' or 'objective', though there are exceptions to this.[7]

III C1 subjective

[a] from transitive verbs

acclaim (*cf: John acclaims . . .; John's acclaim of . . .*)
attack   employ (*cf: in John's employ*)
command   *need*
desire   resolve
dislike

[b] from intransitive verbs

advance   come-back
collapse   *decay*

III C2 objective: from transitive verbs

defeat (*cf: John defeats Fred; Fred's defeat*)
disgust   *surprise*
dismay

IIIC3 subjective/objective: from transitive verbs

aid (*cf: John aids Fred; John's aid to Fred; John comes to Fred's aid*)

arrest	*rebuff*
award	reprieve
murder	*rescue*
praise	*support*

IIID *Miscellaneous phrases*
There are a number of more or less fixed phrases involving zero-derived nouns of various kinds. Examples are:

to be in a (great) *hurry, rush*, sweat
to catch (get) hold (of)
to make *amends*
to be on the boil, the go, the *increase*, the make, the mend, the move, the run, the wane
to be in the know, the swim
to give someone the go-by, the push, the slip, the creeps

4.7 Nouns from other sources

A very few nouns are from particles:

down (= 'grudge', *cf: to have a down on someone*)
in (= 'influence', 'pull', *cf: to have an in*)
out (= 'way out of a difficulty')

A few nouns are from phrases containing verbs, such as *also-ran, has-been, know-how, forget-me-not*.

Notes

1 On this subject, see Jespersen (MEG VI, Chapters 6 and 7, and Marchand (1969), Chapter 5).

2 See Marchand (1963) and (1964) for interesting discussions of ways to determine the direction of derivation in words of this sort. He considers that history is entirely irrelevant, and seeks to account for intuition and to find non-historical justification for decisions where intuition fails. I do not think that all his criteria are successful, and some of the groups set up above actually contradict them. He says for instance (1964, 14), 'Of two homophonous words . . . the one with the smaller field of reference is the derivative', but we see in IC2 for example, that verbs formed from nouns characteristically appear in a greater variety of contexts than those nouns. A *shepherd* looks after sheep only, but one may *shepherd* many other creatures.

3 Many nouns and verbs with the same stem, and some adjectives and verbs, existed together in Old English, the verbs subsequently losing their infinitive endings, for example *bedd, beddian*, 'bed', *pipe, pipian*, 'pipe', *æmetig, geæmtigian*, 'empty'. Most of the verbs mentioned above, which existed in Old English and had corresponding nouns or adjectives, had infinitives in *-ian*. This ending indicates that they were derived at some stage, perhaps before the Old English period, from the nouns or adjectives. But since the derivation took place at a period so remote from the present, I shall not use this evidence as strong support for placing a word in a noun-to-verb group.

4 See OED, and Jespersen (MEG VI 6.7$_9$).

5 Jespersen (MEG VI 6.7$_3$) suggests that some denominal verbs may have arisen in this way.

6 See Rensky (1964) for a discussion of phrases of this kind. Not all such phrases, as he points out, involve derived nouns. The derivation goes the other way in *make a fool* (of)→*to fool*.

7 See Jespersen (MEG V, Chapter 7) for a discussion of nouns and nominalizations of this kind, and the conditions under which ambiguity may occur. Some nouns which we cannot consider as derived (in English), and which may also behave in this way are *capture, custody, memory, photograph, present, ruin, story*.

Chapter 5

Noun compounds

5.1 Compounds and noun phrases

A noun may be premodified by another noun, an adjective or participle, or a nominalization. The resulting sequence may be a free phrase or it may be a compound, in which the premodifying element has lost its independence. If we wish to decide whether the sequences *small talk* and *wet day*, for example, are compounds, we may apply tests to find out whether the first elements are separable from the heads (*cf* the discussion of 'the word' in 1.3 and 1.4 above). Can the adjective be premodified by an adverb? We can say *very wet day*, but not *very small talk;* can it assume the comparative form? *Wetter day* is possible, but not *smaller talk*. Can it occupy the predicative position in a sentence with the head noun as subject? *The day is wet* makes sense, but not *the talk is small*. We can safely conclude that *small talk* is a compound, but that *wet day* is a free phrase. Usually it will be found that institutionalized combinations behave like *small talk* and those which are not habitual collocations are like *wet day*, but this is not always so. *Good (bad) loser* and *good shot*, for example, are well enough established to be felt as compounds in spite of the acceptability of *very bad loser, very good shot*. On the whole however, these tests are reliable in separating sequences that we would like to think of as compounds from those which we feel are free phrases. And usually when we come across an adjective – noun compound in which the first element is premodified on its own account the phrase strikes us as odd; *cf: recognizably human beings* in the following: 'A novel in which recognizably human beings revolve in the world of big business' [*Observer* 19 January 1968, 34/3]. This is clearly an idiosyncratic usage, a blend of *recognizably human* and *human beings*.

If the first element of a nominal sequence is nominal, we can similarly test whether it will take a modifier on its own account. The oddity of *wooden door way, outer door knob, rare book case* may be compared with *narrow door way, brass door knob, mahogany book case.* In the first set of examples, the first element is an appropriate modifier of the second; in the second set it is appropriate to the final element. *Door way, door knob, book case* are seen to be compounds, since we feel that their first elements cannot be modified independently of their heads. Such tests however are not always very helpful. [[*Confirmed bachelor*] *uncle*] and [[*generous*] *bachelor uncle*]; [[*stone pine*] *tree*] and [[*tall*] *pine tree*] are all normal-looking expressions, though in the second example of each pair the noun–noun sequence is premodified as a whole, and in the first the attributive noun alone is modified. And it is perfectly possible to use sequences in which the constituent structure is ambiguous. Is *front door step* to be understood as compound+head noun, or adjective+compound head noun, or is it a telescoping of the sequences *front door, door step,* and possibly *front step*? And compare *car seat belt,* or *sex film club:* 'Their application for possession was contested by the tenant ... who was said to have sub-let part of the premises which was used as a "sex film club" ' [*Evening Standard* 19 February 1970, 1/5].

There is then no easy answer, covering all cases, to the question of 'what is a compound'. In this chapter I have been fairly liberal in including collocations which I felt were to some degree established, and therefore candidates for inclusion in the category. Some of my examples may not be compounds for all readers, but since any attributive-head noun group is potentially a compound and will come to be felt as one if it happens to be used often enough, it is as well not to be too arbitrary in deciding one way or the other. Compound-status can be seen as a matter of degree: *fine art* for instance, is undoubtedly a compound: *very fine art* is not an acceptable phrase. Some speakers might find it possible to add an intensifier to the first element of *fine feathers. Fine point* is more like a free phrase, since *that's a very fine point* sounds normal, even though some speakers might hesitate over *a finer point.* And there is no doubt that *fine sand* is a free phrase.

Compounds may be identified as such by certain other features which may distinguish them from free phrases. Jespersen observes (MEG II, 7.11) that in initial elements of compounds, 'the singular as a rule is used even if the idea is plural'. It is perhaps better to say that the first elements in compounds, for example, *hop-picking* (='the picking of hops'), *tear gas* (='gas which causes tears'), *tooth decay* (='decay of teeth') are grammatically neutral rather than singular. (Notice that this neutrality occurs in stems of complex words generally, *cf: gutless* (='without guts'), *stony* (ground) (='having stones').) It is not always the plural marker that is absent from a first element. In *pigtail* we could say that a genitive *'s* is missing: the corresponding free phrase (with a different meaning) is *pig's tail*. And in *watchdog, workman*, the first words are verbal without verbal endings (cf 'dog that watches', 'watching dog'; 'working man'). Structures like *watchdog*, in which the neutral first elements are verbal, are undoubtedly compounds, since an uninflected verb cannot, except as a kind of citation, as in the '*go*' *signal*, appear as the premodifier of a noun. But where the first element is nominal, its neutrality is not conclusive evidence that it is a compound-element, since nouns in attributive position are in any case often uninflected, cf: *a five-day week, a left-wing plot*.[1] And there are many combinations that we should like to call compounds, whose first elements are not neutral in form, such as *cat's meat, weeping willow, acquired taste*.

Spelling is an unreliable criterion of compound status, since usage varies a good deal. Compounds may be written as one word, as two hyphenated words, or as two separate words, sometimes regardless of the degree of unity that may be felt between the elements. In the following sections I have not adopted any coherent principle as regards spelling, but I have tried where possible to adopt what I feel to be the prevalent usage. In fact, the reader will notice some correlation between accentuation on the first element, and closeness of the two elements in spelling. Compare group IB1, most of whose members have the accent on the second word and are printed with unhyphenated spaces, with, for example, group IA1, most of whose members have the accent on the first word and are printed solid or hyphenated.

Accent is sometimes helpful in deciding whether a noun phrase is a compound. Many compounds are distinguished from free phrases by having the nucleus on the first element. Compare the two examples *bóttleneck, cátgut*, with the phrases *bottle's néck, cat's gút*. In established noun phrases which are used frequently and over a period of time, the nucleus tends to shift from the second element to the first; but this does not always happen. Compounds of certain patterns invariably have the nucleus on the first element (henceforth referred to as compound-accent), for instance verb–object compounds of the pattern verb-*ing*-noun: *chéwing-gum, drínking-water* (IIA1); and all derivational compounds with a zero suffix, for instance *spóonbill* (VIIA2), *bíghead* (IXAb), *húnchback* (IXD3a). Others, like the adjective–noun kind, may have either compound- or phrase-accent. Thus we have *hótbed*, but *hot wár, híghlight*, but *high tréason, cóld cream* but *cold wár, cómmon room* but *common cóld*. Compounds of the participial adjective–noun kind, like *minced méat, inverted cómma, split inf ínitive*, always have phrase-accent.

Some scholars (for instance, Lees 1960 and Marchand 1969) have used the criterion of accentuation on the first element to define the compound; and since compounds are often composed of items which have come together as a result of custom, the two features of 'compound-accent' and 'permanence' may be linked by implication. But, as we have just seen, well-established combinations may be accented as phrases; combinations of the most transient kind, on the other hand, may have compound-accent. *Cf: éscalator-napping* (a compound of the Locative VIC1 group, see below) in the following: 'The senor says ... "If I come across an escalator I lie down, close my eyes and try to guess when the end will come. ..." ... Senor Lobos said ... he is in the import and export business. Escalator napping is just a hobby' [*Evening Standard* 5 May 1971, 5/3].

In some cases, the placing of the accent seems to be dictated by the need to express a contrast. *Wár crime* is a particular kind of crime, *Súnday school* is a particular kind of school, and accordingly, the emphasis in both cases is on the contrasting first element; in *midnight sún*, on the other hand, no contrast is implied, or accentually expressed, since there is only one sun. However, we find *cottage chéese, mountain ásh*, which, since they denote a particular kind of cheese and a particular kind of ash, we might have expected to have accented first elements.

In many cases usage is divided, as with *easy chair* (IX A a), *ice cream* (IX D 3). In the following sections, examples like these are marked with an obelisk (†) following the word.

5.2 Classifying noun compounds

Compounds composed of an adjective followed by a noun are readily distinguishable as a class, though they are not homogeneous in structure; compounds which contain a verbal element linked to a nominal one which is in the relation of subject or direct object to it are also easy enough to identify. *Working man* for instance, is obviously 'a man who works', a verb+subject compound, and *eating-apple* is unambiguously 'an apple which one can eat', a verb+object compound. Compounds containing a verbal element and a nominal one which is not in a subject or direct-object relation to it, like *living-room, pitchfork*, and compounds made up of two nouns, such as *fruit-cake, garden party, bull-ring*, are the ones which present difficulty to the classifier. Two ways of tackling the problem are exemplified in Jespersen (MEG VI, Chapter 8) and Lees (1960, Chapter 4).

Jespersen sets up semantic categories: in *garden party*, the first element indicates the place of the second; in *night train* it denotes the time; in *beehive* and *keyhole* it denotes the purpose, in *handwriting* the instrument, and in *needle-fish* resemblance. In *sand-paper* and *mountain range* it represents something contained in, and characterizing the head element. Jespersen points out that this scheme still leaves him with 'a large residue of compounds which do not fit in anywhere' (8.2$_2$); some 'unclassifiable' examples which he gives are *sunflower, sun-dial, life-boat, conscience money*.

Lees dispenses as far as possible with semantic categories.[2] He extends the principle on which subject–verb and verb–object compounds are classified to all the others, so that *living-room* can be called a 'verb–prepositional object' compound, since the relations of its constituents are the same as they are in the sentence *John lives in the room; pitchfork* would be of the same type, *cf: John pitches hay with the fork. Fruit-cake* can be classified as a 'subject–object' compound, on the basis of *the cake contains fruit, garden party* as a 'subject–prepositional object' compound, *cf: the party is in the garden,* and *bull-ring* as an 'object–prepositional object compound', *cf: John fights bulls in the ring.*

This scheme has its disadvantages. One of them is that it results in the placing together of compounds which one intuitively feels are rather different from one another. The 'subject–object' category for instance would contain *fruit-cake, fruit bat* (*cf: the bat eats fruit*) and *fruit juice* (*cf: the fruit yields juice*). Another is that it separates compounds which we feel are similar in an important respect, such as *garden party* ('subject–prepositional object') *lake-dweller* ('verb–prepositional object', *cf: John dwells on the lake*) and *bull-ring* ('object–prepositional object', *cf: John fights bulls in the ring*), all of which contain a locative element indicating 'place'. The classification that follows has similarities with the one outlined by Jespersen (MEG VI, Chapter 8). The groups are:

I Subject–Verb	VII Resemblance
II Verb–Object	VIII Composition/Form/Contents
III Appositional	IX Adjective–Noun
IV Associative	X Names
V Instrumental	XI Other
VI Locative	

This classification is not a 'tidy' one: that is to say, various different ways of analysing the examples are used. The Instrumental and Locative classes are based on meaning, and include compounds of different grammatical structures, while the Subject–Verb and Verb–Object classes are homogeneous as to structure. The Adjective–Noun class subsumes examples which correspond to a variety of structures and contain a variety of meaning-relations; in this case it seemed desirable to look at these all together and compare them. Compounds containing a genitive *'s* are classed with a type not containing this feature, under the heading of Associative, so that the similarity between, for instance, *lambswool* and *horsehair* may be pointed out.

Some compounds contain more than one meaning-relation. *Car-ride*, for example, may be interpreted as containing a 'locative of place', *cf: John rides in the car*, or an 'instrumental' element, *cf: John rides by means of the car*, and perhaps there is no way of deciding which analysis is the preferable one. *Snowdrift* may be placed with the Subject–Verb compounds on the basis of *the snow drifts*, or with the Composition compounds, since it means 'drift which is made of snow'. In *scrubbing brush*, the second element is the instrument with which the action of the first is performed, but we can paraphrase the compound as 'brush for scrubbing (floors with)', illustrating a 'purpose' relation. This relation of 'purpose', we find, always coexists with another, such as 'instrumental' as in this case, or 'locative' as in *lodging house*, *cf: John lodges in the house*, 'house for lodging in'. And, as we saw in 4.3 above (ID2), 'purpose' is largely a matter of real-life situation. We are more likely to ascribe a 'purpose' meaning to *sleeping pill* (= 'pill which causes sleeping', 'pill for sleeping') than to *laughing gas* (= 'gas which causes laughing') simply because it is more often necessary and desirable to induce sleep than to induce laughter. Therefore it seems best to place these two compounds together under the Instrumental heading, and to regard 'purpose' as a non-basic relation. I have not set up a class of Purpose compounds, even though in some cases the 'purpose' meaning may seem to be more prominent than the one which is considered basic, as for instance in the Contents examples *fire-place, pillow-case*.

Another reason why any classification of nominal compounds seems bound to be unsatisfactory is that individuals interpret particular compounds in different ways. Lees (1960, 123–4) illustrates this very well with the example *witch doctor*, which may be 'a doctor who resembles a witch', 'a doctor who is a witch', or, *cf* Webster (1961), one who detects witches. Evidence for more than one interpretation of this compound is nicely provided by the following: 'Our consternation would be complete when our witch doctor, who evidently should really be called an anti-witch doctor, insisted that each herb he prescribed for us had its own individual incantation . . .' [*Sunday Times* 21 February 1971, 27/4].

A third complication in the exercise of classifying noun compounds is caused by the fact that many of them, such as *screw-driver, plane crash, bus stop*, contain nominalized verbs. This means that, as well as taking account of the relations between the elements of the compounds, we might also classify these nominalized constituents in the manner illustrated in Chapter 4: a 'three-dimensional' classification would be needed to take care of, say, the similarity between *plane crash* and *bus stop*, which are both Subject – Verb (IA1 below) in terms of the relation between the parts, and the difference that we feel exists between them and which is due to the different nominalization-types which they contain. *Crash* is 'result of action' (*cf* 4.6, IIIB2 above), while *stop* belongs to the 'locative' subclass of that group, and is accordingly more concrete in meaning. The following classification is concerned only with the relations between compound-elements, and it ignores the kind of distinction that I have just exemplified between *plane crash* and *bus stop*. To take further instances: among the Verb – Object examples of group IIA2a below which are formed with zero suffix, *scarecrow, turnkey, wagtail*, all 'agents of the action' (*cf* 4.6, IIIA above) are placed alongside *lockjaw*, which is 'result' and *passport*, which is 'instrument'. Of the Verb – Object examples of IIB2, *bootblack* contains an 'agent' nominalization as second element, *cold cure* an 'instrumental' one, and *car park* a 'locative' one. Again, among the examples of VIC2, which are placed together because they contain a 'locative' first element, *bookmark* has an 'instrumental' second element, while that of *home help* denotes a human agent; and similarly with the Verb – Object examples ending in *-er* of IIB3: *screw-driver* and *shock-absorber* have 'instrumental' second elements, while *brick-layer* has an 'agentive' one.

Finally, this classification necessarily ignores much of the 'knowledge of the world' which we bring to the interpretation of compounds. Most nominal compounds require a knowledge of their referents before they can be fully understood, but examples vary in this respect. *Ticket-holder* in the following sentence needs little special knowledge beyond familiarity with the Verb – Object compound pattern: 'Ticket-holders, he added, would be able to get their money back at the box office' [*Evening Standard*]. To understand *scene-stealer*, on the other hand, a compound of the same grammatical make-up, we must know that the interpretation of *scene* varies with the situation, and that *steal* is used metaphorically. In the following pages the reader will find many more examples of differences between compounds placed together, which I have ignored because they seemed less a matter of language than of life.

I SUBJECT–VERB

In these compounds a nominal element is interpreted as the agent of the action denoted by the other, verbal, element. In most examples, therefore, the nominal element is animate, but in a few, like *hovercraft, jump jet, popgun, revolving door*, though the noun is not animate, it still seems most naturally analysed as the subject of the verb.

I A 1 *Noun–verb (zero suffix)*

[a] transitive

bée sting (*cf: the bee stings*)	snáke-bite
fléa-bite	súnburn
gódsend[a]	

[a] *Godsend* was originally not of this type. According to the OED it is a reduced form of *God's send; send* is the obsolete nominalization of the verb *to send*.

[b] intransitive

bús stop	pláne crash
dáybreak	súnset
héadache[a]	súnshine
íce fall	tóothache[a]
lándslide	

[a] *Headache* and *toothache* could also be placed with the Locative compounds (VI), *cf* 'ache in the head'.

I A 2 *Noun–verb (other nominalization)*

[a] transitive

blóod pressure

[b] intransitive

héart failure	populátion growth

I B 1 *Verb(-ing)–noun*

[a] transitive

cléaning lady[a]	línking verb[a]
commanding ófficer	managing diréctor
fíling clerk[a]	mócking bird
governing bódy	seeing éye
helping hánd	

[b] intransitive

falling stár	leading árticle
flýing boat[a]	revolving dóor
flying fish†	sitting dúck
flying sáucer	sliding scále
floating dóck	travelling sálesman
homing pigeon†	weeping wíllow
laughing jáckass	working man†

[a] Notice that Verb(-*ing*)–Subject compounds which have the accent on the first word are, with one or two exceptions, the ones which could have an 'instrument' or 'purpose' interpretation, the -*ing* form being in that case understood as a gerund rather than as a participle, for example 'clerk for filing', 'boat for flying (in)', etc. Compounds in the Instrumental class (V below) are regularly accented on the first word.

Verb(-*ing*)–subject-noun compounds are semantically distinguishable from free phrases of the same form by the fact that in them the present participle has not the progressive aspect characteristic of its use in sentences: a *working man* is 'a man who works', not 'a man who is working'.

IB2 *Verb (neutral)–noun*

[a] transitive

cáll boy	hángman
cópycat	séarch party

[b] intransitive

dríftwood	pláyboy
glów-worm	póp-gun
hóvercraft	túrntable
jump jet†	wórkman
lead árticle	

IB3 *Verb (nominalization)–noun*

[a] transitive

demolítion squad	recéption committee

[b] intransitive

mótion picture

IC *Non-verbal*

The following examples do not contain a verbal element at all, but their head words nevertheless signify, more or less explicitly, agents of an action in which the attributive element is involved as object. They could there-fore be placed also under the Verb–Object heading (II). A *car thief* is 'one who steals cars': this compound could be seen as related to a subject–verb–object structure in which the subject and the verb are combined in one word, *thief*. Similar examples are

cár mechanic	sílk merchant
brÍck mason	trée surgeon
pork butcher†	

Other examples have a head element which is not obviously agentive:

frúit bat (*cf: the bat eats fruit*)
hóney bee (*cf: the bee produces honey*)
sílk worm (*cf: the worm produces silk*)

In *contact lens*† the first element suggests a verb whose subject would be the second element.

II VERB–OBJECT

IIA1 *Verb(-ing)–noun*

chéwing-gum (*cf: John chews the gum*)	rócking-horse
drÍnking-water	smélling-salts
éating-apple	spÍnning-wheel
folding dóor[a]	tálking-point[b]
púnching bag	wéaring apparel
réading material	whÍpping-boy

[a] *Folding door* can also be paraphrased 'the door folds', and this perhaps accounts for its accentual pattern, which is typical of verb(-*ing*)–subject-noun compounds (*cf: revolving door*).
[b] *Talking-point* differs from the others in that the first element represents a verb + preposition (*cf: John talks about (discusses) the point*).

Most of these examples contain a 'purpose' relation: 'gum for chewing', 'water for drinking', and so on.

IIA2 *Verb (neutral)–noun*

dráwstring	scátter cushion
fláshlight	shove-hálfpenny
pláything[a]	slÍde rule
rÍp-cord	stóp-watch

[a] In *plaything* the first element represents a verb + preposition (*cf: John plays with the thing*).

In some of these examples there is a 'purpose' relation: 'string for drawing', and so on.

IIA2a *Derivational compounds with zero suffix*

cease-fire†[a]	scárecrow
cút-throat	shéarwater
dréadnought	spóilsport
lóckjaw	túrnkey
mákeweight	wágtail
pássport	

[a] *Cease-fire* differs from the others in that it is presumably from an imperative structure. The uncertainty in accentuation reflects this difference.

IIB1 *Noun–verb(-ing)*

bóok-binding	háy-making
bríck-laying	hóuse-cleaning
fáult-finding	méter-feeding
fórtune-hunting	múd-slinging
góld-mining	sóul-searching

IIB2 *Noun–verb (zero suffix)*

béll-pull	géar shift
blóodshed	háirbrush[b]
bóotblack	háir-do
cár park	hándshake
cóld cure	róad block
drúg addict[a]	stóne's throw[c]
éngine repair	wáge freeze
éye strain	

[a] In *drug addict* (*cf: John is addicted to drugs*), the verbal element represents a verb + preposition. This example is unusual in that there is no active form of the verb.
[b] The second element of *hairbrush* is perhaps not felt as verbal, but it suggests the action of which *hair* is the object, and seems to fit naturally into this group.
[c] This example is unusual in that its form is that of the Associative compounds of IVA below. It so clearly contains an objective genitive, however, that it is placed in this group.

IIB3 *Noun–verb(-er)*

bríck-layer	scéne-stealer
gráve-digger	scréw-driver
líghtning-conductor	shóck-absorber
nútcracker	shóe-maker
rábble-rouser	tóngue-twister
récord-player	

IIB4 *Noun–verb (other nominalization)*

cháracter assassination	mánslaughter
ínsect-repellant	máil delivery
lífe expectancy	personálity cult[a]
lífe insurance	self-decéption

[a] *Cult* is a verbal noun with no corresponding verb: it was borrowed from Latin *cultus*, from *colere* (= 'to cultivate, respect'), perhaps via French *culte*. *Cultivate*, the approximately-corresponding verb, is from a later Latin derivative of *cultus*.

III APPOSITIONAL

In some rare or nonce compounds, for example *king-émperor, cook-hóusekeeper, historian-politícian, producer-diréctor*, the relation between the constituents could be called coordinative, the whole compound being understood as 'a combination of A and B', though the second element is always likely to appear the more prominent one. (In all the paraphrases given below, A represents the first element of a compound and B the second.) Shakespeare has some compounds of this type, such as *giant-dwarf, uncle-father, aunt-mother*, and Carlyle coined such words as *death-birth, cough-laugh*, but this type of compound is not often found in the general vocabulary. As far as the 'attributiveness' of the first element is concerned, there is perhaps a gradience to be seen in Appositional compounds: in *nation state, city state*, the first elements are a little more 'attributive' than those of the examples given above; in *houseboat* and *prison camp* there seems no doubt that the first element is subordinate to the second. I have subdivided Appositional compounds on the basis of explanatory paraphrases.

III A '*B which acts as, has the function of A*'

buffer státe	master key†
city state†	nation state†
cógwheel	nóse cone
companion volume†	páge boy
féature film	príson camp
fúel oil	sister ship†
géar wheel	student prínce
hándlebar	tárget date
hóuseboat	tenant fármer

III B 1 '*B of which A is a particular instance*'

déath penalty	panic reáction
fóotball game	repáir job
múrder charge	téaching profession

III B 2 The following are similar to those in B 1, but they are almost tautologous: the first element could be used without the second, although in the compound it is understood as being the more specific.

álleyway	fóodstuff
cóbblestone	hédgerow
códfish	páthway
cóurtyard	póckmark
flágstone	

III C *Verb(-er)–noun*

These examples can be paraphrased 'B is an A', and so are placed here, but they might have been put in other classes. *Killer shark*, for instance, could have been called a Subject–Verb compound (*cf: the shark is a killer, the shark kills*); *refresher course* is like some of the Instrumental examples (V) (*cf: John refreshes (his knowledge) by means of the course*).

bóoster shot	killer shárk
carrier bag†	márker buoy
carrier pigeon†	player píano
convéyor belt	refrésher course
ejéctor seat	repeater wátch
fíghter plane	róller skate
founder mémber	wásherwoman

IV ASSOCIATIVE

The label 'associative' covers compounds paraphrasable by 'B is part of A', 'B belongs to A', 'B is typically associated with A', all relationships which may be expressed by means of the genitive 's, though only the compounds under IVA and B actually contain the inflection. Of these, some older compounds have lost the apostrophe; others, like *bullseye*, *lambswool* may be spelt with or without it.

IVA1 'B which is part of A'

búllseye	hógshead
déath's head	lámbswool
drágon's blood	mind's éye
hártshorn	

IVA2 'B which belongs to A'

crów's nest	máre's nest
lion's share†	nó-man's land

In the first three cases above, the paraphrase is of course adequate only if we disregard the normal, metaphorical, meaning of the compounds.

IVA3 'B which is typically associated with A'

beginner's lúck	fóolscap
brewer's yéast	fool's páradise
carpenter's lével	potter's whéel
cat's cradle†	printer's ínk
cát's meat	tailor's chálk
devil's ádvocate	witches' Sábbath
driver's seat†	

Some compounds containing the genitive 's are not easily fitted into either of these groups. *Béeswax*, for instance, is paraphrasable by 'B is produced by A', *cf* the examples under C3 below; *ratsbane* could be interpreted as Instrumental, *cf*: *mousetrap* (VB4).

IVB Noun-s-man

A small number of compounds whose second element is -*man* contain an *s* which may be interpreted as that of the plural.

backwoodsman†	róundsman
pláinsman	spórtsman

The following, according to the OED, were all originally genitival formations, but the *s* has now largely lost its significance and indicates neither
genitive nor plural.

bátsman	húntsman
clánsman	swórdsman
dráughtsman	trádesman

The two senses of *póintsman* in the OED involve different interpretations
of the *s*: 1 (plural): 'A man who has charge of the points on a railway';
2 (genitive or empty): 'A police constable stationed on point duty.'

IV C *Compounds without s*

IV C1 *'B which is part of A'*

bóttleneck	fíngertip
bróomstick	hórsehair
cártwheel	óxblood
cátgut	púmphandle
dóorknob	shírtsleeves
éardrum	télephone receiver
éggshell	whálebone
éyeball	

IV C2 *'B which is associated with A'*

ánt heap	hórse-shoe
bédside	life force†
cáse history	móle hill
city wáll	party líne
dáylight	pláce name
dónkey work	rábbit warren
fólk song	wíll-power

IV C3 *'B which is produced, emitted, derived from, A'*

banána oil	góose grease
cándlelight	móonbeam
cane súgar	sóap suds
chícken fat	

V INSTRUMENTAL

In these examples, one (nominal) constituent denotes the instrument or
cause involved in an action. The other constituent may be verbal, denoting

the action, or nominal, denoting some object or concept associated with the action. In groups A and B the final element is the instrumental one, in C and D the first element represents the instrument.

VA1 *Verb(-ing) – instrument-noun*

[*a*] transitive

báttering ram (*cf: John batters*
    the gate with a ram)
blótting paper
búrning glass
cárving knife
dárning needle
divíning rod
húnting dog
léttering pen

mágnifying glass
prúning hook
réading glasses
rólling pin
scrúbbing brush
stéering wheel
túning fork
wrápping paper

[*b*] intransitive

héaring aid (*cf: John hears with*
    the aid)
láughing gas
living wáge
sléeping pill

snéezing powder
stépping stone
vóting machine
working hypóthesis

VA2 *Verb (neutral) – instrument-noun*

[*a*] transitive

dríve shaft
gríndstone
guíde book
pítchfork
sáwhorse

séarchlight
spýglass
stópcock
túg-boat

The following examples are listed separately, since their first elements appear to be imperative in nature. They are all from the technical language of computer science, in which instructions and orders play a large part.

enáble pulse
hóld facility
ignóre character

inhíbit pulse
tráce routine
wríte head

[b] intransitive

escápe hatch	snéeze-weed
hóbble-skirt	springboard
páss-word	

In most of these A1 and A2 examples there is a 'purpose' relation: *carving knife*: 'knife for carving (meat with)', *pitchfork*: 'fork for pitching (hay with)', and so on.

VA3 *Verb (nominalization) – instrument-noun*

[a] transitive

ignítion key	pléasure boat
insulátion tape	protéction money
percéption mechanism	súction pump

[b] intransitive

navigátion aid	perfórmance drug[a]

[a] *Cf* 'The present crisis has arisen because the distinction has been blurred between outright "performance" drugs – which every trainer knows are illegal – and drugs with genuine therapeutic value' [*Sunday Times* 11 July 1971, 1/5].

VA3 examples containing a clearly-intransitive verb appear to be rare: *to navigate* and *to perform* are both commonly used transitively.

VB *Noun – instrument-noun*

VB1 '*B which prevents, cures, protects against, A*'

cóugh mixture	préssure suit
flý-paper	ráincoat
gás-mask	sún-glasses
mosquíto net	wíndshield
móthball	wórry beads
múdguard[a]	

[a] In *mudguard* the second element should perhaps be considered as verbal (representing a verb + preposition, 'guards against'), but from the point of view of meaning this compound seems most appropriately placed here.

VB2 '*B which is the means of preserving A*'

lífe-boat	sáfety belt

VB3 '*B which causes, promotes, A*'

fertílity rite
hórror film
influénza virus

lóve potion
téar gas

VB4 *Other*

búbble gum
lóbster pot
mílk machine

móusetrap
percússion instrument
tráction engine

In some VB examples the 'purpose' relation is present, for example *cough mixture*: 'mixture for coughs', *lobster pot*: 'pot for catching lobsters in'.

VC1 *Instrument-noun–verb(-ing)*

[a] transitive
    áction painting
    hánd weaving
    ímpulse buying
    ínstrument flying

    léad poisoning
    mércy-killing
    péace-offering
    pícture writing

[b] intransitive
    flý-fishing
    shádow-boxing

    wáter-skiing

VC2 *Instrument-noun–verb (zero suffix)*

[a] transitive
    blóodstain
    fíngerprint
    páper chase

    pínprick
    télephone call

[b] intransitive
    clóg dance
    hánd-spring
    néedlework

    pípe dream
    pówer dive

VC3 *Instrument-noun–verb (other nominalization)*

[*a*] transitive

héat treatment	spin-drýer[a]
léad pollution	stéamroller
líp service	tápe recorder
préssure cooker	

[a] The first element of *spin-dryer* is clearly verbal, since the compound may be paraphrased: 'dryer which works by means of a spinning mechanism'; the accentuation, which differs from that of the other examples in this group, is perhaps related to this syntactic difference.

[*b*] intransitive

fán dancer	métal worker

VD *Instrument-noun–noun*

VD1 '*B which functions by means of A*'

aír gun	hýdrogen bomb
cáble car	mótor cycle
correspóndence course	stéam engine
fóotball	wáter clock
gás stove	

VD2 '*B which is caused by A*'

anxíety neurosis	
báttle fatigue	néttle rash
cóld sore	rát-bite fever
grówing pains[a]	shéll-shock
héat rash	wínd storm
ínsulin shock	

[a] *Growing pains* contains an obviously verbal element, but on grounds of meaning belongs here rather than with the verb(-*ing*) examples.

VD3 '*B which is obtained through using A*'

corn whísky	rye bread†
gás-light	sáwdust
grain álcohol	wheat bread†
maple sýrup	

These may be compared with the examples under IV C3, paraphrased 'B which is produced, emitted, derived from, A'.

VI LOCATIVE

'Locative' includes the notions of 'place where', 'place to or from which', 'time when', 'time during which', and 'situation', the last of which comprehends both 'place' and 'time'. Under 'place' I have not separated 'from', 'to' and 'at' examples, and under 'time', 'at' and 'during' are not distinguished. The locative constituent is nominal. The other constituent may be verbal, denoting the relevant action, or nominal, denoting an object or concept associated with the action. There is some overlap with the Instrumental class: a number of the examples below could also have been placed under V, for example *ironing board: cf: Mary irons on the board* or *by means of the board*. In the A and B examples, the locative element is the final one, in the C and D groups it is the initial one.

VI A 1 *Verb(-ing) – locative-noun*

[a] transitive: *place*

dráwing paper	mélting pot
íroning board	pácking house
láunching pad	

time

cóoking time

[b] intransitive: *place*

díving board	lóoking glass
lánding strip	sléeping bag
líving room	swímming pool
lódging house	tráding post

time

bréathing space	working day†
cóughing fit	

The 'place' examples, and *breathing space* show a 'purpose' relation: *launching pad*: 'pad for launching (rockets from)' and so on.

VI A 2 *Verb (neutral) – locative-noun*

[a] transitive: *place*

báke-house	shów-room
cáll-box	tów-path
chéckpoint	wátch-tower

Further computer examples with imperative first elements (*cf* V A 2 above) are:

place

sáve area	séek area

time

láunch window[a]	wásh-day
páyday	

[a] *Launch window* denotes 'the period of *time* during which it is possible to launch a spacecraft for a particular mission'. With reference to aerospace matters, one may speak of 'a window of three hours'.

'Imperative' examples from computer language are:

ádd time	réad time
compíle time	scán period

[b] intransitive: *place*

dánce hall	thínk tank
péep-hole	wálkway

time

fást day	rúsh hour

A final computer example is *ríse time*.

VI A 3 *Verb (nominalization) – locative-noun*

[a] transitive: *place*

amúsement park	deténtion centre
assémbly line	observátion post
bírth-place	recéption desk
concentrátion camp	sláughter-house

time

complétion date	júdgment day

[b] intransitive: *place*

lábour camp

time

retírement age

Blind spot is unusual in that the first element is adjectival, *cf: John is blind in or at the spot.*

VIB *Noun–locative-noun: place*

ále-house	frúit market
báttle-field	láw court
béar country	lóve nest
bíble belt	penny arcáde
bíscuit factory	téa-room
búll-ring	

time

bédtime	íce age
flág day	

In some 'place' examples there is a 'purpose' relation: *tea-room*: 'room for having tea in'.

VIC1 *Locative-noun–verb(-ing)*

[*a*] transitive: *place*

shóp-lifting	ský-writing

time

spring-cléaning

[*b*] intransitive: *place*

ballroom dáncing	stár-gazing
crýstal-gazing	wíndow-shopping
séa-faring	

time

night flýing

VIC2 *Locative-noun–verb (zero suffix)*

[*a*] transitive: *place*

bóokmark	hóuse arrest
home hélp	

time

night wátch

[b] intransitive: *place*

bóat-ride	móonwalk
fíeld work	nósebleed
hándstand	púb-crawl
hómework	táble talk

time

dáydream	níght work

VIC3 *Locative-noun–verb(-er)*

[a] transitive: *place*

búsh-fighter	schóol-teacher
crádle-snatcher	

time

night fíghter	Sunday páinter
níght rider	

[b] intransitive: *place*

bóg-trotter	míne-worker
búsh ranger	pláy-goer
cáve-dweller	shóp-walker
láke-dweller	street singer†
léaf-hopper	wáyfarer

time

day lábourer	níght worker

VID *Locative-noun–noun: place*

aír speed	lawn ténnis
armchair philósophy	líver fluke
cottage chéese	lóin cloth
dítchwater	mountain ásh
fíeld mouse	néck-tie
héadline	núrsery rhyme
héllhound	pocket hándkerchief
household wórd	séa horse
jáilbird	séat belt

time

afternoon téa

April fóol

bedtime story†

déath duty

evening stár

harvest móon

midnight sún

níght owl

minute steak†

Súnday school

winter wóollies

situation

báth towel

dínner jacket

dréam world

fóg horn

fóotball jersey

shóoting stick

stáge name

wár bride

wár crime

wédding dress

VII RESEMBLANCE

In these examples, the first element denotes something to which the referent of the second is compared. I have not separated compounds containing a verbal element from those made up of two non-derived nouns.

VII A 1 'B which is in the form of, has the physical features of, A'

apron stáge

béll jar

bóx kite

fán vaulting

féather-stitch

hairpin bénd

handlebar moustáche

kídney bowl

píggy bank

pork-pie hát

ríbbon fish

sóapstone

spéargrass

spónge cake

umbrélla tree

VII A 1a Derivational compounds with zero suffix

cóttontail

prónghorn

rázorback

spóonbill

VII B 'B which has some feature characteristic of A'

butterfly táble

gárter snake

hóney dew

mackerel ský

piano accórdion

rázor clam

tíger-lily

zébra fish

zebra cróssing

VIIC1 'B which is like A's B'

cátcall

crocodile téars (='tears like a
   crocodile's tears')

dóg paddle

góoseflesh

hare líp

hórse laugh

máster stroke

pug nóse

VIIC1a *Derivational compounds with zero suffix*

dúckbill

drágonhead

máidenhair

These C examples may be compared with some of the Associative compounds under IV C, since they may be paraphrased 'B which is part of, or is associated with, A'.

VIID *Metaphorical*

VIID1 'B which reminds one of A'

bútcher-bird

demon bárber

dévil-fish

fáther-figure

frógman

grandfather clóck

hérmit crab

pílot-fish

wéaver-bird

VIID2 The following clearly involve a comparison, but are less easy to paraphrase:

ghost town†

lightning decísion

pancake lánding

pincer attáck

rapier wít

sálad days

VIID2a *Derivational compounds with zero suffix*

blóckhead

bútterfingers

égghead

VIII COMPOSITION/FORM/CONTENTS

This group contains compounds in which one element specifies the other in terms of some concrete feature. It is convenient to distinguish the features of 'composition' (A), 'shape or form' (B) and 'contents' (C).

VIII A 1 'B which consists of A'

áir-stream
cómpost heap
físh-cake
íce cube
léaf mould
mud píe

óil slick
peanut bútter
potáto chip
sándbank
snówball
téar-drop

VIII A 2 'B which is made, constructed from, A'

cárpet bag
clay pígeon
fur cóat
iron cúrtain
ivory tówer

rag dóll
rush cándle
sánd-castle
smóke-screen

VIII A 2a Derivational compounds with zero suffix

bráss-hat
cópperplate

léather-jacket
páperback

VIII B 'B which is in the form of A'

bow tíe
bóx camera
chain reáction
fíbre-glass
loaf súgar

páge proof
patch pócket
píg-iron
plate gláss
shéet ice

VIII C 1 'B in which A is a characteristic feature'

bone chína
currant bun †
dúst storm
frúit-cake
háil-storm
hýmn-book
lúng-fish

míracle play
óil-paint
pícture book
sánd-paper
táil-coat
thúnderstorm

VIII C 2 'B which contains, or is meant to contain, A'

béer glass
bírd-cage
cigarétte packet
fíre-place
íce-bag

mátch-box
píg-pen
píllow-case
sált-cellar
wíne bottle

As Jespersen points out (MEG VI, 8.2₃), compounds of this kind may denote receptacles specifically without their contents: a *wine bottle* is usually understood to be empty, in contrast to *a bottle of wine*.

A 'purpose' relation is present in these examples: *fire-place:* 'place for a fire', and so on.

IX ADJECTIVE-NOUN

This class contains compounds of various structures. Under B are examples in which the adjective is related to an adverb, in D the adjective is derived from a verb, and in E it is derived from a noun. The examples in D and E might well be distributed among the classes we have already discussed. However, since the first element of all such examples is formally an adjective, we tend to be influenced by this superficial structure, and to give compounds like *permissive society* (D), and *herbal remedy* (E) a kind of double interpretation. *Permissive society* is both subject–verb (*cf: the society permits* . . .) and adjective–noun: 'society of the permissive kind'; *herbal remedy* is superficially 'a remedy of the herbal kind', and 'instrumental' if we look below the surface: 'a remedy made with, by means of, herbs'. (An alternative paraphrase would be 'a remedy containing herbs'.)

IX A a *Non-derived adjective–non-derived noun*

[i] with compound-accent

cóld cream	híghlight
cómic strip	hót-house
cómmon-room	máinspring
dárk-room	pláinsong
flát-iron	smáll talk
fúnny-bone	tíghtrope
gréy matter	wíld-fowl
hárdboard	wísecrack

[ii] with phrase-accent (including examples in which usage is divided)

best mán	deep spáce	high chair†
big gáme	dry rót	lame dúck
black mágic	easy chair†	magic lántern
blank chéque	fine árt	old hánd
broad béan	foul pláy	
cold wár	free vérse	
crazy páving	hard lábour	

IX A b *Derivational compounds with zero suffix*

bíghead	hárdback
blúebell	héavyweight
blúe-stocking	rédskin
búsybody	stráight-edge
dímwit	

IX B *Compounds corresponding to verb – adverb collocations*

bad lóser (*cf: John loses badly*)	néwcomer (*cf: newly come*)
best-séller[a]	rough ríder
free-thínker[a]	shárpshooter
high-flíer†	wéllwisher
loud-spéaker	

[a] *Best-seller* and *free-thinker* were perhaps linked in their formation with the compounds *best-selling* and *free thought*.

Examples with a zero or other nominalization as second element are:

good shót	slow mótion
near míss	wéll-being
safe cónduct	

Constant compánion is comparable with these examples, although its second element is not related to a verb.

IX C *Adjective–noun stem + -er*

first-níghter	hard líner
flat-éarther	hot-góspeller
four-póster	left-hánder
general practítioner	white sláver

In *first-nighter, general practitioner*, the suffix is an agentive; in *flat-earther, four-poster, hard liner, left-hander*, it is 'characterizing' (*cf* Chapter 2, note 10). *Hot-gospeller, white slaver* are perhaps linked with compound verbs, *to hot-gospel, to white-slave*. *Cf* for the former example: 'Aimee Semple MacPherson still hot-gospelled at her world-famous church' [*Evening Standard* 29 January 1972, 9/2]; see further 7.2 below.

IX D *Verbal adjective – noun*

IX D 1 *Compounds with non-participial adjectives corresponding to verbs*
Some of these might also be placed with the Subject–Verb examples
under I; examples are:

connective tíssue (*cf: the tissue* permissive socíety
 connects . . .) secretive glánd
depréssant effect

Other examples, like

absorbent cótton   evasive áction
creative ímpulse   propellant fúel
digéstive juices   protective cústody

perhaps belong with the Instrumental class, *cf: John evades the enemy by
means of the action. Movable feast* is verb–object, *cf: the feast can be moved.*

IX D 2 *Past participle – noun*

acquired táste[a]   inverted cómma
Authorized Vérsion oiled sílk
chartered accóuntant Promised Lánd
condensed mílk   registered póst
corrugated íron   split infínitive
frozen fóod   tied hóuse
guided míssile

[a] *Acquired taste* is often used in the sense 'taste which must be acquired' rather than
'taste which has been acquired'. A 'has been' interpretation is appropriate for all
the other examples.

These compounds could also be placed with the Verb–Object examples
(II), *cf: John acquires the taste.*

IX D 3 *Reduced past participle – noun*

bómb-site   mínce-meat
hire-car†   púnch card
ice cream†   skim-milk†
mátch-board

Some members of this group developed historically from examples of
the D2 pattern. The OED confirms that *iced cream, minced meat* appeared
earlier than *ice cream, mincemeat,* though *skim-milk* preceded *skimmed milk.*

IX D 3a *Derivational compounds with zero suffix*

áddlepate	húnchback
cráckbrain	

IX E *Denominal adjective – noun*

Structures of this form are particularly difficult to classify. Along with examples like *criminal lawyer*, *political party*, I include those in which the adjective is derived from a classical stem which has no corresponding 'native' nominal form, such as *civil rights*, *local colour*, *public footpath*, *royal family*.

The following are like the Subject–Verb compounds of I:

editorial cómment (*cf: the editor comments*)
presidential véto
scribal érror

They are also similar to the Associative examples of V (*cf: editor's comment*). Other possibly Associative examples are:

civil ríghts (*cf: citizens' rights*)	national débt
industrial revolútion	nérvous system
infantile parálysis	public fóotpath
nasal passage†	royal fámily

Criminal áction and *magnetic néedle* are similar to Appositional compounds (IV), *cf: the action is a crime, the needle is (acts as) a magnet*.

Examples with an Instrumental interpretation are:

chemical wárfare	occupational thérapy
conscientious objéctor	pneumatic dríll
electric líght	póstal service
glottal stóp	tidal wáve
herbal rémedy	

in all of which the first element is the instrument.

The following have a Locative first element:

aquatic plánt	polar bear†
global víllage	solar fláre
local cólour	tropical físh

Musical cómedy is of the type 'B in which A is a characteristic feature', *cf* VIII C 1.

Other examples seem to require more complex paraphrases than have been needed so far:

circumstantial évidence	preferential tréatment
criminal láwyer	racial préjudice
confidential sécretary	sexual deviátion
méntal hospital	sonic bóom
political párty	

Some of these could be seen as based on three-word structures, with an ellipted second element;[3] *confidential secretary* might be explained by a phrase like 'confidential work secretary', *ie* 'secretary who does confidential work' and *mental hospital* by 'mental case hospital', 'hospital for mental cases'. Clearly, all these examples are elliptical in some way. The definition given in Webster (1961) for *circumstantial evidence* runs:

> evidence that tends to prove a fact in issue by proving other events or circumstances which according to the common experience of mankind are usu. or always attended by the fact in issue and that therefore affords a basis for a reasonable inference by the jury or court of the occurrence of the fact in issue.[4]

While a paraphrase for classification purposes need not of course be as full an explanation as this, it seems likely that an adequate one for *circumstantial evidence* would not be easy to formulate.[5]

X NAMES

One kind of compound which I have not attempted to subclassify is exemplified by the following:

Angora rábbit	Prussian blúe
emperor bútterfly	Pullman cár
píne tree	wíndflower

In these, the first element has a naming function. A *pine tree* is simply 'a tree of the "pine" variety'. This particular example might be placed with the Appositional compounds,[6] but since first elements which are names are fairly easily identifiable, I shall say no more about this type of compound.

XI OTHER

It is not difficult to think of compounds which do not fit into any of the classes already discussed. Some examples are:

concert pítch	kitchen gárden
cónscience money	light year†
crádle song	milk tooth†
credibílity gap	nóse dive
dress círcle	séx appeal
éye rhyme	shotgun márriage
fíre sale	télephone directory
gállows bird	tóothmug

Like the examples of the *circumstantial evidence* group, they seem to need rather complex paraphrases. *Conscience money*, for instance, defined as concisely as seems possible, is 'money paid to relieve the conscience by ... restoring ... what has been wrongfully acquired or withheld' [Webster (1961)];[7] *light year* is 'a unit of length equal to the distance that light travels in one year'.

Examples like these show up the limitations of the classification I have attempted in this chapter, which is based on the possibility of supplying a simple paraphrase for each compound. Our understanding of compounds depends on our knowing what it is in the outside world that they denote, and it seems that, in many cases, the first element functions chiefly as a sort of mnemonic device, a reminder of the nature and associations of the object or notion that the whole refers to. For example, we may understand *banana republic* to mean 'a small country dominated by a more powerful one', without knowing that such countries are so called because they are economically dependent on the export of fruit, and on foreign capital. Armed with this information, we may analyse it as an instrument–noun–noun compound, something like *gas-stove* (VD 1). And in *shotgun marriage*, *shotgun* stands for a number of notions, adding up to the idea of 'forced', but once we have the necessary knowledge, this example strikes us as no more complex than an apparently simple and easily classifiable example like *dark-room*. Indeed, perhaps we can interpret *shotgun marriage* as an 'instrumental' example, like *insulin shock* (VD2): 'the shotgun – or a method which calls such an object to mind – is instrumental in bringing about the marriage'; though this interpretation still leaves out a piece of 'knowledge of the world' which is essential to our understanding of the compound. As Sweet very reasonably remarked, in commenting on the grammatical inexplicitness of compounds:

This very vagueness is the chief reason why composition is resorted to: it is only by leaving open the logical relations between the elements of compounds that we are able to form them as we want them without stopping to analyse exactly the logical or grammatical relations between the words we join together, as we might have to do if we connected them together by more definite means, such as prepositions and inflections. (1891, §1560)

This is not to deny, of course, that the logical or grammatical relations are there, but, as we have seen, two or more may be involved in one combination, and, especially if we have previously learned the compound as a whole through meeting it in a context that does not require us to analyse it, such relations may be very much in the background and in some cases not at all obvious, even after introspection.

Notes

1 See Osselton (1962) however, for evidence that noun phrases containing attributives marked for the plural, such as *ideas men, payments deficit, British Standards Institution*, are becoming more common in English.
2 See however Lees (1970) for a treatment of some noun–noun compounds which is based on relations of meaning.
3 Lees (1960, 179, n 67) makes this suggestion.
4 By permission. From Webster's Third New International Dictionary ©1971 by G. & C. Merriam Co, publishers of the Merriam-Webster Dictionaries.
5 For a detailed study of denominal adjective+noun collocations, see Coates (1971). See also Bolinger (1967) on various derived adjective–noun structures.
6 In fact Lees so classifies it. See his Predicate Noun class (1960, 127).
7 See note 4 above.

Chapter 6

Adjective compounds

6.1 Adverb–adjective/participle sequences

Adjectival sequences may present a difficulty similar to that discussed in 5.1 with regard to nominal compounds: we may be undecided whether a particular combination of adverb + adjective or participle is to be regarded as a compound or as a free phrase. Accentuation is unhelpful here, as all combinations of this form, whether fixed or free, are accented in the same way. Spelling is no more reliable than it is in the case of noun compounds as an indication of unity. When we meet a nominal phrase whose elements are joined by a hyphen, we can assume that it is to be understood as a compound. But structures in premodification are often hyphenated, as in *made-to-measure jacket*, *easy-to-read stories*, and the hyphen in adverb–adjective sequences is not necessarily a sign of compound status. Notice the following examples: 'Governor Rockefeller's showing will give his candidacy badly-needed sparkle and credibility' [*Evening Standard* 1 May 1968, 1/1]; ' "The motel is the perfect image of American society," said Malcolm Muggeridge, back in the capital after another wildly-successful speaking tour of the United States' [*Evening Standard* 1 May 1968, 7/5]; 'Perhaps Big Brother was merely getting rid of a too-popular subordinate' [George Orwell, *Nineteen Eighty-Four*, 1949, Penguin 1954, 40]; 'Meanwhile, the English summer pursues its usual fascinatingly-unpredictable course' [*Evening Standard* 3 June 1968, 10/3]. The adverbs in these sequences have an intensifying function; frequentatives like *much* and *often* are also very likely to be hyphenated to a following adjectival element, *cf* 'Golden Boy: Often-heralded, finally imported, Clifford Odets' Broadway musical' [*Observer* 2 June 1968, 21/7]; and manner adverbs also may be so treated: '... a tray full of finely-sharpened pencils' [Gavin Lambert, *The Slide Area*, 1959, Penguin 1963, 9]; 'The rest is sentimental gush carried along on waves of Romberg's sweetly-swelling melodies' [*Evening Standard* 10 June 1968, 4/6].[1] Except for *badly-needed* and *wildly-successful*, these examples are not composed of elements that are especially frequently found together, and the hyphen seems to be irrelevant to their status as compounds or free phrases. In the following sections I have hyphenated compounds where I felt that a hyphen would be appropriate to their use in predicative position. As with the nominal compounds, however, I have not been able to find any consistent rules for hyphenation.

As a test of adjective-compound status, we may ask whether the second element can stand alone as a premodifier; this is the case with the examples I have just mentioned, whereas in other sequences, like *widespread, deep-seated*, it is not. We can say *a widespread feeling, a deep-seated tradition*, but not *a spread feeling, a seated tradition*. Also, in most established – and therefore compound-like – adverb–adjective sequences, the first element is neutral, that is, an *-ly* adverb appears without its suffix. But I have included *newly-wed* in the examples below, since its claim to compound status is supported by the fact that *wed* cannot be independent as a premodifier. We may notice also that even where the first element is neutral, as in *high-priced*, it can take the comparative and superlative endings: *higher-priced, highest-priced*. The last two sequences look less like compounds than the first. The neutrality criterion fails of course with adverbs like *far, half, well, ill*, which do not take *-ly*.

As with nominal compounds, then, we cannot make hard and fast rules to decide which adverb–adjective/participle sequences should be treated as units. If such a collocation is used often enough, it may become institutionalized and will most probably take on a meaning which renders its elements no longer independent of one another. This has clearly not happened with *wildly-successful*, for example, and as clearly has with *half-baked, widespread*. There will obviously be many examples about which we are not sure.

6.2 Accentuation

When an adjective compound (or a sequence containing an adjectival element) is in attributive position, the accent will normally fall on the first element, as in *hánd-picked men, a móth-eaten suit*. In predicative position, the accent is often on the final element: 'the men were *hand-pícked*'. In those cases where the accent remains on the first element in predicative position, as in *the suit was móth-eaten*, I have marked it. Examples like *hand-picked* are left unmarked. Two examples only among those given in this chapter, *mock-heroic* (IA) and the nominal attributive *old hat* (XB) seem to be accented on the second element even in attributive position. The accent is accordingly marked on them. Where accentuation in predicative position appears to vary, I have placed an obelisk at the end of the word. However, the accentuation of adjective compounds seems to be to some extent more variable than that of nominal compounds. Many examples which I have left unmarked may, on occasion, behave accentually like *moth-eaten*, and the obelisk may indicate not only cases where usage is divided, but also those in which I, or my informants, have been unable to decide which is the more likely alternative. Some examples, such as *card-carrying*, *grass-green*, and most of those in group X, seem unlikely to appear as predicatives, but I have disregarded this fact as being irrelevant to the matter of accent.

6.3 Classification of adjective compounds[2]

The classes of adjective compounds set out below are as follows:

I Adjunct–Verb	VI Locative
II Subject–Verb/Complement	VII Comparative
III Verb–Object	VIII Prepositional
IV Appositional	IX Derivational
V Instrumental	X Nominal Attributive

Some of the classes have points of similarity with nominal compound classes. Where verbs as final elements are involved, a compound may of course be nominal or adjectival, since verbal forms may function nominally or adjectivally. With respect to a particular combination, a decision as to whether it is primarily nominal or primarily adjectival may be arbitrary: for instance, both the adjective *time-serving* and the nouns *time-serving* and *time-server* exist, and one cannot say which is derived from the other.

I ADJUNCT–VERB

I A *Adverb–adjective*

évergreen	wide awake
mock-heróic	

IB *Adverb–verb(-ing)*

[a] transitive

far-seeing	long-suffering
hard-hitting	

I have described these examples as 'transitive', but *seeing, hitting* and *suffering* in combination here seem to have become intransitive (without losing their transitive implication). The fact that an adjective normally denotes a state rather than an action, and the presence of an adverb, combine to make the object we would normally expect with such verbs irrelevant. (In connection with *long-suffering*, *cf* the Biblical 'Charity suffereth long and is kind' [I Corinthians XIII].)

[b] intransitive

easy-going	hard-working
everlasting	high-flying
far-reaching	plain-speaking

ICI *Adverb–verb(-ed)* *(active)*

[a] transitive

hard-bitten	well-read

[b] intransitive

high-flown	well-behaved
plain-spoken	

These examples are very similar to those of the preceding *-ing* group. Compare the meanings of *high-flying* and *high-flown*, *plain-speaking* and *plain-spoken*.

IC2 *Adverb–verb(-ed)*

[a] transitive *(passive)*

clean-shaven	new-laid
close-knit	newly-wed[a]
deep-set	quick-frozen
far-fetched	ready-made
first-born	rough-hewn
fresh-cooked	well-dressed
half-baked	widespread
ill-judged	

[a] This compound is of course often used as a noun *cf: the newly-weds.*

[b] intransitive

full-fledged   short-lived
much-travelled

II SUBJECT-VERB/COMPLEMENT

II A *Noun – verb(-ed)*

[a] transitive

communist-infiltrated   mother-dominated
  (= 'infiltrated by communists')   póverty-stricken
fróst-bitten   rát-infested
hén-pecked   rócket-assisted
íce-bound   self-appointed
man-made   self-taught
móon-struck   sún-baked
móss-grown   tailor-made
  (= 'moss-overgrown')   wíndswept
móth-eaten

[b] intransitive

crést-fallen (*cf: the crest is (has) fallen*)
chóp-fallen

II B *Noun – adjective*

cólour-fast (*cf: the colour is fast*)
fancy-free   héart-whole
fóot-loose   héadstrong
fóotsore   thréadbare
héart-sick   top-heavy

As Jespersen suggests (MEG VI, 9.5_1), some of these compounds can be interpreted as 'locative': 'sore at the feet', 'sick in the heart'. *Fancy-free* could also be paraphrased 'free from fancies'.

Some compounds in *self-* may be tentatively included here:

self-complacent   self-important
self-evident[a]   self-righteous

---

[a] This example is possibly also Instrumental *cf* V A below, since it is descriptive of something evident by means of (some feature in) itself.

III VERB–OBJECT

III A *Noun–verb(-ing)*

all-embracing
bréath-taking
cárd-carrying
déath-defying
éye-catching
fréedom-loving
Frénch-speaking
Gód-fearing
hábit-forming
háir-raising

héart-rending
láw-abiding[a]
páinstaking
récord-breaking
self-propelling
self-sacrificing
self-winding
síde-splitting
tíme-consuming
tíme-serving

[a] In *law-abiding* the verbal element represents a verb+preposition, *cf: John abides by the law.*

III B *Noun–verbal adjective*

gérm-resistant
self-assertive

self-congratulatory
self-destructive

III C *Noun–verb(-ed)*

aír-conditioned
brow-furrowed[a]
héart-broken

hídebound
típ-tilted
tóngue-tied

[a] *Cf* 'You sit browfurrowed over jigsaw puzzles' [*Evening Standard* 6 September 1971, 3/3].

These examples, although containing transitive verbs, invite comparison with those of the Subject–Complement group, II B above, *cf: the heart is broken, the tip is tilted.*

IV APPOSITIONAL

Adjective compounds in which there is a coordinative relation between the elements are, like the comparable nominal-compound type, uncommon in the general vocabulary: it is easier to find examples in literature. Shakespeare has such words as *fortunate-unhappy* (used in nominal function), *foolish-witty*, *devilish-holy*, in which there is a contrast between the meanings of the two elements. Other Shakespearean examples are *harsh-rude*, *stubborn-hard*, *sober-sad*, in which the meanings of the constituents are similar. Carlyle coined *grim-taciturn*, *giddy-swift*, and Hopkins *hardy-*

handsome and *wet-fresh*. Outside literary contexts, *bitter-sweet* and *shabby-genteel* have become institutionalized. Nonce compounds like *social-political*, *phonetic-semantic*, in which the adjectives are derived from nouns, are formed more easily than combinations of non-derived adjectives, which seem always to have some 'literary' flavour, *cf: cruel-compassionate* and *humble-surly* in the following: 'The ironic, cruel-compassionate exposition of the everyday life of the English middle classes . . .' [*Observer* 28 April 1968, 28/3]; 'Into this much-admired pantheon of under- and overground heroes . . . Krim, eager for The American Experience, muscled his humble-surly way' [*Sunday Times* 5 April 1970, 31/6].

V INSTRUMENTAL

V A *Noun – adjective*

bomb-happy	séasick
cámera-shy	snów-blind
óil-rich (as in *oil-rich*	trável-weary
millionaire)	wáter-soluble
púnch-drunk	

V B *Noun – verb(-ed)*

áir-borne	páper-bound
ármour-clad[a]	shóp-soiled
bómb-blasted	stone-ground †
drúg-induced	spéll-bound
gín-soaked	spóon-fed
hand-picked	stár-spangled
jet-propelled	tíme-honoured

[a] *Armour-clad* contains a participle which has no corresponding active form.

As with Instrumental nominal compounds, there may be overlap with the Locative class (VI), in which such examples as *air-borne, seasick, shop-soiled* might also be placed.

VI LOCATIVE

VI A *Locative noun – adjective*

brim-full[a]
níght-blind
world-famous[a]

[a] *Brim-full* and *world-famous* express 'extent': 'full to the brim', 'famous throughout the world'.

VIB *Locative noun – verb(-ed)*

country-bred	hell-bent[a]
éarthbound	home-brewed
factory-packed	London-trained
héart-felt	night-scented
heaven-born	world-renowned[a]

[a] *Hell-bent* and *world-renowned* contain participles which have no corresponding active forms.

Foreign-built may be placed here if it is considered elliptical for *foreign-soil built*.

VII COMPARATIVE

In these compounds, the second element is specified by a comparison with some quality characteristic of what the first element denotes. The first element in all cases is nominal.

VIIA *Intensifying*

VIIA1 *Noun – adjective*

crystal-clear (= 'as clear as crystal', *ie* 'as clear as it is possible to be')	jet black
	paper-thin
daisy-fresh	pitch dark
dirt-cheap	razor-sharp
feather-light†	rock-hard
fire-hot	sky high
ice-cold	snow-white

Icy-cold and *silky-soft* seem to belong here, though their first elements are adjectival in form.

It is easy to see how a first element in this kind of compound may become simply an intensifier, as in the following examples which are no longer understood as involving an explicit comparison.

brand new	dog-tired
cock-sure	stock still
dead beat	stone deaf
dead slow	

The OED explains *brand new* as 'new, as if fresh and glowing from the furnace'; *cock-sure*, tentatively is 'as sure as a cock', *dog-tired* is 'tired as a dog after a long chase', and *stock still* is 'as still as a stock or log'.

VII A 2 *Verb(-ing) – adjective*

freezing cold (= 'cold enough to freeze',   scalding hot
   'cold enough to cause (something) to freeze')   shocking pink
hopping mad   wringing wet
fighting ⎫   yawning dull[a]
roaring ⎭ drunk

[a] 'No matter that some of it was yawning dull and overloaded with statistics ...'
   [*Evening Standard* 1 June 1972, 19/2].

Piping hot also belongs here, though it is no longer understood as
involving a comparison. The OED explains it as 'so hot as to make a
piping sound'.

VII B *Particularizing*

VII B 1 *Noun – colour adjective*

ash blond   midnight blue[a]
blood red   nut brown
bottle green   peacock blue
brick red   pearl grey
grass green   sea green
lemon yellow   sky blue

[a] *Midnight blue* is perhaps elliptical for *midnight sky blue*.

VII B 2 *Noun – adjective of 'extent' or 'measurement'*

day-long   skin-tight
knee-deep   shoulder-high
life-long   waist-high
skin-deep   world-wide

VIII PREPOSITIONAL

This is a class of miscellaneous examples, whose elements may be linked
in a paraphrase by a preposition, and which do not fit into the Instrumental or Locative groups. They clearly belong to a number of subgroups, but since institutionalized examples are scarce, I have placed
them all together here.

VIII A *Noun–adjective*

áccident-prone (= 'prone to accidents')	power-mad
blóodthirsty (= 'thirsty for blood')	práiseworthy
class-conscious†	púrseproud
cólour-blind	rent free
hómesick	self-sufficient
penny-wise	wéather-wise
pound-foolish	

Fáilsafe, shátter-proof contain verbal first elements, *cf* 'safe from failure', 'proof against shattering'. As with noun compounds, we find examples which are difficult to paraphrase neatly: *post-free* is elliptical: 'free of postal charges'; *aírtight* means 'so tight as to be impermeable to air'; *word-perfect* cannot be glossed as 'perfect in words': it needs a longer paraphrase, such as 'being in the state of having completely and accurately memorized something consisting of words' [Webster 1961].[3]

VIII B *Noun–verb(-ed)*

canál-built (= 'built for use on a canal')
capácity-filled (= 'filled to capacity')
díamond-cut (= 'cut like a diamond')
móther-fixated (= 'fixated (having a fixation on) one's mother')[a]
sáfety-tested (= 'tested for safety')
séx-linked (= 'linked to sex')

[a] *Mother-fixated* appears to be a backformation (see Chapter 7) from a nominal form, *móther-fixation*.

Táx-deductible (= 'deductible from tax') contains a non-participial verbal adjective.

IX DERIVATIONAL

These consist of a compound noun stem – either noun–noun or adjective–noun – and the adjective-suffix *-ed*. The following are adjective–noun examples.

broad-leaved	open-ended
cross-grained	quick-tempered
good-natured	

One group of Derivational adjective compounds contains a human or animal attribute, mental or physical, as second element:

cool- clear- level- }headed wrong- pig-	big- faint- warm- }hearted chicken-
cráck- féather- }brained háre-	absent- broad- evil- high- }minded narrow- air-
sharp- }eared dóg-	
bright- álmond- éagle- }eyed lýnx-	dim- }witted quick-

bull-necked	short-sighted
double-jointed	straight-faced
lántern-jawed	sure-footed
loud-mouthed	tight-fisted
pigeon-toed	tight-lipped
raw-boned	wasp-waisted
round-shouldered	web-footed

Many of these are metaphorical, and in some cases the compound stem is not current as a compound noun or an attributive–head noun phrase. The combination *long head* used nominally does not mean the same as it does in the adjective compound *long-headed*; and we do not usually talk of anyone having *an absent mind, a pig head, a chicken heart, a wrong head* or *raw bones*, though *clear head, bright eyes, sharp ears* are normal nominal phrases. Possibly some related nominal phrases, like *bull neck, eagle eye, short sight, straight face* have been formed by subtracting the adjectival *-ed* from the adjective compound. *Cf* from *foul-mouthed*: 'Macfugger, a randy and rumbustious redhead with a foul mouth and a rich wife' [*Evening Standard* 20 July 1971, 17/1–2]. Where the first constituent is nominal, as in *lynx-eyed, wasp-waisted*, there is a relationship of 'resemblance' between the elements. The -*minded* compounds however, are an exception to this. (*Cf* the peculiarity of -*minded*, noted in 2.6 above.)

In some adjective compounds ending in -*ed* the second element may be either nominal or verbal, and the suffix therefore either an adjectival or participial one (*cf* 2.6 above). Ambiguous examples are *cándy-striped* (= 'having candy stripes' or 'striped like candy') *deep-rooted* (= 'having deep roots' or 'deeply rooted'), *sugar-coated* (= 'having a sugar coat' or 'coated with sugar'). *Cf* also *chócolate-flavoured, rúst-coloured, colour-prejudiced*: 'Last week's Talkback . . . for example, notched up 100 per cent in answer to the question "Are the British colour prejudiced?" ' [*Observer* 17 March 1968, 32/5].

There appear to be very few examples of Derivational adjective compounds with suffixes other than -*ed* and different relationships between the stem elements. One such is *party-polítical* (= 'concerned with party politics').

X NOMINAL ATTRIBUTIVES

A few adjectival combinations are really nominal compounds or phrases which have become institutionalized in attributive position.

X A *Verb – object – noun*

cátch-penny	lácklustre
bréak-neck	télltale

These are like the Verb–Object nominal compounds in Chapter 5, II A 2; in fact *cut-throat* in that group might well have been placed here since we use it attributively, as in *cut-throat razor* perhaps more frequently now than as a head noun.

X B *Other nominal attributives*

all-time[a]	middle class
bare-back	old hát
floor-length	old-time
frée-lance	one-horse[a]
full-scale	white-collar
long-range	

[a] The examples *all-time, one-horse* seem so unacceptable in predicative use that it would be difficult to say how they might be accented.

6.4 Productivity and use of adjective compounds

Among the various groups of adjective compounds, very generally speaking, three stylistic varieties may be distinguished: established and more or less cliché-like combinations like *long-suffering, heart-broken, star-spangled, tight-lipped;* 'literary' formations which conform to a recognized pattern but are not likely to be much used, and technical compounds. Two examples from a newspaper illustrate the second kind: 'Three new shirts...which were afterwards distributed among the shirt-needy' [*Evening Standard* 11 January 1970, 15/3]; 'The first [thing] was to reorganize Apple, which he performed by wholesale and eagle-sudden dismissals' [*ibid*, 11/3]. Probably the first-mentioned kind of adjective compound is much commoner in everyday speech than the second, nonce, kind, which tends to appear chiefly in writing.

Leech (1966, 137) discussing such formations as *coffee-pot-fresh, shining-clean, fast-foaming, perfect-textured*, says: 'in advertising English, lexical restraints on compound formation are less stringent than elsewhere'. Adjective compounds are certainly common in advertisements; coinages like those just quoted, and others, like *sunshine-flavoured, jungle-fresh, dew-bright, lemon-fragrant*, are recognizably part of the 'diction' of copywriters. But it seems true that the freedom which speakers feel to coin compounds, especially adjective compounds, is not confined to advertising language: it is evident in literature, especially poetry[4] and in some kinds of journalism. We might in any case expect adjective compounding to be less potentially restricted than nominal compounding, since the birth of a new noun is after all dependent on the existence of a corresponding object in the real world, which it names, and many possible nominal compounds would sound very strange to us, because they have no referents. Lees (1960, 121) illustrates this with the meaningless example **examine-cart*, formed on the verb – object pattern of *push-cart* (*cf* Chapter 5, II A 2). Adjective compounds are less limited in this way, though we can of course construct 'impossible' ones, like **law-flavoured, *chocolate-abiding*.[5]

The following quotations provide brief illustrations of the 'literary' use of adjective compounding (italics mine):

> ...younger women in...thin floral dresses clinging with innocent voluptuousness to their long American thighs, sporting generous, *elastic-lipped, perfect-teethed* smiles as advertised by Mary Tyler Moore. Children were everywhere, *band-box neat, fashion-plate cute*, as if newly unwrapped around the corner from cellophane boxes. [*New Statesman* 26 April 1968, 544/2]

... he was palsied of hand and foot and *eye-mad* and *heart-quick* and went from the curse of Ronan *bird-quick* in craze and madness from the battle ... For it is thus that Glen Bolcain is, it has four gaps to the four winds and a too-fine too-pleasant wood and *fresh-banked* wells and *cold-clean* fountains and sandy pellucid streams of clear water with *green-topped* watercress and brooklime *long-streamed* on the current ... He settled and roosted on its slender perch till it bowed beneath him ... not one inch of him from toe to crown that was not *red-prickled* and *blood-gashed*, the skin to his body being ragged and flapping and thorned, the tattered cloak of his perished skin. He arose *death-weak* from the ground to his standing for the recital of this lay. [Flann O'Brien, *At Swim-Two-Birds*, 1939, Penguin 1967, 66–7]

The second passage is of course a burlesque of a certain kind of 'poetic' prose.

Compounds of the third kind, technical formations, are exemplified by *drug-induced, jet-propelled, rocket-assisted*. Further coinages may be found in the language of such specialized fields as computer science; examples are *content-addressed, hardware-detected, implementation-defined, machine-independent, pattern-sensitive*. One reason for the frequency of compounds like these may be the need for the economy and clarity which is desirable in technical descriptions and instructions. An adjective compound is far more compact than a relative clause, '... which is independent of the machine' and so on. Adjective compound patterns, moreover, are fairly 'transparent' and therefore can be used freely without undue risk of ambiguity. It is usually not difficult to understand an adjective compound which we have not seen before: as we noticed in Chapter 5, nominal compounds may be rather different in this respect. Considerations of economy certainly seem to have motivated the compound in the following speech from astronauts in a spacecraft to the Mission Control Centre on earth: 'We're at this time water-critical in the L M [Lunar Module]. We'd like to use as little as possible' [quoted in *Sunday Times* 19 April 1970, 13/8].

Notes

1 In none of these combinations is the hyphen needed to obviate any ambiguity, as it is in, for instance, a pair given by Fowler (1965, 256): *a little-used car* and *a little used car*. Fowler, incidentally – supported by Sir Winston Churchill: '*Richly embroidered* seems to me two words, and it is terrible to think of linking every adverb to a

verb by a hyphen' – considers that hyphens should not be used except where they are necessary.

2 For examples I have freely drawn on Marchand (1969, 84–95), though my classification differs from his.

3 By permission. From Webster's Third International Dictionary ©1971 by G. & C. Merriam Co, publishers of the Merriam-Webster Dictionaries.

4 For numerous examples of literary adjective compounds, see Groom (1937).

5 These are Geoffrey Leech's examples (personal communication).

Chapter 7

Verb compounds and backformation

7.1 Backformation[1]

This chapter discusses a number of different patterns of word-formation which are difficult to separate from one another. It is desirable to treat verb compounds all together, though these are not all formed by the process of backformation, and it also seems best to treat instances of backformation all together, though these are by no means all compound verbs. We may begin by saying that backformation occurs when the formative process from base word to derived word is seen to be reversed: the more complex word comes first and then some element is subtracted from it, resulting in a pair of words which conforms with a base→derived pattern already existing. Thus the verb *to beg* is formed from the noun *beggar*, and this pair corresponds to pairs like *write* (verb), *writer* (noun), *sing* (verb), *singer* (noun), and so on. In some cases, as with *beggar*, a 're-interpretation' of an element in the source word takes place. The ending of *beggar* is not agentive in origin: the word is most probably descended from *beghard* or *beguin*, the names of a medieval brotherhood and sister-hood respectively, deriving from a proper name, *Bègue* [OED s.v. *beggar sb.*] In other cases, as with compound verbs, a different kind of re-interpretation takes place: we do not 'mistake' an element for something which it is not, but we re-analyse the constituent structure of the source word. How this happens is explained in the next section.

7.2 Verb compounds

Verb compounds may arise in three different ways: by backformation from noun or adjective compounds (7.2.1), by zero derivation from noun compounds (7.2.2) and, less often, in the same way as other types of compounds, by linking two words together (7.2.3). Since verb compounds are comparable with noun and adjective compounds in respect of the relations between their elements, they may be given the same kind of classification that is carried out in Chapters 5 and 6. For example, under the Verb– Object heading would come *to giftwrap*, *to sightsee* (7.2.2) and *to test-market* (7.2.3), while the Instrumental group would include *to tape-record* (7.2.1), *to pitchfork* (7.2.2) and *to chauffeur-drift* (7.2.3). I have not set out the examples in this way, however; they are arranged according to the three methods of formation just mentioned, though it would be interesting to find out whether particular patterns are especially favoured in the formation of compound verbs. It would be particularly interesting in the case of the non-derived type of verb compound described in 7.2.3, but examples that we can with reasonable certainty place in this group are not numerous enough to make the exercise of classification sufficiently instructive.

Verb compounds are likely to be written solid or hyphenated; they appear as two separate words much less often than noun compounds. As far as accent is concerned, derived verb compounds follow the pattern of their source constructions; so we have *cáretaker* and *to cáretake*, *mass prodúction* and *to mass-prodúce*. I have therefore not marked the accent on the examples in 7.2.1 and 7.2.2, since accentuation is not relevant to the process of verb compounding. I have however accented the few non-derived examples of 7.2.3.

7.2.1 VERB COMPOUNDS FORMED BY BACKFORMATION

Verb compounds may have nominal or adjectival compounds as their sources. *To globe-trot*, for example, is most probably derived from the nominal *globe-trotter*, or *globe-trotting*. In *globe-trotter*, the *-er* modifies the second element: the whole may be paraphrased as 'one who trots (a trotter) about the globe'. The best way of explaining how the compound verb comes about is to say that a change in the constituent structure of the compound noun takes place, so that the *-er* is seen as belonging, not to the simple stem *trot-*, but to the compound stem *globe-trot-*:

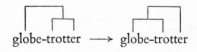

$$\text{globe-trotter} \longrightarrow \text{globe-trotter}$$

The ending may now be subtracted, leaving the compound verb *to globe-trot*. Similar examples are *to brainwash*, *to ghost-write*, *to sleep-walk*. It often cannot be stated with certainty which nominal (or adjectival) form has provided the starting-point for a backformed verb compound. *Brain-washing* seems the most likely source for the first of these three examples, *ghost-writer* for the second; the *-er* and the *-ing* forms for *to sleep-walk* seem equally probable sources. *To free-associate* appears to be from *free association; to hen-peck* and *to spoon-feed* seem most naturally analysed as derived from the adjective compounds *hen-pecked* and *spoonfed*.

In a few cases, the ending which is subtracted is not a nominalizing or participial one, but is re-interpreted as such. *To doublehead* (='of a train, to run powered by two locomotives') is derived from *doubleheader* (='a train pulled by two engines'). In this case there is no re-analysis of constituent structure; *doubleheader* is made up of a compound stem and the 'characterizing' *-er* suffix which is added to nominal stems; it is re-interpreted as the agentive *-er*, and *head-* is re-interpreted as a verbal stem. The adjective-suffix *-ed* may be re-interpreted as the participial *-ed* (*cf: terraced*, 4.3, ID2 and note). *To weatherboard*, from *weatherboarded* is a possible example of this, though it might also have been formed by zero suffix from the noun *weatherboard*.

Further examples of compound verbs formed by the 'subtraction' of a nominal or adjectival ending are

air-condition	mass-produce
book-keep	muck-rake
browbeat	proof-read
caretake	sightsee
gatecrash	spring-clean
gift-wrap	stage-manage
housebreak	tape-record
housekeep	window-shop

Occasionally a new noun may be formed from a verb compound by zero derivation. The noun *house-hunt* is most probably from *house-hunter* or *house-hunting* via a compound verb *to house-hunt*; and *cf* also the nouns *brainwash* and *spy-catch* in the following: 'The great Concorde brainwash' [*Spectator* 14 February 1970, 203/1–2]; 'Italy's most important spy-catch began on the frontier with France on 15 March' [*Observer* 26 March 1967, 1/1]. Some compounds whose second element is a verb with zero nominal suffix, like *sunset* or *bell-pull* (see Chapter 5, I A 1 and II B 2) may well have been formed in this way, since the nouns *set* and *pull* do not occur alone in the same senses. (For this reason compounds like these are described as parasynthetic in 3.4.)

7.2.2 VERB COMPOUNDS FORMED BY ZERO DERIVATION

Section 4.3 above, where patterns of noun-to-verb zero derivation are described, contains a few examples of compound verbs from homonymous compound nouns, which we meet again here, such as *to blue-pencil*, *to sandpaper*, *to snowball*. All the examples which follow immediately might be assigned to one or another of the groups in 4.3.

blue-pencil	pitchfork
cold-shoulder	sandbag
court-martial	shipwreck
handcuff	short-circuit
honeymoon	snowball
machine-gun	wisecrack

7.2.3 VERB COMPOUNDS FROM OTHER SOURCES

Marchand (1969, 100–7) refers to compound verbs as 'pseudo-compound verbs' because of their derivational nature. He says (100) that 'verbal composition does not exist in present-day English'. However, when we find examples of compound verbs which seem not to correspond to noun or adjective compounds of similar form, we may wonder whether verbal composition does not after all exist independently of other kinds. Pennanen (1966, 115) gives the example of the verb *to chain-drink* which seems to have been formed by analogy with *to chain-smoke*, a backformation from *chain-smoker*, and points out (116) that though *to half-choke* and *to half-starve* are probably backformations, other *half-* compound verbs, like *half-turn*, *half-close*, *half-rise*, may be analogical formations. He goes on to make a more interesting suggestion (117), that some verb compounds may be 'so-called inversions with back-formation as back-ground influence'. That is, a verb like *to vólume-expand* may be formed directly, *cf* a phrase like *to expand the volume*, and not from a nominal compound such as *volume-expanding*.

Other examples of (nonce) compound verbs for which corresponding nominal or adjectival forms are not established are *to cathédral-look*: 'She has spent the day exploring various old churches in Périgueux. ... Day of the general mobilization she had been cathedral-looking at Avignon' [Arthur Koestler, *Scum of the Earth*, 1941, 179]; *to cháuffeur-drift*: ' "I feel just like I was in a movie," said Mrs Patrick Nugent, ... as we chauffeur-drifted from Claridges to the Kings Road' [*Evening Standard* 26 November 1970, 3/3]. *To consúmer-test* and *to tést-market* show that we need not specify that inversion occurs, since these are 'subject–verb' and 'verb–object' combinations respectively (*cf: the consumer tests the product; John tests the market*): 'Ivan Pope, aged nine, consumer-tested one of the newest boy's toys for us' [*Evening Standard* 19 November 1971, 19/2]; 'Lightest razor . . . is now being test-marketed by Wilkinson Sword' [*Sunday Times* 20 December 1970, 33/7]. The following examples are from instructions often seen on the labels of clothes, and are presumably compound imperative forms: *hand wásh, cold rínse, short spín, warm íron, hand-hot medium wásh, line drý.*

It could be argued, in support of Marchand's view of compound verbs, that in each of these cases we should assume the existence of a nominal combination, *chauffeur-drifting, test-marketing* and so on, through which these verbs are formed. On the other hand, Pennanen shows conclusively that compound verbs have vastly increased in number in the last two centuries, and it may be that it is now time to recognize a new pattern of compounding which is not derivational.

7.3 Resistance to verb compounds

Verb compounds, however, are still by no means as freely formed as noun and adjective compounds, and are still stylistically marked as more appropriate in informal than in formal use. Jespersen says (MEG VI, 9.7₁):

'Compound verbs of the type *housekeep* are not usual in the Gothonic languages, and are felt to some extent as contrary to idiom.' This may be because of the re-interpretation of structure that has to take place before a verb like *housekeep* can be formed. But even if this is true, we still have to explain why we feel that verbs like *to sandpaper, to snowball*, formed by zero suffix from nouns, are similarly marked stylistically. It may be that the length of these words is relevant here: in general, where derivation by zero suffix is concerned, we prefer to operate with short words rather than long ones.[2] As far as verbs of the kind exemplified in 7.2.3 are concerned – those which it is suggested are formed as compounds in their own right, these are clearly not yet numerous enough to constitute an established pattern. Moreover, the three ways of forming compound verbs cannot be thought of as entirely separate processes, since we are not infrequently unsure which of them is responsible for a particular example.

7.4 Conjugation of complex verbs

An interesting feature of verb compounds appears in cases where the second element is a verb which normally shows some morphological irregularity. It may lose this irregularity in composition. Notice the form of *to drip-dry* in the following, where we might have expected *drip-dries*: 'They're made from polyester and cotton, which feels like cotton but wears like polyester, drip-drys like polyester . . .' [*Sunday Times* 26 July 1970, I, advertisement]. But many verb compounds are attested only in the non-finite forms, for example *to book-keep, to caretake, to sightsee*, for which past tense forms *book-keeped, caretaked, sightseed* seem as unlikely as *book-kept, caretook, sightsaw* (cf the comments in 2.6 and 2.7 above on the role of non-finite forms as intermediaries in the verb-forming process). Incidentally, uncertainty about the conjugating of verbs is not peculiar to compounds of the kind this chapter is concerned with. Zandvoort (1957) gives an example of a verb-particle collocation, *string out*, with a weak past participle: 'We turned and climbed, flying in the same direction as the bombers with the whole squadron stringed out . . .' (228). And the following is an example of a prefix influencing the form of its verb stem. 'One man we heard of had, sadly, to have his hair unwoven (or de-weaved) as he was posted to a country where hair-weaving was unknown' [newspaper 1969].

7.5 Other examples of backformation[3]

The majority of backformed words which are not compounds are verbs. This fact is commented on by Pennanen, who points out (1966, 91):

> Verbs have a peculiar property among the words of the language in so far as they develop round them a number of nominal derivatives: the agent noun, the noun of action, the verbal substantive and the various types of participial adjective. Where there is a verb, we expect to find this family of derivatives attached to it, and conversely, when we come across one or more nominal members of such a family the existence of the corresponding parent verb is taken almost for granted.
>
> This alone gives five different points of departure for an eventual process of backformation.[4]

Nouns ending in *-ion* frequently give rise to corresponding verbs. The verbs *appreciate, abduct, investigate*, all appeared later than the corresponding nouns (cf Jespersen 1935), though it is likely that Latin past participle forms were also involved in the derivation of these verbs. The infinitive *to create*, the past participle *create* (later superseded by *created*) and the noun *creation* all appeared in English at the end of the fourteenth century, and it is hardly possible to say which came first.[5] The verbs *automate, electrocute, intuit, negate, opt, orate* all appeared later than their corresponding nominals in *-ion*. *Destruct* occurs in aerospace language: a *destruct device* is 'a device for destroying space vehicles when safety is threatened'. Hence it is used as a noun, meaning 'the deliberate destruction of a rocket, etc'. (See the Addenda (1971) to Webster (1961).) The verb *to destruct* is recorded by the OED as occurring once, in 1638. *Contraceive* is derived from *contraception* on the pattern of the small group of verbs ending in *-ceive* with nominalizations in *-ception*: 'If the argument of repugnant waste is applied to contraceived eggs and sperm, it can be pointed out that nature is already remarkably wasteful where these products are concerned' [Desmond Morris, *The Human Zoo*, 1969, 153].

Hawk and *sculpt* are from agentive nouns, Old English *hawker* (*hafocere*) and Latin *sculptor*. The endings of *burglar* (corresponding to a medieval Latin word *burglator*) and *coroner* (corresponding to the medieval Latin *coronarius* or *coronator*) are historically only indirectly related to the English agentive ending. The first has given rise to the established *burgle*, the second to the nonce *coroning; cf* 'Coroners began coroning in the 12th century' [*New Statesman* 10 February 1967, 180/3]. *Commentate* dates from 1794 according to the OED, which derives it from *commentator* (1641), but in the modern sense of 'to provide a running commentary' it has been re-derived from the modern sense of *commentator; cf* 'I wonder the BBC doesn't put on Lévi-Strauss to commentate at Silverstone' [*Listener* 15 February 1968, 198/3]. *Reminisce* and *enthuse* are from the nominal forms *reminiscence* and *enthusiasm*.

A now obsolete adverbial suffix, *-ling*, which appears in *darkling, grovelling*, was re-interpreted as a verbal ending, to produce the verbs *darkle, grovel*. A similar-looking recent example is *gangle, cf* 'Ronald Pickup gangles his way suspendingly through this lark' [*Evening Standard* 19 June 1968, 5/2–3]. *Gangling* was originally not an adverb but a participial adjective, from a non-existent verb *to gangle*, explained by the OED as a frequentative of the now only dialectal verb *to gang* (='to go'). The Addenda (1971) to Webster (1961), however, lists *gangle* (='to move in an awkward ungraceful manner') as backformed from *gangling*. The OED compares *gangling* with the noun *gangrel* in its sense of 'a lanky, loose-jointed person'.

Some prefixed forms involving backformation have come into existence through a re-interpretation of structure like that described for compound verbs in 7.2.1. The verb *to non-cooperate* contains a prefix which is normally only added to nouns and adjectives, and we can imagine a process like this:

non-cooperation ⟶ non-cooperation ⟶ non-cooperate

cf ' "I had to leave the college when Gandhi ordered us to non-cooperate. I spent the best of my student years in prison," said Jagan' [R. K. Narayan, *The Sweet-Vendor*, 1967, 33]. Nominal prefixed forms which are clearly backformations are *unsurprise* and *illogic*, which contain negative prefixes not normally attached to nouns; *cf* 'our utter unsurprise' [*Listener* 28 March 1968, 415/2]; '[Those] . . . who . . . condemn scientists who cooperate in CBW are often accused of illogic' [*Listener* 11 July 1968, 36/2].

Like verb compounds, backformations of all kinds, unless very well established, are more frequently found in informal than in formal language.

Notes

1 For a detailed study of this subject, see Pennanen (1966).
2 This aspect of zero derivation has been noticed by several scholars: Bladin (1911, 51), Biese (1941, 247), Pennanen (1966, 111 n).
3 See also Jespersen (1935), Jespersen (MEG VI, Chapter 29), Pennanen (1966), Marchand (1969, Chapter 6).
4 Lakoff (1970, 55–66) discusses the postulation of hypothetical verbs such as *to critique, to mote,* corresponding with the nouns *critique, motion,* which behave syntactically like nominalizations, and he points out (85) that the OED occasionally sets up hypothetical verbs, for example *to ablute,* explaining the participial form *abluted.* This verb is described by the OED as 'not otherwise found'. *Cf: gangling,* mentioned above, which the OED derives: 'f. as if **gangle*'. Lakoff further comments (85–6) that backformed verbs such as *to aggress,* from *aggression,* may be acceptable to some speakers and not to others, and (88–90) that this area of the vocabulary is particularly fluid and susceptible to change.
5 See Reuter (1934) and comments by Marchand (1969, 256–8) on the subject of verbs formed from borrowed past participles.

Chapter 8

Compounds containing particles

8.1 Compounds with a particle as first element[1]

Compounds containing particles may be nominal, adjectival, verbal or adverbial, and an arrangement of examples according to word-class is not entirely convenient, since many nouns have corresponding verbs and participial adjectives and it may be interesting to look at these together. Thus, corresponding to the noun *úpset*, we have the verb *to upsét*, and the participial adjectives *upsétting* and *upsét*. In the following sections I have noted such correspondences. Opposite the nominal example *úpset* (I B 1) a note mentions the two adjectives and the verb; these three words therefore do not appear in their appropriate sections. This arrangement should not be taken to indicate which words are basic and which derived, since here we are concerned only with the occurrence of compounds with particles. Where the non-particle element is a derived word, however, this is noted by means of subgrouping. For nouns like *outcome* (I B 1) or *play-back* (V C) which contain nouns derived from verbs, and for a few like *bypass* and *upset* which have homonymous verbs, the kind of classification carried out in Chapter 4 would be appropriate, and some of the examples in this chapter will already have been met there.

As in Chapters 5 and 6, an obelisk indicates uncertain accentuation.

8.1.1 NOMINAL

In a few cases there may be doubt as to whether we should consider a combination of particle and noun a compound or a free phrase. Thus, while *áfter-effect*, *óuthouse*, *óvercoat* are accented as compounds and are clearly established combinations, *after years*, *down platform*, *through train* are not usually so accented and could be considered as free phrases. As far as nominal constructions are concerned, this question only arises with compounds of class I A, in which a non-derived noun is the second element and the particle functions to some extent like an attributive adjective. As in Chapters 5 and 6, I have not attempted to define the notion of 'compound' with any strictness, but have included combinations where I felt them to be established collocations.

I A *Particle – non-derived noun*

To say that the particle 'functions like an attributive adjective' is a little misleading, since its adverbial or prepositional nature is not lost in the combination. An *after-effect* is 'an effect occurring after (as the result of) something', and the first element here retains its prepositional aspect, as if we understood the compound as elliptical for, say, *after-illness effect*. Similarly, a *down-stroke* is 'a stroke down(ward)', and the first element retains its adverbial sense.

áfter-effect	áfter-life
báckground	báckwater
cóunter-attack[a] (& verb *cóunter-attack*)	counter-intélligence
	counter-írritant
counter-éspionage	cóunter-proposal
cóunter-example	counter-reformátion

[a] These examples, with the exception of *counter-example* and *counter-intelligence*, in fact contain a second element derived from, or corresponding to, a verb; but they nevertheless seem to belong here, since there could be no corresponding verb-particle collocations. A *counter-proposal* is 'a proposal, something proposed, which is counter, opposed, to some earlier proposal'. *Counter-* also appears prefixed in 'opaque' words like *counterpart, counterpoint*, and attached to bound stems, as in the verbs *countermand, countervail*. Words of this kind were borrowed into Middle English from French.

cróss-current[a]

[a] *Cross-* is a shortened form of *across*, itself derived from *in + cross* (noun); in some uses of this element it is difficult to decide whether we are dealing with the locative particle or with the noun *cross*. *Cf: cross-piece, cross-road*, which may be analysed as 'piece (road) forming, or being part of, a cross' as well as 'piece which lies across...'. *Cróss-stitch* seems best interpreted as 'stitch in the form of a cross'.

dówn-stroke

fórearm[a]	fórehead
fóredeck	

[a] *Fore* is not often found as an independent word; it is so used however in (for instance) nautical contexts (*cf: he went fore to check his instruments*), and so I have treated it as a particle rather than a prefix.

ín-group   ín-road

off-chance†   off-licence†[a]

[a] *Off-licence* is elliptical (= 'off-premises licence', 'an establishment licensed to sell liquor to be consumed off the premises'). It should probably be considered as originally attributive (from *off-licence shop* or *establishment*).

óuthouse   óutpost

óut-patient   óut-tray (= 'out-going letters tray')

óvercoat   óverdraft

óverdose   óverlord

úndercarriage   úndertone

úndercurrent   únderworld

únderdog

IB *Particle – nominalized verb*

Here, as in other sections in this chapter which involve nominalizations, I have not distinguished between nouns derived from transitive verbs and those from intransitive verbs. I have however attempted to separate those combinations that correspond to a verb–adverb or verb–preposition–noun collocation as used in a sentence, from those that do not.

IB1 *Particle–verb (zero suffix)*

[a] a verb–adverb/preposition collocation with related meaning exists

býpass (& verb *býpass* IIIA)

dównfall   dównturn

dównpour

ínput (& verb *ínput* IIIA)   íntake

óutburst   óutlay

óutcome   óutlook (*cf: lóok-out* VC

óutcry   = 'prospect')

óutfall (*cf: fáll-out* VC)   óutput

óutfit (& noun *óutfitter* IB2
   & verb *óutfit* IIIA)

óverhang (& adjective *over-*   overspill
   hánging IIB1 & verb
   overháng IIIA)

únderpass   únderwear

úpkeep   úpstart

úplift (& verb *uplíft* IIIA)   úpthrust

thróughput

[*b*] no verb–adverb/preposition collocation with related meaning exists

óffprint (& verb *óffprint* III A)   óffspring
óffshoot

ónset

óverkill (& verb *overkíll* III A)

úpset (& adjectives *upsétting*   úptake
  II B 1, *upsét* II B 2 & verb
  upsét III A)

Some of these B 1 examples may be seen as parasynthetic (see 3.4 above). There are no nouns *hang, set, take* which have senses relatable to the compounds *overhang, onset, intake,* so that the stems of these compounds may be seen as taking 'simultaneously' the prefixed particle and the zero suffix.

I B 2 *Particle–verb(-er)*

[*a*] a verb–adverb/preposition collocation with related meaning exists

backslider† (& verb *backslíde* III A)
býstander
ónlooker (*cf: looker-ón* V A)

[*b*] no verb–adverb/preposition collocation with related meaning exists

óutrider

óverseer (& verb *oversée* III A)

underachíever (& verb *underachíeve* III A)   únderwriter (& verb
úndertaker   *underwríte* III A)

Outsíder is a derivational compound, from *outside* and the non-agentive -*er*.

I B 3 *Particle–verb (other nominalization)*

[*a*] a verb–adverb/preposition collocation with related meaning exists

áfterthought
óutpouring
úpbringing   uprising†

[*b*] no verb–adverb/preposition collocation with related meaning exists

forebóding

ínbreeding (& adjective *inbred* II B 2)

overabúndance (& adjective
over-abundant II A)

overcompensátion (& verb
overcómpensate III A)

overexcítement (& adjective *over-
excited* II B 2 & verb *overexcíte*
III A)

over/underexpósure (& verb *over/
underexpóse* III A) ·

úndergrowth
undertáking (& verb *undertáke* III A)
uphéaval

fóresight

ínfighting

overindúlgence (& adjective
indulgent II B 1 & verb
overindúlge III A)

óversight

óver/únderstatement (&
verb *over/understáte* III A)

IC *Particle–noun derivational compounds with zero suffix*

áfterbirth

fórenoon

ín-law[a]

óverall

úndergroundb

afternóon

óverheadb

[a] *In-law* is of course a shortened form of *mother (etc) -in-law*.

[b] *Overhead* and *underground* are from attributive–head phrases, as *overhead costs*,
underground movement or *underground railway*.

About-face† (& verb *about-face*†, = 'to face about, *ie* in the opposite
direction') is presumably from an imperative phrase.

8.1.2 ADJECTIVAL

The question of deciding whether a combination is a compound or a free
phrase may arise in the case of adjectives in *over-*. The OED [s.v. *over-*
28] notes that this element 'can be prefixed at will to any adj.' and points
out its similarity to the adverb *too* and its ambiguous status as between
word and word-element in such sequences as *not over-obliging*, *not over-
burdened with*. It seems arbitrary perhaps to make a distinction between the
two combinations in the following: 'Nevertheless, the pattern of the too-
compliant male and the over-dominant female is so common that it

accounts for a great deal of marital disharmony' [*Evening Standard* 12 July 1968, 8/1–2]. Marchand (1969, 118) points out that *over-* may be less closely bound to its stem than other prefixed particles and quotes 'many underdeveloped countries are over, not under, advised' [*Economist* 19 January 1952, 118]. Compare also the quotation in 6.3, IV: '. . . under- and over-ground heroes . . . '. (This comment applies of course to *under-* as well as *over-*.)

Among particle compounds generally, it is noticeable that *over-* and *under-* often appear prefixed to the same stem (*cf* IB 3 above). In many cases the *over-* compound has prompted the coining of the *under-* one (*cf* OED s.v. *under-* 10c), though with the example *over-ground* just mentioned, the prompting has gone the other way. The following nonce formations exploit the *over-/under-* opposition in adjectival particle compounds: 'when Johnson actually went, McCarthy looked quite naked, though still perfectly composed and, as the Washington Post put it, "under-whelmed"' [*Observer* 7 April 1968, 21–7] (see also the Addenda (1971) to Webster (1961) for the verb *to underwhelm*); 'His backers . . . were said to be underjoyed by collections which failed to please private clients' [*Sunday Times* 15 August 1971, 8/4].

For the principle on which accent marks are assigned to adjective compounds see 6.2; and notice that a few particle compounds may take the accent on the second element even in attributive position. In such cases, the accent is marked on the second element.

II A *Particle – non-derived adjective*

| overdue | over/under-ripe |
| overlong | oversensitive |

II B 1 *Particle–verb(-ing or other adjectival ending)*

[*a*] a verb–adverb/preposition collocation with related meaning exists

counter-intuitive

íngrowing

offputting

óncoming	óngoing
óutgoing	outstánding
óutlying	

underlying (& verb *underlíe*
   III A)

[b] no verb–adverb/preposition collocation with related meaning exists

overbéaring[a] (& adjective
  over-borne II B 2)
overwhélming   overwéening[a]

---

[a] *Overbearing* and *overweening* are the present participles of the obsolete verbs
overbear and *overween*.

II B 2 *Particle–verb(-ed)*

[a] a verb–adverb/preposition collocation with related meaning exists

abóve-mentioned
býgone
dówncast   dówntrodden
inbuilt (*cf: built-in* II A)   inborn
outdated (& verb *outdáte* III A)   outstretched
overgrown

[b] no verb–adverb/preposition collocation with related meaning exists

overcast   over/underfed (& verb *over/*
over/underdone   *underféed* III A)
                                overwrought

Úndersigned† is regularly used in nominal function: *the undersigned* (= 'the
person who signs his name at the end of a document').

II C *Particle–noun(-ed)*

downhéarted
outmóded
overcrowded   over/undersexed
overjóyed   over/undersized
over/underprivileged   over/understaffed

Some of these examples are parasynthetic, for example *downhearted*: the
forms *downheart* and *hearted* do not occur. *Overcrowded* on the other
hand may be analysed as *over+ crowded*.

8.1.3 VERBAL

III A *Particle–verb*

The existence of comparable verb–particle collocations is noted where relevant.

backdáte	backpédal
backfíre	bácktrack
counteráct	cóuntersign
cóunterbalance	
foredóom	forestáll
foreshádow	
offlóad	offsét

Out- as a prefix to verbs usually has the meaning 'to surpass', 'to excel in':

outgrów (also, more commonly, = 'to	outlíve
develop to the point of having no further	outmanóeuvre
use for', *cf* verb *grow out of*)	outshíne
outguéss	outstríp
outlást	out-tálk

Over- appears in a number of verbs, with various meanings.[2] In the following it has the sense of 'do to excess' and for some examples there are corresponding verbs in *under-* (= 'do insufficiently').

overchárge	overlóad
overdó	oversímplify
over/underéat	oversléep

In the examples below the particle has the sense of 'upset':

overbálance	overthrów (& noun *óverthrow*
oversét	IB 1)
	overtúrn (*cf* verb *turn over*)

In *overclóud*, *overspréad* it conveys the notion 'cover' (*cf* verbs *cloud over*, *spread over*). In the following it means 'pass over a boundary':[3]

overflów (& noun *óverflow* IB 1,	overstép (*cf* verb *step over*)
cf verb *flow over*)	overshóot
overréach	overtáke
overrún	

In *overpówer*, *overrúle*, *overtówer* (*cf* verb *tower over*), the particle conveys the meaning 'above', either literally or metaphorically. Words in *under-* meaning 'below' are

undercút	underpín
underlíne	underséll
undermíne	

Other senses of *over-* are seen in *overhéar*, *overhául*.

updáte	upgráde
upénd	upróot (*cf* verb *root-up*)

III B *Particle–noun (zero suffix)*
This class contains *out-* examples in which the sense of the particle is the same as that in the *out-* group of III A, *ie* 'to surpass'.

outdístance	outgéneral
outfáce	outnúmber
outflánk	outwít

Outsmárt is a rare example containing an adjectival stem. Some of these examples may be considered parasynthetic: there is no verb *wit* for example, except in the context of *out-*.

Shakespeare contributed to this class with his 'outHerods Herod' [*Hamlet* III ii], 'out-villaind villanie' [*All's Well that Ends Well* IV iii]. The OED gives a number of phrases formed on this pattern with the general meaning 'to outdo the agent in his own sphere or work', the majority from the seventeenth and nineteenth centuries. There are also phrases of this form in *over-*, for example 'over-Gospell the Gospell', 'over-Macphersoning Macpherson' [OED s.v. *over-* 22b, 1647, 1826].

8.1.4 ADVERBIAL AND ATTRIBUTIVE

IV *Preposition–noun*
With combinations of preposition and noun used adverbially, we may be in doubt as to whether we have to do with compounds or free phrases.

They are quite freely formed and their elements often seem rather loosely bound together, *cf* 'their doings off-screen and on were matters of concern throughout the world' [*Radio Times* 2 September 1971, 6/1]. Some established examples are

inland[a]

on-line ⎫
off-line ⎬ (computer equipment)

outdoors

overnight   overseas

upcountry   upstairs
upstage (& verb *upstáge* by zero
    suffix, = 'by staying upstage, to
    make an actor face away from
    the audience', hence 'to steal
    the show from someone').

[a] *Inland* in attributive position has the pronunciation /ˈɪnlənd/.

The examples just given perhaps seem more compound-like than

down hill   down town

under cover   under water

All such phrases are frequently used attributively, as in *undercover operation, underwater swimming.* Those which end in *-s* sometimes lose this in attributive position: *outdoor games;* but *an upstairs room.* Some prepositional phrases are not at all compound-like when used adverbially, but have nevertheless become established in attributive use:

in-flight (movie)   in-service (training)

on-course (bookie)

Cross-country (running) and *off-peak* (travelling) are preposition–noun combinations which are more likely to be used attributively than adverbially.

Those combinations which regularly appear after a copula verb vary as between complement and adjunct: *overweight*, for example, seems more adjectival, *off-beam* more adverbial. Some further examples are

abóveboard

off-beat	off hand
off-colour	off key
over/under-age	underhand
over/under-arm	

up-to-date

Examples in which the combination has acquired a non-literal meaning, like *aboveboard*, *off-colour*, *underhand*, are more likely to seem adjectival than those in which such a meaning-shift has not taken place, like *over-age*, *upcountry*.

All these IV combinations are really not different from the nouns under I C above, except as regards their function in sentences.

8.2 Compounds with a particle as second element

8.2.1 NOMINAL[4]

V A *Verb(-er) – particle*

diner-óut	passer-bý
hanger-ón	runner-úp
knocker-úp	whipper-ín
looker-ón	

V B *Verb(-ing) – particle*

dressing-dówn	summing-úp
going-óver (= 'thorough inspection')	tálking-to[a]
lying-ín	washing úp

---

[a] *Talking-to* is unusual in that its particle can normally function only as a preposition. The accentuation reflects this.

All the examples in V A and V B have corresponding finite verb–particle collocations.

VC *Verb (zero suffix) – particle*

[a] a verb–adverb/preposition collocation with related meaning exists

bláck-out	híde-out
bréak-down	pláy-back
buíld-up	pláy-with[a]
cóme-back	prínt-out
dróp-out	púsh-over
fóllow-up	sénd-off
gó-between[a]	sét-back
hánd-out	táke-off
háng-up (& adjective *hung up*	wríte-off
VIA, = 'having a hang-up',	wríte-up
'anxious')[b]	

[a] *Go-between* and *play-with* are unusual in that they contain a particle which can normally function only prepositionally. For the latter example, *cf* 'The notorious Hefner pad turned out to be a sedate Victorian mansion crammed with modern playwiths – abstract paintings and wide screen projector' [*Observer* 11 February 1968, 23/5].

[b] For the corresponding verb, *cf* 'I think like a white man, and when I get out into the world, that is maybe going to hang me up a bit' [*Evening Standard* 17 November 1971, 27/3].

Here we may note a few examples containing an adverb which is not a 'core' particle as defined in 3.3.

blów-hard	gét-together
come-hither† (= 'an enticing invitation'	knów-how
also attributive, = 'seductive')	sáy-so
díe-hard	stánd-still

Examples whose second constituent is, or was once, a prepositional phrase are *líe-abed*, *stáy-at-home*, *stíck-in-the-mud*.

[*b*] no verb–adverb/preposition collocation with related meaning exists

brúsh-off	háng-over[b]
cóme-down	láy-by
dím-out (= 'partial darkness', by analogy	móck-up
with *bláck-out; cf* also *brówn-out* and	préss-up
whíte-out, = 'a weather condition in an	shów-down
arctic area in which only dark objects	téach-in (see 13.4.1
are discernible')	for further -*in*
flásh-back	examples)
fráme-up[a]	thrów-back
gréy-out (= 'transient dimming of vision',	túrn-over
cf: réd-out, = 'physical condition causing	
reddening of the vision')	

[a] Corresponding to *frame-up*, the verb *to frame* occurs without the particle.
[b] Corresponding to *hang-over* there is the participial adjective *hung-over* (= 'suffering from a hang-over'), *cf* 'And then Ravitch, hung-over, came from his room, . . . his look guilty' [Saul Bellow, *Herzog* 1964, Penguin 1965, 146].

Many compounds of the V C type occur attributively, as in *a put-up job, a take-over bid*. Nouns like *clíp-on, pín-up, róll-on, sée-through* are most probably derived from attributive-head phrases from which the head noun has been dropped. *Cást-off, dúg-out, grown-úp, léft-over* contain past participles (*cf* group VIA below), and seem likely to have been attributives originally. But according to the OED, the head noun *cast-off* appeared a little before the attributive, the noun *dug-out* as head preceded its attributive use by some sixty years, and the noun *left-over* appeared at the same time as *left-over flowers*. *Léft-offs* (= 'old clothes'), however, is late nineteenth-century, whereas the phrase *left-off clothes* appeared about a hundred years earlier.

Group VC appears to be very much larger than V A or V B, but nonce compounds of all three groups are frequently found. Examples are: (V A) 'Reading about some people's major prejudices, I broke off – I am a great breaker-off these days – to ask myself what my own prejudices were' [*New Statesman* 24 December 1971, 886/1]; 'happy dabbler in seaside pools and ardent grubber-up of mossy trifles' [*Sunday Times* 26 September 1971, Magazine 22/1] – *cf* Shakespeare's 'snapper-up of unconsidered trifles' [*The Winter's Tale* IV iii]; '. . . a nation of traders, and shopkeepers, and improvisers, and muddlers-through' [*Sunday Times* 20 February 1972, 56/6]; 'Richard Dadier, sizer-up of women . . . walked to the bench and took a seat' [Evan Hunter, *The Blackboard Jungle*, 1955,

Panther 1957, 7]; (VB) 'drugs, alcohol, escapism, dropping out and all kinds of hippyism' [*Evening Standard* 5 June 1971, 9/1]; and *cf* 'the gunning down of another Kennedy', 2.7 above; (VC) 'the central talking point has been the political bounce-back of Mr Harold Wilson' [*Observer* 28 July 1968, 3/2]; 'Two families that face split-up' [*Evening Standard* 8 June 1971, 15/6, headline].

8.2.2 ADJECTIVAL AND OTHER

VI A *Past participle–particle*

browned off	líved-in[a]
cheesed off	pút-upon
clued up	run down

[a] *Cf: this house doesn't look lived-in*, in which the participial combination is distinct from the passive of *to live in* (something), as in *this house is lived in by ten people*.

As with the nominal combinations of V above, nonce formations are very common.

VI B *Other adjectival combinations*

far out	way out
hard up	well off
uptight[a]	

[a] This example belongs here in spite of its superficial resemblance to the II A group (*eg: overdue*). The particle *up* is here playing an adjective-like role, whereas the adverb/adjective *tight* is acting like a particle. A fairly recent Americanism (= 'anxious, indignant, tense, obsessed about something'), it appears to be comparable to an expression such as '(tied) up tightly'; *cf* 'He is totally cool or very uptight, depending on your point of view. The latter school says: "He's like a high-powered executive who doesn't show his feelings, but he's seething inside" ' [John Wilcock, *The Autobiography and Sex Life of Andy Warhol*, 1971, 49]. (The Addenda (1971) to Webster (1961) gives 'being in financial difficulties' as another meaning of this word.)

VI C *Other*

Among miscellaneous examples not yet mentioned are the adverbial *flat out, head on*; the nominal *hígh-up* (= 'person of high rank'), *lów-down* (= 'inside knowledge'), *sún-down, sún-up*. These do not represent productive patterns; the last two are idiosyncratic in formation.[5]

8.2.3 VERBAL

Combinations of verb and particle are of course extremely numerous in

English; but these have been described for the purposes of this book as belonging to syntax rather than to word-formation (see 1.4 above), so they will not be discussed any further here.

Notes

1 See Jespersen (MEG VI, Chapter 9) and Marchand (1969, 108–21); also for many examples, OED s.v. *out-*, *over-*, *under-*.
2 See Jespersen (MEG VI, 9.7₂) who comments on the 'series of related senses' in which *over-* is used in verbs.
3 See Jespersen *ibid*.
4 See Lindelöf (1937) for various examples, and a brief history of this pattern.
5 The OED suggests that *sun-down* may be a shortening of the combination *sun-go-down*, and that *sun-up* was formed by analogy with it.

Chapter 9

Neo-classical compounds

9.1 Native and borrowed elements

Neo-classical elements[1] productive today may be well-established ones which are compound-elements in the classical languages, and which have been current in English for some time. Among these are the *-cide* of *insecticide, pesticide*, which came into the language via French in the fourteenth century with *homicide*; the *-cracy* of *meritocracy*, which appeared in the sixteenth century in *aristocracy*, and the *poly-* of *polythene*, which appeared in the early seventeenth century with *poly-angle* and *poly-tragicke* (= 'containing many tragedies'). As Marchand points out (1969, 188), *pseudo-* as a compound-element is first recorded in Wyclif's works, and it was used as a word on its own from the fourteenth century on. Under *pseudo*, quasi-*adj*. (*sb.*, *adv.*) the OED quotes, among others, Wyclif (*c* 1380): 'Hou men shal know siche pseudoes', and Reginald Pecock (*c* 1449): 'So manye pseudo or false Apostlis.'

Other neo-classical elements have only recently come into use as parts of compounds, like *chem-*, from a Greek word which appears in English in *alchemy* (1362);[2] *chemigraphy* (a process of etching on metal) is a recent compound containing it. Another fairly new neo-classical compound-element is *vibr-*, from Latin *vibrare* (= 'to vibrate'), as in *vibraphone*. With many such recent compound-elements the distinction between native and classical, or neo-classical, becomes difficult to make. *Chem-* and *vibr-* might well be considered as formed from our words *chemical* and *vibrate* rather than from classical antecedents. Webster (1961) has adopted the label ISV (= 'International Scientific Vocabulary') for many modern coinages. This label 'recognizes that the word as such is a product of the modern world and gets only its raw materials, so to speak, from antiquity' (7a). Some neo-classical word-elements in fact have no connection at all with Latin or Greek, though they may be 'classical' in form. *Benz-*, for example (as in *benzocaine*) is from *benzoin*, a word derived ultimately from an Arabic expression. Other neo-classical elements which are classical in origin, but correspond to English words are *disc-*, as in *discophile* (= 'one who is devoted to the study and collecting of phonograph records'), *immun-*, as in *immunology*, *puls-*, as in *pulsimeter*, *pulsojet*, *turb-*, 'turbine', as in *turbo-jet*, *vert-*, as in *vertiport* (= 'an airport for vertical take-off and landing planes'). *Eur(o)-* as in *Eurocrat* (see 13.5.1), *Euro-dollar* and *Euro-market* has been formed from *Europe*: this form seems to have displaced *Eur-*, as in *Eurasian*, and the unwieldy *Europæo-* (both nineteenth-century), though we still use the word *Europocentric*.

Since English contains such a large proportion of classical borrowings and has acquired a facility for using them in new coinages, it may be difficult to decide what is a 'hybrid' – that is, a word composed of a mixture of classical and native elements. (The term 'hybrid' is also used for words like *television*, which contain borrowings from different sources, in this case Greek and Latin, but I shall not discuss these here.) In spite of the long-standing hospitality of English to words and word-elements of foreign origin, hybrid words have often been condemned in strong terms. Fowler distinguishes two kinds of 'malformations' – hybrids and 'abortions . . . in which all the elements belong indeed to one language, but are so put together as to outrage that language's principles of word-formation' (1965, 253).[3] Elsewhere (48–9) he discusses 'barbarisms' – words 'formed in an unorthodox way', but admits that there are difficulties in the way of avoiding such words: 'We may lack the information that would enable us to decide whether any particular word is or is not a barbarism. This is indeed obtainable from a competent philologist; but life is not long enough to consult a competent philologist every time one of the hundreds of dubious words confronts us; nor yet is it long enough for an *ad hoc* course of Latin and Greek grammar.'

Neo-classical compounds in which the first element is a combining form and the second a full English word, such as *aero-navigation*, *auto-suggestion*, *megadeath* (= 'one million deaths'), *physiotherapy*, *porno-journalism*: 'The shelves are bulging with books, magazines, and porno-journalism' [*Sunday Times* 1 March 1970, 6/4], are more frequent than compounds in which the native or naturalized word precedes the combining form, such as *addressograph*, *insecticide*, *jitterscope* (= 'an oscilloscope for measuring jitter, *ie* distortion in a television picture'), *speedometer*. This may be partly because some words do not fit entirely comfortably into the role of first element of a neo-classical compound. The first element of *insécticide*, for example, has its accent shifted from the first syllable to the second, and *speed* /spiːd/ in *speedómeter* /spɪdˈomətə/ has its long vowel shortened and changed preceding the nuclear *-o-*. Fowler remarks (1965, 254): 'The wordmakers have missed an opportunity with *meter*; we have an English METER that we use in *gas-meter* and *water-meter*; why could they not have given us *flood-meter* and *speed-meter* . . . instead of our present monstrosities?'

A few compounds of neo-classical form appear to be composed wholly of native elements, linked by a combining vowel. An example is *resistojet*: 'The Applications Technology Satellite now in orbit carries an experimental electrothermal engine called a resistojet' [*Science News* 28 January 1967, 95/3]. We can see a progressive 'naturalization' process in the three examples *kleptomania*, a compound made up of two Greek elements, though *mania* is also an independent word in English, *discomania* (= 'love of phonograph records'), whose first element is also homonymous with an independent English word, and *Beatlemania*, which dispenses with the combining vowel – the second syllable of *Beatle* serves instead – and which could well be classified as a native compound. Pound (1951) notes as a 'verbal novelty' the frequent use of medial *-o-* in trade names, pointing out however that such coinages as *Talk-O-Phone* appeared as early as 1912. Among more recent American examples which she cites are *Teach-O-Filmstrip, Diffuse-O-Light, Wool-O-Rugs*. And Praninskas (1968, 29) notes that 'the second most frequent pattern [of modern American trade names] consists of units formed of two components joined by an arbitrarily chosen "binding" or stem vowel'. Some of her examples are CLAMP-O-FRAME, ICE-O-BOX, ROLL-A-MAGIC, SELECT-O-SPEED. In such trade names as *Dial-A-Cab, Dial A Job, Recordacall* (Telephone Answering Machine), *Rent-a-Phone, Rentavilla*, the medial vowel is the indefinite article, but the formations have possibly been influenced by neo-classical compounds with combining vowels.

A feature of many modern neo-classical compounds which might bring objections from followers of Fowler is the variations of form which can be seen in different instances of the same element. We find for example *basifixed* (= 'attached at or near the base') beside *basonym* (= 'the earliest name of a taxonomic group or entity'); *cathodography* (= 'photography by cathode rays') beside *cathoscope* (= 'an instrument for exhibiting the optical effects of X-rays'); *dosemeter* and *dosimeter* (both = 'an instrument which measures radiation dose'); *evaporimeter* and *evaporometer* (both = 'an instrument for measuring the quantity of a liquid evaporated in a given time'), and *evapotranspiration* (= 'loss of water from soil by evaporation and transpiration'); *gravipause* (= 'the point between two planets where the gravity of one equals that of the other') and *gravitometer* (= 'an instrument for measuring specific gravities'). It seems likely that in time the preferred forms of these elements will establish themselves and there will be greater uniformity.

9.2 Classification of neo-classical compounds

It was suggested in 3.2 that neo-classical compound-elements may be combined into structures analogous to those of native noun and adjective compounds.[4] They may be for example verb–object, like *agriculture*, from Latin *agricultura*, translatable as 'field-cultivation', or *homicide*, from Latin *homicidium*, 'man-slaying'. *Basifixed* is a locative participial-adjective formation similar to *earthbound*. And compare some miscellaneous examples in the following passage:

> We may suffer from *nephropathy* (disease of the kidney), *nephralgia* (pain in the kidney), ... We may undergo the surgical operations of *nephrotomy* (a cutting of the kidney), *nephrectomy* (a cutting out) ... We might like to invent a few more terms ourselves. The kidney can suffer the processes of *nephrothermolysis* (being cooked) and *nephrophagy* (being eaten)! (Flood, 1960, xiii)

An attempt to classify neo-classical compounds as the native compounds of Chapters 5 and 6 have been classified would present difficulties however. It is of course necessary to translate a neo-classical compound in order to paraphrase it, and many elements have only approximate translation-equivalents. Also, it would perhaps be misleading to assume that we understand and form these compounds just as we do native ones. We may coin *nephrotomy* from the Greek *nephr-*, *nephros*, 'kidney' and *tom-*, *tomos*, 'cutting', but the result is hardly as transparent as *kidney-cutting* would be, and therefore not nearly as useful as a model for similar formations. Accordingly, the examples mentioned have been chosen to illustrate different elements in use rather than the various combinations of elements.

We can however distinguish a class of Appositional neo-classical compounds, which, unlike those so far mentioned, are mainly adjectival. A detailed history and analysis of this type of compound is to be found in Hatcher (1951), and I shall comment briefly on her findings here. Appositional compounds of Greek and Latin elements as we know them are entirely a post-classical development. Hatcher distinguishes two semantic groups, the 'name' group, for example *Indo-European*, and the 'appellative' group, for example *politico-religious*. The name type had its fore-runners in the sixteenth century when dictionaries appeared with titles like *Lexicon Graeco-Latinum*; the word *Gallo-Belgicus* (='pertaining to both France and Belgium') also appeared in a book-title in the sixteenth century, and Hatcher suggests that this word was in some sense a development from such classical, non-appositional, nominal compounds as *Gallo-Graeci* (='Gauls living in Greece'). Appositional name adjectives did not however appear in English until the nineteenth century, with *Indo-European* (1814) as the first example. They are now common enough: examples are *Anglo-Russian*, *Austro-Hungarian*, *Malayo-Polynesian*, *Turco-Iranian*. To *Indo-Chinese* (1842) corresponds the nominal *Indo-China* (1886). *Anglo-Saxon* (1610), as the OED points out, originally meant 'English Saxon' (as opposed to 'Old Saxon'), and later, having been applied to Old English as a whole, not just the Saxons and Saxon dialects of Old English, was 'erroneously' interpreted as 'Angle+Saxon'.

The appellative type of appositional adjective compound, Hatcher concludes, is descended from the Renaissance *comico-tragicus*, which was 'inspired' she suggests (79) by Plautus' coinage *tragicomoedia*, revived in the fifteenth century as *tragico-comoedia*. Terms connected with fields of learning, like *physico-chemical* (1664), *historico-geographical* (1738), followed, and later, in the nineteenth century, words like *sphero-cylindrical*, containing a first element that is nominal, not adjectival. The adjective *sphericus* existed and would have been available for a compound *spherico-cylindrical*, but apparently the simpler form was preferred. From, or corresponding to, appositional adjectives, nouns have occasionally been formed: *physico-chemist* (1866) from *physico-chemical*, *biochemistry* (1902) from *biochemical* (1867), *naso-pharynx*, cf: *naso-pharyngeal* (both nineteenth-century), *theologico-politician*, cf: *theologico-political* (both seventeenth-century). Of such appositional noun compounds as *cupro-nickel*, *hydro-carbon*, *nitro-cellulose*, Hatcher says 'there can be no doubt that [they] are to be ultimately explained by the adjectival pattern ... *talco-chloritic*, *zinco-aluminic* etc' (163).

A point which Hatcher makes (149) about some of these appositional compounds is that they may be used ironically or facetiously, and the following very recent examples support this. 'Of course there is no medico-scientific conspiracy afoot' [*Sunday Times* 1 March 1970, 11/4]; 'What solemn, didacto-modernistico-Revolutionary tract, one wondered, would *The Occupation* turn out to be?' [*Sunday Times* 8 August 1971, 21/7]; 'he wrote a mixture of almost faux-naif flatness with often dissonant poetico-rhetoric' [*Listener* 14 March 1968, 346/1]; 'And these Big Boys are sure the last general election in Britain went their way. I was ... surrounded by these politico-businessmen who were cheering like VE-day' [*Observer* 8 November 1970, 11/8].[5]

9.3 A historical note

I have dealt comparatively briefly with the subject of neo-classical compounds, perhaps too briefly when one considers their prominent role in word-formation today. (Further examples of complex words containing neo-classical elements will be found in 12.6 and 13.5). But perhaps the majority of such formations are in learned and technical fields. Some technical vocabularies are almost entirely made up of them (see 14.5 below). The reasons why this has come to be so are nowhere better discussed than in Jespersen (1905, Chapter 6), and I conclude by quoting a relevant passage from that work:

> When the influx of classical words began, it had its *raison d'être* in the new world of old but forgotten ideas, then [at the beginning of the Renaissance] first revealed to medieval Europe. ... But as times wore on, the ideas derived from classical authors were no longer sufficient for the civilized world, and, just as it will happen with children outgrowing their garments, the modern mind outgrew classicism, without anybody noticing exactly when or how. New ideas and new habits of life developed and demanded linguistic expression, and now the curious thing happened that classical studies had so leavened the minds of the educated classes that even when they passed the bounds of the ancient world they drew upon the Latin and Greek vocabulary in preference to their own native stock of words.[6] (§120)

So that the nineteenth-century writer Henry Rogers, in an essay on the preponderance and superiority of the Anglo-Saxon element in the English language, has to admit: 'we know nothing that would be gained but ridicule if we were to substitute "bone-knowledge" for "osteology", or "shell-craft" for "conchology", or "ship-skill" for "the art of navigation" ' [*Edinburgh Review* October 1839].

Notes

1 The OED distinguishes between 'combining forms' – first elements of neo-classical compounds – and 'endings' – second elements. Examples are: 'Micro- . . . repr. Gr. μῑκρο-, comb. form of μῑκρός small . . .'; '-scope, an ending representing mod. L. -scopium (f. Gr. σκοπεῖν to look at, examine').

2 The history of the element *chem-* is complicated: two Greek words, χημία, *chemia*, 'Egypt', and χῡμεία, *chymeia*, 'pouring, infusion', are involved in it. See OED, s.v. *alchemy* and *chemic*.

3 Exactly sixty years before this edition of Fowler's book, however, Jespersen wrote: 'It should be remembered ... that ... correctness in one language should not be measured by the yard of another language' (1905, §119).

4 For a classification of Latin compounds, see Johnson (1931). His categories are Dependent (*aquæductus*), Descriptive (*æquilibrium*), Possessive (*æquinoctium*) and Prepositional (*intervallum*).

5 Compare Browning's

> As long I dwell on some stupendous
> And tremendous (Heaven defend us!)
> Monstr'-inform'-ingens-horrend-ous
> Demoniaco-seraphic
> Penman's latest piece of graphic.
>   ['Waring']

6 A notable exception to this is the vocabulary of computer technology, which makes considerable use of native compounds, and of zero derivation, and has accordingly a familiar and almost colloquial flavour. A few examples are mentioned in Chapters 5, 6 and 8.

Chapter 10

Clippings and acronyms[1]

10.1 Clipping

This term refers to the process by which a word of two or more syllables (usually a noun) is shortened without a change in its function taking place. *Advertisement, examination, gymnasium, laboratory, photograph, professor,* all have commonly-used clipped forms: *ad,* or *advert, exam, gym, lab, photo, prof.* Clipped words are generally used in less formal situations than their full-length equivalents: they indicate an attitude of familiarity on the part of the user, either towards the object denoted, or towards the audience. There do not seem to be any clear phonological or graphological rules by means of which we might predict where a word will be cut. Most often the first syllable is retained, and sometimes the first two. Since however it is mostly three- or four-syllabled words that are clipped, and since these are likely to be of French or classical provenance, the retained syllables are often not the nuclear ones. This is the case with *exam, gym, lab* (British pronunciation), *prof* above; *advert* contains the nuclear syllable of the full form, but the nucleus is shifted in the clipping to the preceding syllable.

The following are examples of clipped adjective–noun phrases: *perm,* from *permanent wave, pub,* from *public house, op,* from *optical art, pop,* from *popular music, prefab,* from *prefabricated structure,* with shifting of the nucleus as in *advert, zoo,* from *zoological garden.* From *perm,* a verb (= 'to treat hair with a permanent waving process') has been formed. Another example of a clipped verb is *con* (= 'to swindle'), from *confidence trick.*

Maths and *specs* retain the final *s* of the full forms *mathematics, spectacles; turps,* from *turpentine,* has acquired an *s.* Other 'irregular' clippings are *bike,* from *bicycle, mike,* from *microphone,* and *pram,* from *perambulator.* Clipped forms which have a *-y* or *-ie* suffix are *Aussie,* from *Australian,* *bookie*, from *bookmaker*, *commie*, from *communist*, *hanky*, from *handkerchief*, *movie*, from *moving picture*, and *telly* (or *tele*) from *television*.

Examples (all nominal) which represent the final part of a word are *bus*, from *omnibus*, *cello*, from *violoncello*, *copter*, from *helicopter*, *phone*, from *telephone*, *plane*, from *aeroplane*; in each case the missing part is the one which bears the nucleus in the full word. In rare cases, a clipping consists of the middle part of a word, as with *flu*, from *influenza*, *fridge*, from *refrigerator*, and *script*, from *prescription*, *cf* 'He added: "I've known of several doctors who will give you a script (prescription) for the stuff without question if you put a pound on their desk"' [*Evening Standard* 26 March 1970, 8/1–2].

Clippings show various degrees of semantic dissociation from their full forms. Words like *mob*, from *mobile*, shortened from the Latin *mobile vulgus*, and *pants*, from *pantaloons*, are now no longer felt to be clippings, since the longer forms are not used. (*Mob* and other clipped words are deplored by Swift in *The Tatler*, No 230, 26 September 1710, as evidence of 'a natural Tendency towards relapsing into Barbarity, which delights in Monosyllables'.) *Curio* (= 'object valued as a curiosity') and *fan*, from *fanatic* (= 'admirer', 'enthusiast'), have acquired meanings rather different from their full forms and are also not felt to be shortenings. It seems likely that such examples as *lunch*, *movie*, *pram* are on the way to independence, since *luncheon*, *moving picture*, *perambulator* are now not much used. Instead of the clippings being familiar or colloquial, the full forms have acquired a formal, even slightly pedantic flavour.

10.2 Acronyms

Acronyms, words formed from the initial letters of a phrase, have been on the increase since the beginning of the twentieth century. Many originated during the two world wars, and many have been formed as short names for government agencies[2] and international organizations. Acronyms may be pronounced as words, for example *Unesco*, or as series of letters, for example BBC. Occasionally they are given 'pronunciation-spellings', for instance *deejay* (= 'D.J.', = 'disc jockey'), *emcee* (= 'M.C.', = 'master of ceremonies'), *okay* (= 'O.K.'), *veep* (= 'V.P.', = 'vice-president'). More than one letter of a word in the full expression may be included in the acronym and then we have formations like those mentioned in 10.1. An example is *binac* (= 'binary automatic computer'). Sometimes the full expression is devised so that its initials form an acronym which is appropriate to it in some way, such as MAGIC (= 'Machine for Automatic

Graphics Interface to a Computer'), or PILOT: 'A new kind of typewriter for severely handicapped people has been developed at Queen Mary's Hospital, Roehampton. It is called PILOT. Patient Initiated Light Operated Tele-Control' [*Evening Standard* 23 February 1968, 18/2].

In specialist technical fields, where much use of this kind of naming is made, sets of acronyms with a common ending, or 'suffix' may be found. The field of computer science has provided such a 'family', with the ending -*ac*, as in *binac*, *maniac* (= 'mathematical analyser numerical integrator and computer'), *ordvac* (= 'ordnance variable automatic computer'), *radac* (= 'rapid digital automatic computing system'), *radiac* (= 'radioactivity detection, identification and computation'). *Radar* (= 'radio detection and ranging') was the first member of a series with the ending -*ar*: *colidar* (= 'coherent light detection and ranging'), *hipar* (= 'high power acquisition radar'), *ladar* (= 'laser detection and ranging'), *secar* (= 'secondary radar'), *sodar* (= 'sound detecting and ranging'), *sofar* (= 'sound fixing and ranging'), and *sonar* (= 'sound navigation and ranging'). The following quotation gives examples of another such family:

In addition to masers [microwave amplification by stimulated emission of radiation] and lasers [light amplification by stimulated emission of radiation] the names rasers, irasers, uvasers, xasers and gasers are also being used. Indeed, another one has recently been jocularly proposed – 'dasers', standing for 'darkness amplification by stimulated emission of radiation'! [*Times Educational Supplement* 3 December 1965, 1228/4]

10.3 Clippings and acronyms with other processes

Compounds of clipped elements occur, such as *Amerind* (= 'American Indian'), *biopic* (= 'biographical picture'): 'Personally . . . I find that *Star!* . . . leaves me as cold as most Hollywood bio-pics' [*Observer* 21 July 1968, 29/3]; *diamat* (= 'dialectical materialism'): ' "What did you study at the University?" "History, literature, diamat, and culture in general" ' [Arthur Koestler, *The Age of Longing*, 1951, 155]; *hifi* (= 'high fidelity'); *psywar* (= 'psychological warfare'): 'The lieutenant parroted every cliché of modern psywar; the Vietcong can only keep their support through fear . . .' [*New Statesman* 3 March 1967, 282/2]. These compounds fall within the range of complex words that I call blends (see 11.4 below). Examples made up of more than two elements are *alnico* (= 'an alloy of aluminium, nickel and cobalt') and *tacsatcom* (= 'Tactical Satellite Communications').

Initials and clipped elements may combine with full word-elements, as in *adman, alsifilm* (*alsi-*, = 'aluminium' and 'silicate'), *con-man* (= 'swind-ler'), *D-day, g-force* (= 'gravity force'), *op art, pop art*. In the following, a nominal acronym has become a verb: 'finally he made contact with a Battle class R.N. destroyer that was N.A.T.Oing down the Lebanese coastline' [Len Deighton, *The Ipcress File*, 1962, Panther 1964, 49].

The Addenda (1971) to Webster (1961) has the verb *to lase* (= 'to emit coherent light'), backformed from *laser*, and Pennanen (1966, 35 n) notes some backformed acronyms – singular forms of acronyms which have plural significance and happen to end in *S* – for example *AT*, = 'a mem-ber of the ATS ('Auxiliary Territorial Service'), *WREN*, or *Wren*, = 'a member of the WRNS ('Women's Royal Naval Service'). WAAF ('Women's Auxiliary Air Force') perhaps on analogy with acronyms like these, acquired a plural *-s* in popular use, *cf: she's in the Waafs*.

Notes

1 For discussions of these see Jespersen (MEG VI, Chapter 29), Marchand (1969, Chapter 9) and Wells (1956).
2 In America during the presidency of F. D. Roosevelt, these earned the nickname of 'alphabet soup agencies'.

Chapter 11

Morphemes, phonaesthemes and blends

11.1 The term 'blend'

So far, in the review of word-formative patterns with which Chapters 4 to 10 are concerned, nothing has been said about the range of complex words to which I shall give the general name of blends. The following examples provide some indication of what I include in this range.

[a]	squirl (n)	'a flourish or twirl in handwriting' [OEDS]
	flimmer (v)	'to burn unsteadily' [OED]
[b]	smog (n)	'a fog made heavier and darker by smoke' [Webster 1961]
	contrail (n)	'streaks of condensed water vapor created in the air by an airplane or rocket esp. at high altitudes – called also *vapor trail*' [Webster 1961]
	balloonatic (a, n)	'(one who is) balloon-mad' [OED]
	aerobatics (n)	'spectacular flying feats and evolutions (as rolls and dives)' [Webster 1961]
[c]	folknik (n)	*cf* 'anyone who can master three chords, grow a beard and sit heavily on a stool can be a folknik' [New York *Times* 8 May 1966, Magazine 32/3–5]
	straightnik (n)	*cf* ' "Straightniks" (also known as normals) in New York City are always trying to assimilate, to be a little colored, Jewish, gay, etc' [Alan Rinzler, ed, *The New York Spy*, 1967, 388]
	scribacious (a)	'given to, or fond of, writing' [OED]; *cf* 'Heraud is a loquacious, scribacious little man' [Daniel Webster, letter to W. E. Emerson, 1846]
	verbacious (a)	*cf* 'he was not verbacious by nature and was not used to communicating with his father' [John Bratby, *Breakfast and Elevenses*, 1961, 30]

The words in this list may appear at first sight to be a miscellaneous collection, but all of them may strike the reader as being unusual in some way. The examples under [a] contain elements which may remind us of other words similar to them: the beginning of *squirl* recalls *squiggle* and *squirm*, and the remainder is found in words like *swirl, twirl, whirl*. The *fl-* of *flimmer* seems to be similar to that in *flare, flame, flicker*, while the *-immer* is recognizable in *glimmer* and *shimmer*. The [b] words are more like compounds. *Smog* is made up of parts of *smoke* and *fog; contrail* is a telescoped form of *condensation trail; balloonatic* is a combination of *balloon* and *lunatic. Aerobatics* is from the neo-classical element *aero-* and the second part of *acrobatics*. The examples under [c] are suffixed words: but the *-nik* of the first two reminds us particularly of the word *beatnik*, and the *-acious* of the last two, with their sense of 'over-communicative', recalls *loquacious*. In this chapter, we shall glance at some words of the [a] type; Chapter 12 is about blends of the [b] type, while Chapter 13 contains a detailed examination of some sets like those of [c]. Here I shall try to show what it is that the three groups have in common.

11.2 Morphemes

So far, in describing how words are built up, I have referred to 'free forms', like the constituents of *blue-print*, and 'bound forms', like the first and last constituents of *uneatable*; and I have used the terms 'stem' (*eat*), 'prefix' (*un-*) and 'suffix' (*-able*). Now I shall discuss the structure of the word in different terms, and show how words are broken down into smaller units, and how such units are recognized.

By comparing words with one another, we can identify the parts that compose them. An element *-dom* can be identified in *kingdom, stardom*, since there is no difficulty in recognizing *king* and *star* as forms which can occur by themselves or with other elements (as in *kingly, stardust*); from *wrapped, dropped*, a form, *-ed*, can be abstracted. Such fragments, which cannot be further broken down, are morphemes, 'free' (*king, star*) or 'bound' (*-dom, -ed*). Every word is analysable into one or more morphemes, with nothing left over.[1] To speak more strictly, the segments themselves may be termed morphs (or allomorphs), representing the abstract units, morphemes. A morpheme may be defined, then, as a unit representing one or more morphs, which occur in different contexts with exactly the same meaning and function. The morphemes *king, star, -dom* are each represented by one morph, but the 'past tense' morpheme has various morphs, *-ed* (/t/) in the words *wrapped* and *dropped* (/ræpt/, /drɒpt/),

-ed (/d/) in *bothered*, and forms which are not so easy to represent graphically in *took, cut, were*. The morpheme *herb* has one morph, which appears in the words *herb* and *herbal*; but the morpheme *accident* has the allomorphs *áccident* and *accidént-* (in *accidental*). Similarly, *muscle* is represented by the allomorphs *muscle* and *muscul-* (in *muscular*).

The definition I have given of the morpheme relies on meaning, but it is sometimes inconvenient to talk about the meaning of a morpheme. The *bil-* of *bilberry*, for instance, has no identifiable meaning by itself, but since undoubted morphemes like *blue, black* can be substituted for it in the context *-berry*, we can call *bil-* a morpheme. The parts of *receive, concur, resist* have no meaning for us, and from this point of view such words are indivisible units; but their parts do appear in some other contexts, such as *deceive, recur, consist, desist*, and on these formal grounds *re-, -ceive, -sist, -cur* can be considered morphemes. On the other hand, although the *fl-* of *flare, flame, flicker* seems to have a meaning which can be roughly stated as 'moving light', the remainders of these words, *-are, -ame, -icker*, have no claim to separate status at all (although we can tentatively recognize the first of these in *glare*). It would therefore be awkward to say that *fl-* represents a morpheme, even though we can argue that it has a kind of meaning.

In general, however, morphemes can be identified easily enough. The most central and productive word-formative processes, compounding and derivation, are concerned with combinations of established morphemes and groups of morphemes. New words like *bounce-back, unputdownable, stratoscope* are new combinations of familiar morphemes, each of which makes a more or less constant and predictable contribution to new contexts. We do not find new words containing elements like *-sist, -ceive, -cur*, because these fragments have no identity for us outside the small group of words in which they appear. Having detached them, so to speak, we should not know what to do with them. It has been suggested therefore, in particular by Bolinger (1948), that the most reliable proof of morpheme status should be the potentiality of an element to enter new combinations. Thus, the innovatory analogy by which the pattern of *cavalcade* allows us to coin *motorcade* is placed on the same footing as the preservative analogy which is responsible for the appearance of established segments like *un-, -able, -scope* in more conventional new words. As de Saussure put it:

if living units perceived by speakers at a particular moment can by themselves give birth to analogical formations, every definite redistribution of units also implies a possible expansion of their use. Analogy is therefore proof positive that a formative element exists at a given moment as a significant unit. (1916, 170)

However, if we took the ability to appear in new contexts as incontrovertible proof of morpheme status, we should find that words of the kind exemplified under [a] and [b] in 11.1 would present difficulties in morphemic analysis. We might say for instance that *smog* is a compound, since the coining of *smog* shows that *sm-* and *-og* have acquired morph status. But now we would be faced with all sorts of exceptions and irregularities of 'lexical' morphemes. The morpheme *smoke*, we would have to say, is represented generally by the morph *smoke*, but in this one context (preceding the 'irregular' morph *og* representing the morpheme *fog*) it appears as *sm*. As another illustration of the complications which would arise, we may look at the group of words modelled on *hotel*, on which a linguist (Olsson 1964) has attempted to impose morphemic order. Beginning with *motel*, he suggests that this word could be analysed *m-otel*, since *-otel* is the fragment which it has in common with *hotel*; or *mo-tel*, on the pattern of *mo-ped*, an analysis supported by *quadru-ped*, *ped-al*; or *mot-el*, in line with *mot-or*, of which the ending can be compared with that of *accumulat-or*. This last analysis, he says, is preferable because of the semantic association of *motel* with *motor*. The elements thus distinguished Olsson calls 'minimum operative units'. *Boatel* and *floatel* share the element *-otel* (a 'rhymeme') with the other two, though *boat* and *float* are clearly morphemes. He concludes that a new suffix, *-el*, should be set up. However, another member of the group which he does not consider, *lorry-tel*: 'Opening Soon – the Dockside Lorry-Tel. ... lorry-drivers ... will have the opportunity to put-up at a luxurious "Lorry-Tel"' [*Evening Standard* 30 December 1964, 15/1–2] upsets this solution. In fact, it seems better simply to accept the irregularities and to say that in these words *hotel* is represented by various shorter substitutes – *-otel*, *-tel* or *-el* – which I shall call splinters.[2] Words containing splinters I shall call blends. Usually splinters are irregular in form, that is, they are parts of morphs, though in some cases there is no formal irregularity, but a special relationship of meaning between the splinter and some 'regular' word in which it occurs. Thus I shall call *transceiver* (='transmitter-receiver') a blend, because its parts *trans-* and *-ceiv-* do not simply represent the morphemes *trans-* (='across') as in *transalpine*, *transformer*, and *-ceiv-* as in *deceiver*, *perceiver*, but they stand for the relevant parts of the words *transmitter* and *receiver*. Similarly, *folknik* and *scribacious* may also be called blends of a sort, since their suffixes, though they cannot be said to represent *beatnik* and *loquacious*, seem to have a closer relationship with the endings of these words than with those of, say, *nudnik* (see 13.3.4) and *fallacious*.

New morphemes may of course arise from old ones in the course of time. In Chapters 7 and 10, two processes which can involve the splitting of previously indivisible forms have been mentioned. Some backformations like *burgle*, *beg*, have resulted from a change in the morphemic constituency of *burglar*, *beggar*; and some clippings, like *exam*, *bus*, *pub*, were originally parts of longer morphemes. As far as backformation is concerned, de Saussure's view of analogy is enlightening: the coining of the verbs *burgle* and *beg* is proof that *burglar* and *beggar* were understood at the time as bimorphemic words. In the case of clipping, however, the shorter form simply stands for the longer one, and a word which gives rise to a clipping need not be an analysable one.

11.3 Phonaesthemes

To return to the examples of 11.1, the first two, *squirl* and *flimmer*, are representative of a fairly large group of words in English, many of which have to do with sound or movement of some kind. Although such words cannot easily be analysed into constituents, they seem typically to be composed of an initial consonant, or consonant cluster, and an ending. Sometimes only one 'element' may be recognized in other, similar words. Compare the words in the following groups: *crick, crinkle, crabbed, criss-cross, cramp*, in which the *cr-* seems to contribute something 'crooked' in each case; and *stump, thump, clump*, which share an ending with the significance of 'dull impact'. To elements like these, which in word-groups varying in size of membership have a more or less discernible identity, Firth (1930, Chapter 6) gave the name of *phonaestheme*.

It is difficult to estimate how important a part phonaesthemes play in the formation of words. It has been shown for various languages that often the names of things or concepts which are likely to be connected in the minds of speakers have developed some corresponding likeness of form. Malkiel for instance (1966, 350–1) comments on the group of Latin adjectives denoting physical defects, which contain a medial vowel *a*, such as *caluus* 'bald', *mancus* 'maimed', *strabus* 'squinting'. This group, he suggests, may have influenced the displacing of *obesus* and *pinguis* 'fat' by *crassus*. Again, he points out (351) that a group of Spanish and Portuguese words with no precise common meaning, but with 'a narrow spectrum of fluctuating denotations ranging from "ungainly" and "clumsy" to "silly", "deranged", and "lazy"' have in common a medial *o*. In English (and related languages) we can point to, for instance, the *n-* of negative words. Bolinger (1940, 67) draws attention to a comparatively new (and marginal) member of the group, *nuts*; the American *nix* (from German *nichts*) belongs here too, of course. Another example which Bolinger gives is the *v-* of *violent, vitriolic, vituperative, vicious, venomous*, and other words associated with ill-temper.

Such group resemblances are in many cases difficult to pin down. To demonstrate that they have had any influence on the shaping of words, or, negatively, on the disappearance of words which could not be aligned with them, seems impossible. But the existence of such groups in various languages indicates that, as Malkiel puts it, a few words which share some formal and semantic feature can become 'through gradual rapprochement, the central section of a magnetic field toward and into which lexical items less neatly tailored, hence more isolated, are almost irresistibly attracted' (1966, 352). As a nineteenth-century philologist commented: 'The soul is by nature no "Sprachvergleicher" [comparative philologist] and but an indifferent morphologist. It knows nothing of the *history* of forms, but knows them as they *are* – in their relations to each other' (Wheeler 1887, 5). We can point to many pairs of words which may have arisen partly through such attraction. Jespersen (1922, 389) cites, among others, *claw* and *paw; twig* and *sprig; rim* and *brim*. For one member of each of these pairs at least, there is something baffling about the etymology. This process of attraction is obviously so gradual, and so inextricably linked with other developmental factors, that we can know little of how it works. We can only record the facts that reveal it, and point to the numerous cases in which words standing for associated things and ideas have somehow come to look alike.

With the 'sound/movement' part of the vocabulary, however, we are more conscious of the forces at work; the groups are more easily perceived, and indeed we not infrequently coin new words on their patterns. Some examples are: *squeelch:* 'The squeelch and buzz of the windscreen wipers continued steadily as he made up his mind' [Len Deighton, *The Ipcress File*, 1962, Panther 1964, 184]; *shumbling:* 'The click-click of the wind in the Indian corn, plucking at the coarse leaves, shumbling them' [Lawrence Durrell, *Clea*, 1960, Faber 1961, 46]; *wrankles, grangles:* 'My mother, the ladies, such talk, every afternoon you'd hear great wrankles and grangles over . . . sewing cloth' [Jack Kerouac, *Doctor Sax*, 1959, 14]; *sploopsing:* 'I come sploopsing to a no-good end and wake up' [*ibid*, 20].

Opinions have differed considerably about what exactly is the impetus behind formations like these. Terms like 'sound symbolism', 'echoism', 'onomatopoeia' are often used in a way which takes for granted, but does not explain, their implications. Have certain sounds an intrinsic appropriateness to certain meanings, or are sound-meaning links in all cases simply a matter of established expectancy, like the connection between a certain note and the expectation of food which Pavlov established in his dogs? Firth takes the latter view, dismissing sound symbolism as 'a fallacy' and onomatopoeia as 'misleading' (1951, 194). The objection to the term 'sound symbolism' is that it implies a comparison of impressions from different senses, a matter of which too little is known. Von Humboldt, for instance, leaves a great deal unexplained when he says 'language chooses to designate objects by sounds which . . . produce on the ear an impression resembling the effect of the object on the mind' (quoted by Jespersen, 1922, 396). 'Onomatopoeia' has suffered some disrepute because too much has been claimed for it. Once a linguistic form and a meaning are associated with one another, it can be very difficult not to think of the two as essentially appropriate to each other. Words like *crack, growl, roar, squeak* seem to be especially suited to their meanings; but in fact, when spoken, they are not very much like the sounds they denote – though it seems that if certain sounds in such words are pronounced with some exaggeration, the argument for onomatopoeia becomes more convincing: *cf* an advertisement (seen April 1969) for a life assurance company featuring a picture of a lion and the legend 'Grrrrrowth for your savings'.

The four words just mentioned – *crack, growl, roar, squeak* – are among the examples of which Ullmann (1962, 84) states: 'The referent itself is an acoustic experience which is more or less closely imitated by the phonetic structure of the word.' Such phenomena Ullmann sees as universal, and not to be accounted for across languages by common origin or mutual influence. 'Comparative philologists', he warns, 'must be careful to eliminate such correspondences while trying to adduce evidence for historical kinship or influence' (86). Firth, on the other hand, not believing in 'sound symbolism', considers that the common sound-sense correspondences ('habits') of different languages provide important evidence for linguistic kinship (1930, Chapter 7). Confining our attention to English, it seems safe to say that certain sounds are particularly appropriate to suggest certain physical effects, and will do so if they occur in words whose meaning invites the suggestion.[3] Such effects are most clearly those of sound. It would be hard to deny the direct suggestiveness of *bubble, splash, sizzle, whisper*, for instance, although that of *scamper*, *scuttle; totter, dither; flame, flare, flicker,* is rather more elusive. New coinages like those mentioned above, *squeelch, shumbling,* and so on, indicate that words of this kind should be mentioned in an account of word-formation; some of them at least may be seen as composed of more than one element.

11.4 Compound-blends

The examples under [*b*] at the beginning of 11.1 are, much more clearly than those under [*a*], premeditated formations. Such blends can be seen as contracted forms of compounds, and may be compared with the compounds of Chapter 5. Consciously-formed blends, unlike the *squirl, flimmer* kind, appear to be essentially a twentieth-century phenomenon (at any rate, in written language). A few nineteenth-century examples are recorded, and rather fewer for the sixteenth to eighteenth centuries (see the examples in 12.1 below). The OED records very few factitious blends, and indeed does not recognize 'blending' as a process in the derivations it gives. Compare the following assortment of explanations which it gives for words which by my definition are all blends:

Amerind	contraction for *American Indian*
brunch	A 'portmanteau' word f. BREAKFAST and LUNCH
cablegram	f. CABLE *sb.*+-GRAM, by superficial analogy with TELEGRAM ...
catalo	f. CAT(TLE+BUFF)ALO
dictaphone	irreg. f. DICTATE+-*phone* as in GRAMOPHONE
extrality	Syncopated form of EXTRATERRITORIALITY
squarson	A jocular combination of SQUIRE *sb.* and PARSON
solemncholy	Fancifully f. SOLEMN *a.*, after *melancholy*
stalloy	App. arbitrarily f. ST(EEL)+ALLOY

Today we are used to new and unusual-looking words, and the influence of press and radio ensures that almost every neologism, however transient, which occurs in a communication meant for the public, leaves behind it some record of its existence. Some of the examples in Chapter 12 may already be obsolete, and many cannot have been used very frequently. But taken all together, they reveal patterns which are more orderly than the eccentric appearance of individual items might suggest.

11.5 Group-forming

We have noticed groups of words containing 'phonaesthemes', which are linked in both form and meaning; the [c] examples of 11.1, *folknik* and *straightnik*, *scribacious* and *verbacious*, indicate another way in which groups of words associated in form and meaning may grow up. Under this heading of 'group-forming' may also be mentioned cases in which there has been a purely formal addition to a suffix. The *n* of words like *botanist*, *pianist* has found its way into *tobacconist*. The diminutive suffix *-let* is from the French *-ette*, which acquired its *l* from stems ending in *l* to which it was attached; the suffix *-ness* is descended from a Germanic element *-assus* which acquired its *n* in a similar way. In the ending *-cade*, of *motorcade*, a new formal element, *c*, and a new element of meaning, both from *cavalcade*, have augmented the original suffix *-ade* (see 13.6.1).

Developments of this kind, occurring chiefly with suffixes, have been variously referred to as 'adaptation', 'secretion', 'irradiation'. As Malkiel points out (1966, 323) 'comparatively seldom does a given affix descend from a succession of older phases without lateral interferences which, if sufficiently powerful, amount to actual blends'. As we shall see in Chapter 13, sometimes such formal and semantic developments of word-elements take place over comparatively short periods: *-cade* for example has been active chiefly in the twentieth century, and the formations with *-nik* that I shall look at have appeared since the middle nineteen-fifties. And we shall also see in Chapter 13 that not only suffixes, but occasionally prefixes, and also 'lexical' elements, can spread from word to word to form groups, undergoing in the process some change of meaning.

Notes

1 For discussions of morphemic analysis see, among others, Harris (1951, especially Chapter 12), and more briefly, Robins (1964, 5.5) and Lyons (1969, 5.3).

2 A term borrowed from Berman (1961).

3 For a brief account of onomatopoeia and the ways in which it achieves its effects, see Leech (1969, Chapter 6).

Chapter 12

Compound-blends

12.1 Introductory: pre-twentieth-century examples

In this chapter I shall discuss at greater length blends of the kind exemplified under [b] in 11.1, which are like compounds in their make-up. They do not constitute an important kind of word-formation – in fact, compound-blends are rather rarely used – but it is interesting to notice the patterns on which they are formed and to compare them with the patterns of conventional compounds. And it is worth asking whether compound-blends as a class have anything in common apart from the formal characteristics – the morphological irregularities – by which we identify them; whether there are notions which they express more readily and appropriately than other kinds of complex word, and varieties of language in which they are especially likely to appear. Here, for the sake of convenience, I shall refer to compound-blends simply as 'blends'.

In 11.4 I remarked that almost all blends with a compound-like structure are twentieth-century coinages. The following are a few exceptions. In the sixteenth century appeared Dean Colet's *blatterature*: 'That Fylthiness and all such abusion which the later blynde worlde brought in, whiche more rather may be called "Blatterature" than literature' [*Statutes for St Paul's School, c* 1512]; and Robert Greene's *niniversity*: '[I] will make a shippe that shall hold all your colleges and so carrie away the Niniuersitie with a fayre wind, to the Bankeside in Southwarke' [*The Honorable History of Friar Bacon and Friar Bongay, c* 1590]. Another blend of Greene's is *foolosophy* – spelt *foolosophie* [*The Defence of Conny Catching,* 1592]; and Sir Thomas Chaloner uses *foolelosopher*: 'Such men therfore, that in deede are archdoltes, and woulde be taken yet for sages and philosophers, maie I not aptelie calle theim foolelosophers?' [*The Praise of Folie,* 1549, EETS 1965, 10]. The seventeenth century produced *knavigation*: 'For my part, I wish so well to Nauigation and discoueries, that I could wish such complaints to be but calumnies, and to be the knauiga-tions of false discouerers' [Samuel Purchas, *Pilgrimage*, 1613, 579], and Francis Lodwick's *universalphabeth* [*c* 1670]. *Clantastical* is an eighteenth-century example, noted by Samuel Pegge (*Anecdotes of the English Language*, 1803, 1844 edn, 210) as 'ingeniously invented by a maid-servant... which she contrived should express both *fantastical* and *clandestine*'. From the nineteenth century we have *astronography: Astronography or Astronomical Geography with the use of globes*, the title of a book by E. Willard, 1856; Charles Dickens's *wiglomeration:* 'He's a ward in Chancery, my dear. .... They will all have something to say about it; they will all have to be handsomely fee'd, all round, about it; the whole thing will be vastly ceremonious, wordy, unsatisfactory, and expensive, and I call it, in general, Wiglomeration' [*Bleak House*, 1858, 58–9]; and *balloonacy:* 'We live in an age of balloonacy' [*Daily Telegraph* 19 February 1864; OED s.v. *balloon sb.*[1] 10].

We might also remember Lewis Carroll, to whose explanation of words in 'Jabberwocky' [*Through the Looking Glass*, 1872, Penguin 1971, 221–3] we owe the term 'portmanteau word' which has since been often used to refer to blends. In the dialogue between Alice and Humpty Dumpty which follows the verse

'Twas brillig, and the slithy toves
Did gyre and gimble in the wabe:
All mimsy were the borogroves,
And the mome raths outgrabe.

the words *slithy* and *mimsy* are explained as made up of *lithe* and *slimy*, and *flimsy* and *miserable* respectively. 'You see [says Humpty Dumpty] it's like a portmanteau – there are two meanings packed up into one word.'

These examples indicate that in past centuries those who coined and used blends did so most often for the fun of it; most of the blends re-corded from the Renaissance onwards are puns and terms of mockery. It was not until well into the twentieth century that blends began to appear in appreciable numbers, and to be noted and discussed as a separate phenomenon, a pattern of word-formation that could on occasion pro-duce serious and permanent additions to the vocabulary.

12.2 Formal characteristics

A blend may be composed of two elements which are splinters, like *ballute* (from *balloon* and *parachute*): 'When the vehicle drops to an altitude of approximately 100,000 feet...a top-shaped Ballute (balloon-parachute)...will be released' [*Science News* 4 June 1966, 438/2]. In *escalift* (from *escalator* and *lift*) only the first element is a splinter; the second is a full word: 'A research team in Geneva has "mated" a lift to an escalator and produced a remarkable hybrid device with the advantages of both. Lifts can hoist small numbers very rapidly; escalators can carry large numbers rather slowly. The Battelle Institute's new escalift will hoist large numbers fast' [*Observer* 5 June 1966, 13/5]. In *needcessity* (from *need* and *necessity*) the second element is a splinter and the first is a full word: ' "Is this necessary?" said Jeanie... "A matter of absolute needcessity," said Saddletree' [Walter Scott, *Heart of Midlothian*, 1818, Chapter XX].

Many blends show some degree of haplology, that is, the overlapping of vowels, consonants or syllables, as in the following examples: *privilegentsia* (from *privilege* and *intelligentsia*): 'But one can gain an equally clear impression of the alienation of the worker and peasant classes from the owning privilegentsia in the press of the countries directly concerned' [Robert Conquest, in Milovan Djilas, *The New Class*, 1957, Unwin 1966, 8–9]; *motel* (from *motor(ist)* and *hotel*); *latensification* (from *latent* and *intensification*, = 'intensification of a latent photographic image by chemical treatment'); *selectorate* (from *select* and *electorate*): 'Do the voters return the man they really want to Parliament? Not exactly; when the parties pick their candidates the choice is determined by only a handful of people, in secrecy, and under various pressures. This is the Selectorate' [*Sunday Telegraph* 1 October 1967, 8/3–4].

When one constituent echoes in some way the word or word-fragment it replaces, a punning effect is the result. We have already noticed *foolosopher*, echoing *philosopher*; other examples are *fakesimile*, echoing *facsimile*: 'Old maps, old countries, genuine fakesimiles' [D. J. Enright, 'Empire Games']; *icecapade* (= 'spectacular show on ice'), echoing *escapade*: 'She is...the kind of girl you would expect to see as a star in an icecapade' [*Evening Standard* 3 October 1962, 15/6]; *scrollduggery*, echoing *skulduggery*: 'Scrollduggery. The first scrolls from the Dead Sea caves, discovered by a Bedouin goatherd in 1947, subsequently came into the possession of a Bethlehem trader... He and other dealers have since made fortunes from them' [*Observer* 13 November 1966, Magazine 19/3–4]. The effect of word-play may be achieved when syllables simply overlap, as in *balloonatic* (11.1); *shamateur* (from *sham* and *amateur*, = 'in sport a player who is classed as an amateur, while often making money out of his play like a professional'); *sexcapade:* 'I am a playwright. I have written tragedies, comedies, fantasies. I have made private movies out of *Justine* and other eighteenth-century sexcapades' [V. Nabokov, *Lolita*, 1955, Corgi 1961, 314]; *Yiddiom:* 'A number of expressions ... strike me as probably Yiddish in origin. ... The extent to which these "Yiddioms" are current in America varies widely' [*American Speech* 18, 1943, 43].

It seems difficult to make any generalizations about the shapes that splinters are likely to assume. They may be severed from the source word at a morpheme boundary, as in *transceiver* (11.2); or at a syllable boundary, like *cessity* in *needcessity*, or *cute* (from *execute*) in *electrocute*. Or boundaries of both kinds may be disregarded, as with the constituents of *brunch* (from *breakfast* and *lunch*) or *zebrule* (from *zebra* and *mule*). One point we may notice about the shapes of blends is that many are reminiscent of the neo-classical type of compound, although they may not contain a neo-classical element. For example, *escalift, medicare* (from *medical* and *care:* the name for the U.S. government's scheme for the public financing of medical costs), *ruddervator* (from *rudder* and *elevator*), *breathalyser* (from *breath* and *analyser*), all echo the stem+vowel+stem pattern of neo-classical compounds, which is perhaps becoming established as a preferred shape for neologisms.

Most of the words mentioned in this chapter will not be found in dictionaries and are not in common use. Many appear in the quotations between inverted commas. One reason for the lack of popularity of blends may be the problems of comprehension which they present. Many blends are puzzling until one has met them in context, or learned where their constituents come from. And two other difficulties not infrequently arise with blends: how to spell them and how to pronounce them.

Variations in spelling arise in cases where there is an overlapping of syllables which happen to be spelled differently in the two source words. Wavering between single and double consonants occurs in *guestimate/guesstimate* (from *guess* and *estimate*, = 'an estimate based on conjecture'); *swelegant/swellegant* (from *swell* and *elegant*), *opinionaire/opinionnaire* (from *opinion* and *questionnaire*, = 'a questionnaire designed to elicit views on matters of opinion'). Other differences in the spelling of a shared syllable are seen in *botel/boatel* (from *boat* and *hotel*, = 'hotel for boat-travellers' or 'hotel on a boat'), *revusical/revuesical* (from *revue* and *musical*), *slantindicular/slantendicular* (from *slanting* and *perpendicular*). Silent letters occurring in a source word may be felt as inappropriate in a blend, as in *bomphlet* (from *bomb* and *pamphlet*, 12.3) and *solemncholy* (from *solemn* and *melancholy*, 12.4), which has the variants *solemcholy* and *solemncoly*. The influence of the neo-classical pattern stem-*o*-stem is probably responsible for the variants *travelator/travolator* (from *travel* and *escalator*, = 'a moving pavement'), and *motordrome/motodrome* (from *motor* and *hippodrome*, = 'a track or course for spectators at races or tests of automobiles').

The pronunciation of blends presents greater problems. This was confirmed by a small experiment in which I asked some half-dozen informants to read a list of forty blends collected from written language – chiefly newspapers and magazines, and afterwards to read sentences containing the blends in contexts which clarified their derivations and meanings.

Aside from difficulties arising when a splinter accidentally resembles a quite unconnected morpheme, as in *squireshop* (/ˈskwaiəʃəp/, from *squire* and *bishop*, = 'a bishop who is also a squire'), whose second element is likely to be associated with *shop*; and *bushler* (/ˈbʌʃlə/, from *usher* and *butler*), whose first element appears to be *bush* (/buʃ/), the greatest difficulty in pronouncing blends is in deciding which syllable should take the primary accent. My informants found this kind of difficulty with well over half the examples I asked them to pronounce.[1] *Tangemon* was pronounced, with hesitation, in a variety of ways – /ˈtæŋəˌmɔn/, /ˈtændʒəˌmɔn/, /ˌtæŋˈgiːmən/ – out of context, by my informants, who did not realize that the constituents are from *tangerine* and *lemon*. There was less hesitation over this word when it was seen in context, but there was still uncertainty as to where to place the accent. The first and last syllables of *hurricoon* (from *hurricane* and *balloon*, = 'a balloon sent into a hurricane to record information about it') are nuclear in their source words, and informants could not decide which should be nuclear in the blend. Another example in which there was a conflict between two nuclear syllables was *thermistor* (from *thermal resistor*). Informants were also puzzled by *ballute* (from *balloon* and *parachute*), which contains two originally non-nuclear syllables, and by *anecdotage* (= 'garrulous old age'), in which *dot* is nonnuclear in *anecdote* but nuclear in *dotage*. *Skinoe* also caused hesitation, *cf* 'Mr Alexander Wozniak . . . was making good progress today in his 260 miles "walk" on the river Thames. . . . He is using skinoes (miniature canoes which fit the feet). He hopes to introduce skinoeing into Britain as a sport' [*Evening Standard* 29 December 1966, 13/4]. This blend, composed of *ski* and *canoe*, seems to pose an insoluble accentuation problem, since, if the resemblance to *canoe* is to be preserved, the first syllable must be unaccented: /skiˈnuː/, and this obscures the fact that the first element is *ski* /skiː/.

12.3 Nominal compound-blends

Compound-blends can be classified on the basis of the relationships between their elements in the same way as ordinary compounds, although
uncertainties and ambiguities may be greater because of the missing
elements; is *guestimate*, for example, an appositional combination of *guess*
and *estimate*, or an adjective–noun contraction of *guessed estimate*? In this
section and the following one I shall give a few examples of blends
under some of the headings of Chapters 5 and 6.

A Subject–Verb example is *screamager* ('screaming teenager'): 'The
Rolling Stones are on a high stage, and below on a low stage are 34 burly
bouncers facing a wooden barricade and 4,000 screamagers' [*Daily
Express* 12 August 1964, 6/5].

Verb–Object blends are *breathalyser* ('breath analyser'), *bus-napper*
('bus kidnapper'): '. . . my daughter concluded that some kind of "bus-
nappers" must be hard at work in the district. We should dearly like to
know what they do with the kidnapped buses' [*Evening Standard* 16 June
1969, 5/4]; *keytainer* ('key container', 'a small case for carrying keys');
passenveyor ('passenger conveyor'): 'The Passenveyor . . . could carry
60,000 people an hour at a speed of about 11½ miles per hour . . . a passenger conveyor which could roll round corners, navigate slopes, all at
18 ft off the ground' [*Evening Standard* 24 February 1966, 10/2]; *sexploitation* ('sex exploitation'): 'Mr H said his movies would be in no sense
sexploitation films, any more than "playboy" is a girlie magazine, and
this brought happy laughs' [*Observer* 7 September 1969, 7/2].

Appositional blends of the coordinative kind are much more common
than the incidence of corresponding full compounds might lead us to expect. We have already noticed *ballute* ('balloon–parachute', 12.2), *brunch*
('breakfast–lunch'), *escalift* ('escalator–lift', 12.2), *ruddervator* ('rudder-
elevator'), and two examples mentioned in Chapter 11, *smog* ('smoke-
fog,' 11.1) and *transceiver* ('transmitter–receiver' 11.2). Other examples
are *compander* ('compressor–expander'), and *elevon* ('elevator–aileron').
Examples denoting animals and plants which are hybrids are *catalo*, or
cattalo ('cattle–buffalo'), *liger* ('lion–tiger'): 'Daisy, a Salt Lake City zoo
tigress, gave birth to the first known liger (offspring of a female tiger, a
male lion) ever born in the U.S.' [*Time*, Atlantic edn, 17 May 1948, 13/2];
zebrule ('zebra–mule'); *celtuce* ('celery–lettuce'), *plumcot* ('plum–apricot'),
tangemon ('tangerine–lemon'). A few coordinative noun blends are combinations of synonymous words, like *needcessity* ('need–necessity', 12.2),

insinuendo ('insinuation–innuendo'): 'I hate his nasty insinuendoes' [Samuel Butler, *The Way of All Flesh*, 1903, Methuen 1965, 235].

Appositional blends which are not coordinative, that is, in which the first element specifies or qualifies the second, are *bromidiom* ('bromide idiom', 'a commonplace or hackneyed expression, or notion'), *refujews* ('refugee Jews'): 'Rarely had he come into contact with people who could correct ... his delusions about an England brought to decadence and catastrophe by a small group of what he called "Refujews"' [Francis King, *The Widow*, 1957, Penguin 1961, 136]; *shamateur* ('sham amateur', 12.2), *slanguage* ('slang language'), *squarson* ('squire–parson', 'a land-owning parson, a parson who is also a squire'): 'Round about this time [1700] it was rather a fashion, particularly among the better-off clergy (the squarson, for instance) to bring back cedar saplings from Lebanon' [*Times* 10 October 1964, 10/6].

Blends that could be classified as Instrumental are *automania* ('automobile mania', 'mania caused by automobiles'): 'Marc has what you might call automania. He is mad about fast cars' [*Evening Standard* 8 February 1968, 10/4]; *beermare* ('beer nightmare', 'nightmare caused by beer'): 'so in the morning I wake from the scream of beermares' [Jack Kerouac, *The Subterraneans*, 1958, Deutsch 1960, 31]; *contrail* ('condensation trail', 11.1), *cf* 'She ... was back – almost before her cigarette smoke had eddied away in the air. She breathed out a contrail of it like a shared confidence' [*Evening Standard* 23 March 1965, 8/4–5]; *stimulighting* ('stimulation lighting', 'stimulation caused by lighting'): '"Stimulighting" was introduced by the Americans a short while back. This was an increase in hours of lighting to stimulate more activity in the pullet and encourage her to lay more eggs' [*Observer* 1 March 1964, 21/5–6].

The following contain a Locative element: *chunnel* ('channel tunnel'): 'A channel tunnel? Of course. As quickly as possible. Britain has needed one for a century. My newspaper christened the project "The Chunnel". The word has stuck in the minds of the British people' [New York *Times* 17 November 1957, Magazine 55/1]; *daymare* ('day nightmare', 'distress while awake like that experienced in nightmare'); *nightscaping* ('night landscaping'): 'Nightscaping boasts that it creates "by means of light and shadow after dark, as charming a picture of your garden as landscaping by day." Also it "discourages prowlers"' [*Observer* 28 May 1967, 30/8]; *seavacuation* ('sea evacuation', 'evacuation by sea'): 'Parents Say "Speed Up Seavacuation"' (headline) 'Parents applaud the seavacuation scheme for their children' [*Daily Express* 25 June 1940/5]; *telegogue* ('television demagogue'): 'An Expert Views the Telegogues ... the prime burden of winning votes via TV will fall on the eleven politicians shown here' [*Observer* 27 September 1964, Magazine 14/1–2].

Bomphlet ('bomb pamphlet', 'pamphlet like a bomb') could be analysed as a Resemblance blend, *cf* 'Three years ago the Rev Mary Webster... distributed copies of what has come to be known as "The Bomphlet" ' [*Observer* 21 November 1965, 12/4]. In the following, earlier, quotation, it means presumably 'pamphlet dropped like a bomb, as a bomb is dropped': 'Bomphlets, coined by Mr A. P. Herbert, ... describes the leaflets dropped over Germany by the RAF' [H. L. Mencken in *American Speech* 19, 1944, 8].

Plastinaut ('plastic astronaut') is a Composition compound: the first element is the material from which the second is made: 'The Air Force is building 3 mansize plastic dummy astronauts – it calls them plastinauts – for biological studies of radiation above the atmosphere' [newspaper 1961, quoted in *American Speech* 39, 1964, 144–6].

Adjective–Noun blends are not uncommon, for example, *bit* ('binary digit'), *permalloy* ('permeable alloy'), *positron* ('positive electron'). *Guestimate*, *privilegentsia* ('privileged intelligentsia', 12.2) and *spam* ('spiced ham') may be analysed as participle–noun structures. Blends containing a derived adjective as first element are *medicare* ('medical care', 12.2), *nuplex* ('nuclear complex'): 'The broad idea of the project is to build large nuclear-powered industrial complexes – or "nuplexes" – to help to feed a hungry world by making the deserts bloom' [*Observer* 15 June 1969, 16/5]; *submarisle* ('submarine isle'): '... an undersea island which could house a base for submarines or drilling equipment for off-shore wells. The United States Navy, it was learned today, has shown considerable interest in Mr Buckminster Fuller's idea. He calls the structure a "submarisle" ' [*Daily Telegraph* 16 March 1972, 13/7–8].

Blends of the punning type mentioned earlier in this chapter are usually not easily classifiable in this way, since the combinations lose much of their point when 'taken apart'. In addition to those already mentioned – *anecdotage*, *balloonatic*, *fakesimile*, *foolosopher*, *scrollduggery* – some other examples are *beerage* (from *beer* and *peerage*, = 'prominent and wealthy brewers'): 'The hero, a disenchanted son of the beerage, is the narrator' [*Evening Standard* 3 September 1968, 10/4]; *chattire* (from *chat* and *satire*): '*Variety* ... coined the word "chattire" for Braden's show ... It implied a lack of bile ... "I prefer to persuade rather than shock," he says' [*Observer* 7 November 1965, 23/5]; *Mummerset* (from *mummer* and *Somerset*, a term descriptive of 'stage rustic'): 'Ask a photographer (Sikh) where Nirad Chaudhuri lives. He pushes his turban forward and scratches his head like a Mummerset man' [Dom Moraes, *Gone Away*, 1960, 67]; *singspiration* (from *sing* and *inspiration*, = 'a song service featuring the group singing of hymns'): 'Churches of the east capitol group . . . held a "singspiration" Sunday evening . . . Sacred music and choruses made up the evening's program' [American newspaper 1943, quoted in *American Speech* 19, 1944, 77].

12.4 Adjectival compound-blends

These are of the Appositional, coordinative type, like *clantastical* ('clandestine–fantastical', 12.1). Other examples are *alphameric* ('alphabetic–numeric', 'consisting of both letters and numbers'), *hydramatic* ('hydraulic–automatic'), *respectaburban* ('respectable–(sub)urban'): 'Riverside Street running off to hide itself in the rich respectaburban wildhouses of Fraternity presidents of Textile' [Jack Kerouac, *Doctor Sax*, 1959, 5–6]. Examples composed of synonymous elements are *attractivating* ('attractive–captivating'): 'Attractivating: that's how you'll feel in the newest, softest, liveliest fabric made from Courtauld's Celaire' [advertisement, 1966]; *boldacious* ('bold–audacious'), a dialect word: '. . . gettin' more boldacious an' ondacent wi' ivery step' [Q, *Troy Town*, 1888, xi; EDD, s.v. *boldacious*]; *fantabulous* ('fantastic–fabulous'): 'Everything about her's so *bright*, the green of her housecoat thing and the red of her nails, and the blond of her hair. FANTABULOUS is the only word' [Gavin Lambert, *Inside Daisy Clover*, 1963, Penguin 1966, 38]; *swelegant* ('swell–elegant'): 'We've thrown open the swelegant Hilton Roof Restaurant' [*Evening Standard* 3 July 1967, 6/5–6, advertisement]; *solemncholy* ('solemn–melancholy'): 'Maybe I hadn't ought to talk about Mrs Haydock and her Solemncholy Seventeen in that fresh way' [Sinclair Lewis, *Main Street*, 1920, 114–15]. As some of these blends show, adjectival synonyms are often combined for the purpose of emphasis; cf 'Robert Benchley's new mirthquake, colossapendous, stupeficent, magnossal' [New York *Times* 13 January 1938, quoted in *American Speech* 13, 1938, 239].

12.5 Verbal compound-blends

These are rather rare; unlike any of the verbal compounds of Chapter 7, they are coordinative. Examples are *baffound* ('baffle–confound'), a dialect word: 'Thou'd baffound a stoop [post]!' EDD, s.v. *baffound; galvanneal* ('galvanize–anneal'), *meld* ('melt–weld'), cf 'The university is keen to meld with the local community' [*Observer* 10 October 1965, 4/7]; *smothercate* ('smother–suffocate'), another dialect word: see EDD, s.v. *smothercate*, and 'It's hot and I'm smothercating, though I suppose there's worse things at sea. The impression was of a coffin with lid on tight' [Alan Sillitoe, *Key to the Door*, 1961, 243].

12.6 Neo-classical compound-blends

In these examples, the neo-classical element is present in its entirety, and the other constituent is the splinter; though overlapping may occur. As with full compounds, the neo-classical element is most often the initial one. Examples (all nominal) are *aerobatics* ('aero-acrobatics', 'spectacular flying feats'), *cf* 'Ability to perform aerobatics ... gives a pilot confidence' [OEDS, s.v. *aero-*, 1923]; 'Bats whirled past me in their crazy aerobatics' [John Wain, *Nuncle*, 1960, 239]; *aquacade* ('aqua-cavalcade', = 'a water spectacle'), *astrodemic* ('astro-epidemic'): 'Just possibly some of these bugs – if there are any – could be brought back to earth, escape, and come to life again. Given a few mutations while away, they could punch holes in our natural defences and start an "astrodemic" among men or animals or plants' [*Observer* 20 July 1969, 7/3]; *electrolier* ('electro-chandelier'), *multiversity* ('multi-university'): 'Berkeley, a campus with 27,000 students, and part of a "multiversity"' [*New Statesman* 15 January 1965, 65/3].

Blends in which the neo-classical element is the final one are: *appestat* (from *appetite* and *-stat*, = 'the neural centre regulating the appetite'), *calligraphone* (from *calligraph(ic)* and *-phone*): 'The pictures below may lead to a new aid for teaching deaf children to speak. They are produced by a "calligraphone" – a device ... to represent the sounds of speech' [*Observer* 12 January 1964, 12/8]; *dictaphone* (from *dictate* and *-phone*), *oceanaut* (from *ocean* and *-naut*): 'Commander Jacques Yves Cousteau, the French underwater explorer, has caught the imagination of French scientists with his announcement of plans for a new submerged house in which six oceanauts will live next summer' [*Observer* 1 November 1964, 12/8]; *travelogue* (from *travel* and *-logue*).

12.7 Contamination

Among the coordinative examples we have noticed in this chapter are *insinuendo*, *needcessity*, *boldacious*, *baffound*, *smothercate*, all of which seem to have arisen in dialect or 'uneducated' speech. They exemplify the type of blend which apparently results from the confusion of synonyms or words related in meaning. Many scholars have recognized only this presumably unintentional kind of blending, or as it is sometimes called, 'contamination'. The originator of this term was Herman Paul, or his translators, whose definition appears in the OEDS [s.v. *contamination* 1c(*b*)]: 'By "contamination" I understand the process by which synonymous forms of expression force themselves simultaneously into consciousness, so that neither of the two makes its influence felt simply and purely: a new form arises in which elements of the one mingle with elements of the other' (1886, 160).[2]

We should perhaps distinguish (in theory) between the contamination which arises because words are imperfectly known, or unfamiliar, and that resulting from 'slips of the tongue'. The dialectal examples appear to represent the former; it is the latter kind of contamination which Paul is defining. Blends of synonyms may arise quite often in speech, but they are quickly forgotten unless noted down by an interested observer.[3] A few which I have heard now and then are *subservile* (from *subservient* and *servile*), *diswrought* (from *distraught* and *overwrought*), and *aggranoying* (from *aggravating* and *annoying*). This last has been current at least from the beginning of the century: Pound (1914, 52) notes that it was 'given diffusion by its employment on the vaudeville stage, 1912'.

Examples of apparently unpremeditated blends also arise in hasty writing. The following are taken from examination answers written by training college students: *barallels* (from *barrels* and *parallel*, perhaps not coordinative like the rest): 'I think this is a very effective image for railway lines do indeed resemble the barallels of a shotgun'; *climatic* (from *climactic* and *dramatic*): 'By using this type of setting the author allows the reader or playgoer to relax, not really expecting anything of a climatic nature to happen in this serene setting'; *distruption* (from *disruption* and *destruction*): 'When the distruption of his mine seems probable, Charles Gould thinks only of its preservation'; *sombriety* (from *sobriety* and *sombreness*): 'A picture of Victorian sombriety is well laid here, with "melancholy streets in a penitential gait of soot".'

12.8 Some blends in use

As we have seen, coordinative noun blends which are consciously formed are likely to be names of 'mixtures' or hybrids (*escalift*, *brunch*, *liger*, *plumcot*); and coordinative adjective blends are often coined for the sake of emphasis. Blends with other structures turn up not infrequently in scientific and technical contexts, where names for new things are often required. Among the examples cited are *compander*, *elevon*, *nuplex*, *stimulighting, submarisle.* Since they break the rules of morphology, blends have an attention-catching quality which makes them appropriate for trade names and other words in advertising copy.[4] Examples of trade name blends are *dictaphone, keytainer, permalloy, spam. Cf* also *compucessories*: 'COMPUCESSORIES ... a new word? Yes! ... We've just coined it to describe those Data Processing Accessories *we* at PCA delight in designing, and without which *your* computer cannot function with full efficiency' [newspaper advertisement, February 1967]. Other words from advertising are *attractivating* (12.4) and *stimulotion* ('stimulating lotion'): 'Stimulotions for refreshing and stimulating' [magazine advertisement, May 1966].

Writers with a more serious literary purpose may use blends for their capacity to surprise. Two literary examples that have been mentioned are D. J. Enright's *fakesimile* (12.2) and Jack Kerouac's *beermare* (12.3). Many blends in literary contexts which are not puns are resistant to analysis. When we read Jack Kerouac's description of a river: 'old gloor-merrimac figalitating down the dark mark all spread' [*Doctor Sax* 1959, 127–8], or, in the same work, of 'houndmasters of the Francis horn, phantom-grieved, golupally in their shrouds' (106), of 'the rawmous clouds' (202), 'the smoony snow night' (170), 'the grown up gulpitude' (202), we are prompted to interpret the unknown words in the light of known words with something similar in their shape which fit the contexts in some way. But, as with the sound/movement words like *squirl, sizzle, flicker,* discussed in 11.3, we often cannot point with certainty to the source words.

The best-known practitioner of literary blending is of course James Joyce, in *Finnegans Wake,* in which the invented words are 'bound over to carry three score and ten toptypsical readings' [*Finnegans Wake,* 1939, 20]. Joyce's blends have definite source words, often many more than two. A. Walton Litz (1964, 74) says: 'In breaking down the structure of words [Joyce] overcame ... the linear nature of language'; Litz shows (91) how, in the word *Everscepistic,* for example, [*Finnegans Wake* 536], descriptive of the book's central character, HCE, Joyce means to combine *Everest, sceptic, septic* and *pistic* (= 'pure', 'of, or relating to faith'). Joycean blends are bound to their contexts – one could hardly use his inventions elsewhere – and there is frequently no obvious semantic link between the source words of the splinters which are combined. Though blended, the elements remain separate. *Everscepistic* has no 'meaning' as a unit; it is simply a compression of four disparate notions.

This 'atomized' quality sets Joycean blends apart from those which we have been looking at in this chapter, and from compound words generally.

Leech (1969, 44), discussing what he calls 'the "concept-making" power of neologism', points out: 'If a new word is coined, it implies the wish to recognize a concept or property which the language can so far only express by phrasal or clausal description'. And of course, if the word is a blend, novel also in its form, the point is made even more forcibly. Newspaper competitions asking for new words 'expressive of well-known but hitherto wordless states or plights', to quote one of them [*New Statesman* 22 June 1962, 918/2–3], show clearly the feeling that innovations in form are most appropriate to express new notions. The competition referred to above yielded, among others, the blends *proletentiousness* (= 'a tendency, especially in modern literary and artistic circles, to boast of real or imagined working-class origin') and *telephoria* (= 'belief, induced by commentators and news readers, that essentially all is right with the world').

A final example, together with a comment from its coiner, will illustrate further the point about 'concept-making': ' "Education for Creation" as a title for the book ... seemed clumsy. That is how the word EDUCREATION was born: to fill a need. The need for one word to signify a new growth-oriented concept of education' [Paul Ritter, *Educreation*, 1966, xiv].

Notes

1 This problem was noted by Praninskas (1968) in connection with trade names. She comments: 'Haplologies and replacement of partials or bound forms by free forms in compounding cause problems in stress placement which sometimes seem insurmountable to the native speaker. More than one informant has refused to try to pronounce CALEMONA, CIRCOLAIR, FEATHAIRE, HAP-P-NUT (when peanuts were in evidence), NYLONGE (a nylon sponge) and SERV-ICE' (35).
  Among other blends which caused hesitation or embarrassment in my experiment were *fanzine* (from *fan(atic)* or *fantasy*, and *magazine*), *squadrol* (from *squad* (car) and *patrol* (wagon)), *rockoon* (from *rocket* and *balloon*), *zebrule* (from *zebra* and *mule*), *permalloy* (from *permeable* and *alloy*), *jetomic* (from *jet* and *atomic*). With all these, there was uncertainty about where to place the nucleus. Examples which presented other difficulties were *loosy* (from *loose* and *easy*): /luːsɪ/ or /luːzɪ/? and *celtuce* (from *celery* and *lettuce*): /seltəs/ or /seltʊs/?
2 *Cf* also Bergström (1906) and Jespersen (1922, 312–3).
3 Bolinger (1961b) comments on some examples of this kind of contamination in a more general context of questions of association and memory, and discusses how these bear on the relationship of form to meaning.
4 For more about 'copywriter's licence', see Leech (1966, especially Chapter 20).

Chapter 13

Group-forming

13.1 Prefixed and suffixed elements

This chapter will examine in more detail some aspects of the group-forming tendencies in word-formation that were touched on in 11.5, and exemplified by words in -*nik* and -*acious*. When we look at words from the point of view of how they fall into groups, linked formally by a common element and semantically in that they refer to a particular province of 'real life', we find that the most interesting developments involve suffixed elements rather than prefixed ones. It happens that a great many of our prefixes are of Latin or Greek origin, and are much used in forming scientific words; whereas our suffixes are more often of native origin, or have come into the language via French. They have been in the language longer, and are more frequently employed in the general vocabulary. The sense-groups into which prefixes fall show a different general pattern from the sense-groups of suffixes. The largest groups of prefixes are: the 'negative, privative and reversative' group, with *a-*, *de-*, *dis-*, *ex-*, *in-*, *non-*, *un-*; that of 'number', for example *bi-*, *demi-*, *multi-*, *poly-*; 'time', for example *ante-*, *pre-*, *post-*; 'size', for example *mega-*, *micro-*, *mini-*; and 'place', for example *ante-*, *ex-*, *mid-*, *supra-*. These categories are fairly well defined ones, and have shown less tendency to acquire extra nuances of meaning than some of those which are the province of suffixes, like 'collectivity', for example *-dom*, *-ery*, *-ship;* or 'agent', such as *-arian*, *-eer*, *-ician*, *-ist*.

A possibly general difference between prefixes and suffixes is that prefixes are characteristically less 'integrated' with the stems to which they are attached than are suffixes. It is perhaps worth quoting here Sapir's general-linguistic comments on prefixing and suffixing. He observes (1921, 67–8) that prefixing is far less common than suffixing in the languages of the world; he feels (127, n 10) that the difference between the two processes needs greater emphasis, and comments: 'In the more highly wrought prefixing languages the word is apt to affect us as a crystallization of floating elements, the words of the typical suffixing languages ... are "determinative" formations, each added element determining the form of the whole anew.' He adds, however, 'It is so difficult in practice to apply these elusive, yet important, distinctions that an elementary study has no recourse but to ignore them.'

It may be rash not to follow Sapir's advice here, but I shall try to illustrate these suggestive remarks from English. Three prefixed elements, *sub-* as in *sub-cylindrical* (= 'nearly cylindrical'), *near-* as in *near-saint*, *semi-* as in *semi-formal*, all mean something like 'approximating to'; two suffixes, *-ish* and *-like* have the same meaning. But in the pairs *monkish*, *monklike*, and *childish*, *childlike*, the suffixes are seen to be subtly different: the words with *-ish* have a depreciative shade of meaning which is absent from the *-like* words. Such shades of meaning occur quite often with suffixes, which tend to be 'influenced' by their stems in ways which prefixes do not. *-ish* may have acquired this faint nuance, which is not perceptible at all in many *-ish* words, through the influence of stems like *churl-*, *fool-*, *fiend-*, to which it was early attached.

As another example, compare *pseudo-patriot* with *patrioteer*, both meaning 'one who is not genuinely a patriot' (*cf* 3.2). But the second word seems to be much more of a unit than the first. *Pseudo-* is a productive element, and has been since before the Renaissance, with words like *pseudo-Christ* (c 1380), *pseudo-politician* (1628), *pseudo-zealot* (1680) *pseudo-ascetic* (1711), and so on. *-eer* has been productive since the Renaissance, or before; neutral in *cannoneer*, *volunteer*, it later formed *pulpiteer*, *sonneteer*, words which carried a suggestion of charlatanry. Having acquired from words like these a flavour of dishonesty, it subsequently appeared in more strongly 'dishonest' words like *profiteer*, *patrioteer*, *racketeer*. And, as Jespersen points out (MEG VI, 15.5₂), the suffix has developed a 'preference' for stems ending in *t*. This is readily apparent from the examples given in 13.3.3 below. *Pseudo-* words on the other hand, do not fall into groups in this way; there is no trace in them of the 'stamping' of semantic or phonological preferences on it which is so noticeable in the case of *-eer*.

One obvious advantage which suffixes have over prefixes in the forming of associations between words is that words containing the same suffix rhyme with one another, and rhyme is a powerful way of linking words together. We are used to it in poetry; a poem can impose a temporary link between rhyming words.[1] Marvell in the following lines emphasizes the contrast between *dust* and *Lust*:

... your quaint Honour turn to dust
And into ashes all my Lust.
      ['To His Coy Mistress']

And in Browning's lines, the intractable quality of a glutinous substance
is somehow reinforced by *mutinous:*

Save when at noon his paunch grew mutinous
For a plate of turtle green and glutinous
      ['The Pied Piper of Hamelin']

We occasionally find this kind of rhyming situation in prose. It is easy
to see why Shaw coined the word *proprietariat*, from the context in which
he places it: 'an arena in which the Proletariat and the Proprietariat face
each other' [*The Intelligent Woman's Guide to Socialism*, 1928, 223]; and
in the following quotation from Southey, we have a hint as to how the
suffix *-arian* could have acquired a slight pejorative nuance in some words,
along with a preference for stems ending in *t:* 'If the Utilitarians would
reason and write like you, they would no longer deserve to be called
Futilitarians' [OED, s.v. *futilitarian*, 1827]. Bolinger (1940, 72), commenting on 'pairings' of words, says: 'How often our writers have used
the phrase "to *banish* the mists" – because it suggests *vanish! Pendulous*,
for all its Latin origin, is a more vivid word in some contexts than *dangle*,
probably because it has been enriched by *tremulous*. ... *Ravage* is more
devastating than *raze* or *despoil* because of the overtone *savage*.'
    Prefixes have the advantage of alliteration, another 'poetic' means
of linking words, which is of course fully utilized in Old English poetry.
In modern English, however, the effect of the alliteration of prefixed words
is to a large extent counteracted by the fact that the prefix is frequently
unaccented or only secondarily accented. However, Bolinger (1940, 69–70)
points out that we do find a few sets of words linked semantically by prefixes,
or prefix-like elements. He mentions the *del-* of *delight, delicious, delicate*
and the nonce word *delovely;* the *irre-* of *irreparable, irresistible, irregardless*,
which carries a suggestion of 'utterly'; the *ob-* of *objectionable, obnoxious,
obtrusive*. These elements, as it happens, are more properly regarded, not
as prefixes but as 'prefixoids', since they have only a tenuous identity
for us.[2] To these examples may perhaps be added the *de-, des-, dis-* of
verbs with a 'disagreeable' meaning, like *detest, despair, despise, disdain,
disgust.*[3]

13.2 Stems and suffixes

The examples in the following sections illustrate the ways in which a suffix may develop a preference for a stem of a certain shape and/or a certain kind of meaning. It has often been noticed how frequently the addition of a nuance of disapproval is involved in the semantic development of words. As we shall see, this has happened with each of the four suffixes examined in detail in 13.3. This kind of semantic shade is one of the most noticeable and easily identifiable components in the meaning of a word. For instance, among the considerable number of nominalizations in -ery in English – *archery, bravery, embroidery*, and so on, there is a subset of words denoting some kind of 'sharp practice', and examples readily come to mind: *chicanery, jiggery-pokery, knavery, pettifoggery, skulduggery, thievery, treachery, trickery*. It is words like these which were probably responsible for the choice of suffix in the hostile terms *popery, whiggery*. On the other hand, some words in -ery which might have joined this set, have not done so: we might have expected *machinery* to acquire a sense akin to *machinations*, but according to the OED it has never been so used.

A set with perhaps a slightly pejorative sense is that of -acious. Among the many formations with this suffix, the general meaning of which is 'given to', 'inclined to', 'abounding in', as in *capacious, vivacious, voracious*, a small group which has to do with 'communication' may be distinguished. *Linguacious* (1651) is the earliest of these; it was followed closely by *loquacious* (1667), *scribacious* (1677): 'We have some letters of Popes (though not many; for Popes were then not very scribacious . . .)' [OED, s.v. *scribacious*]. Jespersen (MEG VI, 19.7₇) cites *gossipaceous* [sic], from Darwin (1888); Berrey and Van Den Bark (1943) give *gabbacious*, and finally we have *verbacious* (11.1). It is interesting that all of these words, with the exception of *loquacious* have been used very rarely, yet the pattern has persisted through three centuries.

Some suffixes, or combinations of suffixes, we may surmise, are too specialized in meaning, and therefore too restricted in the kind of stems they are likely to have, to acquire new shades of meaning. Stems of -iana (as in *Johnsoniana*) for instance, are almost entirely confined to proper names. -ness, on the other hand, may be affixed to any adjective to form an abstract noun, and it is probably too general in application to develop subgroups. But it seems impossible to make predictions about what kind of suffix will show semantic developments through interaction with its stems. One suffix which might have been expected to form some distinct subgroups is -dom, which has been quite productive in the last two centuries,[4] and appears with a wide range of stems, a great many of them human nouns. But although some observers have remarked on a tendency to form disparaging words, such as *old fogeydom, nazidom*, there are many which are not disparaging. The groups of *-dom* words that may be distinguished are very closely linked with one another. Givón (1967a, 24–30) in a detailed examination of the sense-developments of this suffix, distinguishes such senses as 'tenure of office' (*popedom*), 'system' (*priestdom*, = 'the rule or dominion of priests') and 'geographic' (*kingdom*). He indicates the very complex ways in which such senses combine and interact in *-dom* words. The suffix does not seem to have developed any preference for stems of a particular shape: it is equally likely to appear with long stems (*bachelordom*) or short ones (*fandom*).

Finally, in this introductory section, it is relevant to notice how group-forming tendencies operate in our everyday use of language. A study of writing done in haste, in the training college examination papers mentioned in 12.7 above, yielded numerous examples like the following: '. . . a suggestion of delicacy and feminacy in "such lightness in her footfall"', where the influence of *delicacy* has prevented the choice of *femininity*; 'it makes the reader aware of the almost insectile smallness of humanity against the implacable forces of nature', in which the unusual word *insectile* instead of the more common *insect-like* was perhaps prompted by such words as *reptile, puerile, infantile, futile*; 'the proliferance of words like "blood" and "death" throughout the play always keep a feeling of terror in the audience', in which words like *abundance, preponderance*, possibly *exuberance*, are behind *proliferance*. Lastly, a spoken example reported in a newspaper: 'We can't send helicopters out today because they can't be used in blizzardous snow' [*Evening Standard* 4 March 1970, 1/1], in which the choice of *blizzardous* was evidently suggested by *hazardous*.

We can compare the way in which stems and affixes interact within the word with the way in which words interact within the sentence. McIntosh points out (1961, 327–8) in a general discussion of the collocation of words in sentences, that words have a certain 'potential of collocability' and the edges of this range of tolerance are not precisely definable. The range of collocational possibilities of an adjective, for instance – an example which he mentions is *molten* – is represented in part by the inventory of nouns which it may qualify. The native speaker knows how to use *molten*, and he knows how to extend the range of nouns that may occur with it in various ways, by metaphor and by associations of various kinds. The illustrations for this word in Webster (1961) include: 'molten lead was poured . . .'; 'the molten sunlight of warm skies'; and 'seething . . . he set himself to compose a molten political pamphlet'. We have no difficulty in understanding that the 'glowing' implications of a phrase such as *molten lead* appear in the second example, and the (metaphorical) 'heat' in the third. In considering the behaviour of word-elements – stems and affixes – we have to do with similar matters of collocation and extension of range, though usually the ranges involved are extended gradually, step by step through successive words, without such metaphoric leaps as I have just exemplified. We shall see in the following sections how not only suffixes (13.3) but compound-elements (13.4 and 13.5) and splinters (13.6), when they become productive, may acquire different 'strands' of meaning from the word-contexts in which they occur, and may then pass these on to new contexts.

13.3 Suffixes

In the following sections I shall examine four 'personal' suffixes. The first three, *-arian*, *-ster*, and *-eer*, are similar in many ways; they have been productive in English for hundreds of years and there is much evidence in the OED to help in reconstructing their development. The fourth, *-nik*, has been productive only for a very short time and very recently; the examples illustrating it are taken mainly from newspapers and are probably mostly ephemeral. However, an advantage in examining very recent words is that intuitions about them may be first-hand and not based on possibly incomplete documentary sources; and I think it is possible to see in *-nik* words the same kind of developments as we find in the more established suffixes. In tracing the activities of these suffixes through their periods of productivity, we shall see how instructive it is to list words containing a common element, and to consider their meanings and chronological sequence. In this way we may learn something about the range-extending processes of word-elements, and about how and why new words are formed.

13.3.1 –ARIAN

In the sixteenth century, when words in *-arian* first began to appear in English, they were often adapted from Latin words in *-arius*. Thus, *Trinitarian* (1565)[5] is from sixteenth-century *trinitarius*, from *trinitas*, 'trinity', + *-an*. But Latin words in *-arius* were also anglicized as words in *-ary:* thus we have *millenarian* (1631) and *millenary* (1550), from *millenarius;* and *disciplinarian* and *disciplinary* (1585) from medieval Latin *dis-*

ciplinarius. This means that some *-arian* words can be considered as derived from English words in *-ary*, with the addition of the suffix *-an*, or *-ian:* the OED derives *necessarian* (1777) from *necessary+-ian.* There is also the possibility of the influence of French words in *-aire*, which had the same Latin source, *-arius*. Thus, the OED describes *egalitarian* (1885) as 'after F. *égalitaire*'. Quite early, however, 'irregular' coinages came about, showing that *-arian* very quickly acquired an identity of its own as a suffix. The OED derives *predestinarian* (1638) from the verb *predestine+ -arian;* and other seventeenth-century words not related to Latin words in *-arius* or English words in *-ary* are *pulpitarian* (1654), and Milton's *anti- quitarian* (1641). In spite of these and many like them, we still find dis- approval of such irregularity expressed as late as the nineteenth century: in 1819 we hear of someone being 'more shocked as a grammarian at the word [*humanitarian*] than as a divine at the sect' [OED, s.v. *humanitarian*]; and in 1875 Gladstone refers to *establishmentarian* as a 'barbarous word' [OED, s.v. *establishmentarian*].

Attempts to keep the derivations of *-arian* words as tidy and uniform as possible may have results which run counter to our intuitions about the words. When *sectarian* appeared in the language (1654), there was a word, *sectary*, from which it could be considered as derived, and the OED so derives it. But now that *sectary* is no longer much used, it is natural to see *sectarian* as a combination of *sect+-arian.* The OED's derivation of *necessarian* from *necessary+-ian* obscures the fact that by this time, 1777, the suffix *-arian* was well enough established to have been felt as a con- stituent of the word. We cannot of course know how an eighteenth- century speaker 'felt', but this impression is supported when we come to consider *-arian* words collectively, and the semantic groups into which they fall: *necessarian* fits very well into one of them. The OED derives *doctrinarian* (1747) from an unattested Latin form **doctrinarius;* Webster (1961) says it is a modification of French *doctrinaire,+-ian.* But although the religious order, The Brethren of Christian Doctrine, whose name gave rise to the word *doctrinarian*, originated in France, the word *doctrin- aire* does not appear in English until the nineteenth century. And as we have seen, by 1747, there were numerous precedents in English to justify a derivation *doctrine+-arian* without the mediation of Latin, a derivation also supported by the fact that *doctrinarian* falls naturally into a semantic group of *-arian* words. Another word which may be derived in more than one way is *totalitarian* (1928) which the OED derives from *totality+-arian*, whereas Webster (1961) explains it as from *total+itarian* (as in *authori- tarian*); in this explanation it has obviously been influenced by meaning.

In examining -*arian* words which have been in the language for a long time and have acquired more than one meaning, we find that, for different meanings, different derivations may be appropriate. Thus, the OED derives *unitarian* in its theological sense (1867, = 'one who affirms the impersonality of the Godhead, especially as opposed to an orthodox Trinitarian') from modern Latin *unitarius*+ -*an;* in its nineteenth-century philosophical and political senses however (for example, = 'an advocate of national or political unity'), the derivation is given as *unit-y*+ -*arian.* *Proprietarian* in 1776 meant 'an advocate or supporter of proprietary government in the N. American colonies', and as such the OED derives it in the 'regular' way from *proprietary*+ -*an;* in its nineteenth-century sense (1866, = 'a stickler for propriety') it is derived from *propriety*+ -*arian.* In a third sense, as used by Shaw, *cf* 'sending proletarian winners of scholarships to proprietarian public schools' [Webster (1961), s.v. *proprietarian adj*], Webster (1961) derives it from *proprietariat* on the analogy of the pair *proletariat/proletarian* (*cf* the quotation from Shaw in 13.1).

The stems of -*arian* words have more than one characteristic formal feature. Most contain two syllables or more; a number of them end in *n*, like *disciplinarian, doctrinarian.* This latter 'preference' was probably determined by the many words derived from Latin numerals which found their way into English, such as *millenarian, octogenarian, centenarian.* But the majority end in *t*; many correspond to words in -*ity*, like the stem of *Trinitarian*, but others, like *societarian, libertarian, vegetarian, packetarian* (1882, = 'one of the crew of a packet-boat') have stems with different *t* endings. This last example does not belong to any semantic group of -*arian* words: it seems likely that *packet* attracted the suffix simply because of its shape – two syllables, ending in *t*. *Binitarian* (1908) has even acquired a *t* to make it conform to the prevalent pattern, *cf* 'There are Trinitarians, Binitarians, Arians, and Unitarians' [OEDS, s.v. *binitarian*, 1908]. Perhaps because *agrarian, librarian, grammarian* consist of a monosyllable+ -*arian*, these words do not seem to belong to the set of those I have already mentioned. But a few stems, though monosyllabic, which end in *t*, proclaim their membership of our -*arian* family: *sectarian, tractarian, strictarian, fruitarian* and *nutarian* (see below).

In some cases, a pair of -*arian* words has been formed from what is etymologically the same stem, one form containing the characteristic *t*, the other not. Examples are *sabbatarian* (1613) and *sabbatharian* (1719); *necessarian* (1777) and *necessitarian* (1798); *ubiquarian* (1737) and *ubiquitarian* (1640). These have flourished side by side, but in each case the -*t*- form seems to have been more widely used.

We find small sets of words whose stems have greater similarities of form. Similarity of meaning may not be involved, as with *latitudinarian* (1662, = 'one who practises latitude, especially in religious matters'), *valetudinarian* (1703, = 'a person in weak health, especially one who is constantly concerned with his own ailments'); *attitudinarian* (1754-6, = 'one who studies and practises attitudes') and *platitudinarian* (1855). A quotation which the OED gives for the last-mentioned example shows the force of rhyme in word-formation: 'As much need to be on their guard against platitudinarianism as against latitudinarianism' (1887). Another little group, formed after *utilitarian* (1781), contains *futilitarian* (1827) and *beautilitarian* (noted by Pound (1914, 44) as used in the magazine *Good Housekeeping* March 1911, 281).

One of the largest semantic groups into which *-arian* words fall is that of terms referring to those who hold moral or political beliefs, such as *egalitarian*, or *necessitarian* (= 'one who maintains that all human action is determined by the law of causation'). This group grew naturally out of the earliest group, denoting members of religious groups or sects, such as *sabbatarian*, *sacramentarian* (1535), *Trinitarian*, *unitarian*. Perhaps because people often used these words in referring, not to themselves, but to others, and because religion and politics are matters about which people feel strongly, very many *-arian* words have an uncomplimentary shade of meaning. However, in some cases we need to be careful in assigning such a nuance, because, for a word current in the past, we may not be able to decide whether this simply depended on the individual writer's view, or whether it was a constant feature of the word. But it does seem that *-arian* had acquired such a shade of meaning even in the seventeenth century, and this is supported by the way in which Milton introduces his coinage *antiquitarian*: 'I shall distinguish . . . the hinderers of Reformation into 3 sorts, 1. Antiquitarians (for so I had rather call them then Antiquaries, whose labours are usefull and laudable)' [OED, s.v. *antiquitarian*]. (It is worth noticing also that Milton chose the *-t-* form rather than *antiquarian*.) While many *-arian* words have never had any uncomplimentary use, for example *humanitarian*, the suffix certainly has what Jespersen calls a 'taint' (1922, 388), which may or may not be active; *cf* 'The tractarians, if without offence we may so call them' [OED, s.v. *tractarian*, 1839].

Another shade of meaning or taint which the suffix has acquired is that of 'strict or narrow-minded (believer in certain tenets, or enforcer of certain policies)'. A study of quotations illustrating *-arian* words shows that adjectives such as *strict*, *stiff*, *uncompromising*, *stern* frequently qualify them. A nucleus of words in the 'strict' group consists of *authoritarian*

(1879), for which the illustrations in Webster (1961) include the adjectives *strict* and *uncompromising; disciplinarian*, originally (1585) a name for a political-religious group of Puritans, later 'one who enforces (strict) discipline' (1639); *doctrinarian*, the name of first a religious, then a political group, and later, 'a person devoted inflexibly to a particular doctrine', *cf* 'A stiff and doctrinarian politician of the Whig school' [OED, s.v. *doctrinarian*, 1878]. For *sectarian* in its sense of '(bigoted) adherent of a sect', a frequent qualifier is *narrow;* for *uniformitarian* (= 'an advocate of uniformity'), the OED quotes 'The procrustean work of a miserable uniformitarian' (1890). Also in the 'strict' group are *proprietarian* in the sense 'a stickler for propriety': the OED quotes 'the rigid pro-prietarians' (1866); *strictarian* (1867) and *totalitarian* (1928).

In some words which do not so obviously belong to this group, we can see a tendency to occur with the same kind of adjective or to have the same flavour. Thus, a frequent qualifier of *sabbatarian* is *strict;* others are *rigid, precise, stiff*. The OED's quotation of 1899 for *universitarianism* has an implication of 'rigidity': 'At the risk of being accused of classicism, or universitarianism, I must confess that I do believe in a certain amount of classical work.' The system of religious opinion contained in *Tracts for the Times* (1833–41) which gave rise to the main sense of *Tractarian* (1839) was a rather High-Church and non-liberal one; we learn from a writer in 1892 that there were competing forms of the name: 'Lawless in formation, certainly, is *Tractarian*; and yet it will live in history, to the exclusion of *Tractite, Tractuist* and *Tractator*, all of which have been proposed in its stead' [OED, s.v. *tractarian*]. Clearly, among the advantages of *tractarian* are the sense of 'sect', the 'strict' taint, the stem ending in *t*, and the echo of *sectarian*.

The fact that one word can suggest another of similar form and, usually, related meaning, is demonstrated by the frequency with which two or more *-arian* words occur in the same context. We have already noticed several instances of this. A break-away subgroup, presumably from the 'moral or political beliefs' group, is that inspired by *vegetarian* and having to do with 'beliefs about diet'; *cf* 'We flee from before the face of vegetarianism, fruitarianism' [OEDS, s.v. *fruitarian*]; 'Why do they call that thing they gave me nutsteak? Nutarians. Fruitarians' [James Joyce, *Ulysses*, 1922, Bodley Head 1937, 154]. Also in this group is *dietarian* (1880); *meatarian* and even *sea-foodetarian* have been coined in the twentieth century.

Another example of a pair in the same context is the following: 'It is only these two types, the sentimental humanitarian and the sentimental brutalitarian, whom one hears in the modern babel' [OEDS, s.v. *brutali-tarian*, 1909]. There is a little 'semantic field', or system, consisting of *humanitarian* (1819) and its opposite *brutalitarian* (1904), *animalitarianism*, which contrasts with a different sense of *human* (= 'the view that animals are more natural, happier and admirable than human beings'), and a near-synonym of *humanitarian*, *charitarian* (1858).

Another little system of *-arian* words can be diagrammed thus:

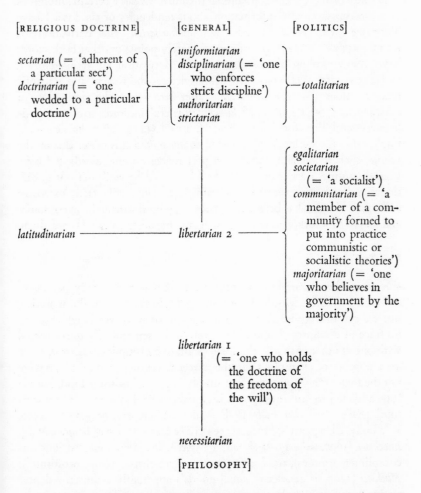

(The vertical lines join antonymous or contrasting words or groups of words, and the horizontal lines join words or groups of words which are similar in meaning.)

I have dealt in this very detailed way with -*arian* in order to point to some of the forces at work in word-formation, and the difficulty of pinning them down and being precise about them. It seems likely, for instance, that the affinities of suffixes for stems of a certain shape is a more potent force in deciding patterns of word-formation than has hitherto been recognized by most grammarians.[6] The subject deserves a much more thorough and scholarly investigation than is possible here.

A study of the OED's derivational formulas reveals a certain amount of tacit and unsystematic information about tendencies of the kind I have illustrated with -*arian* words. For *authoritarian*, the derivation 'f. AUTHORITY+-ARIAN; *cf: trinitarian*' merely points out that both words have corresponding nouns in -*ity*; the derivation of *futilitarian*, 'f. FUTILITY, after UTILITARIAN' acknowledges the formal and semantic links, as does that for *strictarian:* 'after *sectarian*'. The derivation of *equalitarian*, 'f. EQUALITY: *cf: humanitarian* etc' indicates some semantic likeness, and that for *brutalitarian*, 'f. BRUTALITY, after *humanitarian*' implies that the semantic relationship to *humanitarian* is close. But on the whole, such tendencies, trends and preferences among words as I have been discussing are not of the kind which could be easily set out in dictionaries. Sometimes they are not readily apparent until a fairly extensive collection of items has been made; they may be dormant in one instance and active in another, according as form, meaning or use favour them.

13.3.2 -STER

-*ster* is another example of a suffix which has formed many pejorative and non-pejorative words side by side. The former are in the majority, but we can distinguish three or four groups of such words which carry no trace of disapproval, and in fact seem to be semantically unconnected with one another. As far as the main pejorative group is concerned, there are a number of examples from the sixteenth century, though these were not the first.[7] One is *gamester*, first simply 'a player' of some kind, but via 'one addicted to amorous sport', it appears in Shakespeare as= 'a prostitute' [*All's Well that Ends Well* V iii]. Others are *bangster* (*c* 1570, = 'a bully, a braggart'), *lewdster* (1598), [*The Merry Wives of Windsor* V iii], *smockster* (1607, = 'a go-between, a bawd'), *whipster* (1598, various uncomplimentary uses), and *hackster* (1581, = 'cut-throat, pimp, prostitute'). *Huckster* (1200, = 'retailer of small goods') apparently acquired a depreciative meaning as early as 1400, according to the OED.

A group of nineteenth- and twentieth-century formations denoting 'criminal' of various kinds probably received an impetus from *shyster* (1856, = 'one who is professionally unscrupulous, especially in the practice of law or politics'). The ending of this word is a 'suffixoid' rather than a real suffix (see note 2 at the end of this chapter): the word is thought to be from the name of a nineteenth-century American lawyer, Scheuster, whose name lives because it happened to fall into line with the still productive process which produced, for example, *trickster* in 1711, and *prigster*, current since 1688 in various depreciative meanings, and used in 1807 as = 'thief, pilferer'. Later came *ringster* (1875, = 'a member of a political or price-fixing ring'), and *gangster* (1896). In the twentieth century appeared *mobster* (1918), *bankster* (1932, = 'a profiteering banker', see Jespersen MEG VI, 15.1₃) and many other probably transient coinages, such as *gypster*, *thugster*, *crimester*. A very recent member of this group is *fraudster:* 'A team of fraudsters swindled London post offices out of £168,000 . . .' [*Evening Standard* 5 June 1972, 6/1].

Various other words with this suffix hover on the fringes of respectability, such as *boomster* (1879, = 'a speculator'), *cf* 'The trickery and usurpation . . . of the leading boomster' [DAE, s.v. *boomster*]; *dopester*, (1916) and *tipster* (1862), both meaning 'forecaster of (sporting) events', *cf* 'today's newspaper tipsters – who much prefer being called racing correspondents' [*Sunday Times* 25 April 1971, Magazine 42]; and *jobster*, one of whose senses links it with the *ringster* group: 'one who gives or takes jobs in public service for political favours' (1879).

A different group of *-ster* words which seems to be related to the 'criminal' group is that to which we could give the general label 'one possessing inferior skill at some (artistic) pursuit', of which the earliest example seems to be *penster* (1611, = 'a petty writer, a literary hack'). Ben Jonson uses the otherwise respectable *songster* in a way which suggests contamination by depreciative *-ster* words:

For Silke will draw some sneaking Songster thither,
It is a ryming Age, and Verses swarme
At every stall
          ['An Elegie', *Under-Wood*, 1640]

Others are *rhymester* (1719), *daubster* (1853, = 'a clumsy painter') and *dabster*, originally (1708) 'an expert or dab', but used by Browning in a sense which puts it in this group:

lines
Which every dabster felt in duty bound
To signalize his power of pen and ink . . .
['Prince Hohenstiel-Schwangau', 1871]

Tennyson uses *tonguester* in a similar way:

. . . lowly minds were madden'd to the height
By tonguester tricks
['To Mary Boyle', 1889, ix]

Webster (1961) defines *wordster* as 'one that is adept in the use of words, esp. in an empty or bombastic manner', and *pulpster* is noted in Wentworth and Flexner (1960) as = 'a writer, editor, or publisher of "pulp" '.

Possibly this group has in the past received some impetus from similar words in *-aster*, current mainly in the seventeenth century. Examples are *criticaster* (1684, = 'a petty or inferior critic'), *poetaster* (1599, = 'a petty or paltry poet'), *philosophaster* (1611, = 'a shallow or pseudo philosopher'), *politicaster* (1641, = 'a petty, feeble, or contemptible politician'). The suffix *-aster* is unrelated to *-ster*: it is from Latin, and the meaning illustrated in these examples developed from the meaning 'incompletely resembling'.

Three groups of *-ster* words without any element of depreciative meaning are:

1 Twentieth-century examples connected with music or art: *bopster, coolster, hepster* (= 'devotee of jazz'), *jivester, swingster; opster* (= 'practitioner of optical art') and *popster* (= 'practitioner of pop art'): 'It would seem that two older artists have been curiously misunderstood – Albers by the "opsters" and Duchamp by the "popsters" ' [*Saturday Review* 1965, quoted in *American Speech* 41, 1966, 141].
2 Synonyms of *joker: punster* (1700); *jokester, funster* (nineteenth-century); *japester, gagster, quipster, prankster.*
3 Words meaning 'vehicle': *speedster* (1918, = 'a fast vehicle'), *roadster* in its latest sense, 'type of car' (1922); *jeepster* (1948, the name of a sports car) and *dragster* (c 1950, = 'a car built or adapted for drag racing').

A recent use of *speedster* is interesting, since it suggests some contamination from the *gangster* group: 'MP urges: Jail the M-way fog speedsters' (headline) 'Long prison sentences for drivers who speed in fog on motorways were demanded in the Commons today ... ' [*Evening Standard* 17 March 1972, 1/5].

This is by no means a complete picture of the past and present behaviour of -*ster* in English. Many words are recorded only in dictionaries of slang, and it would be difficult to ascertain the nature and extent of their use. Of twentieth-century coinages, Lubbers (1965, 465) comments that 'the lingo of sports, music and the underworld' has provided the largest number.

The suffix is attached only to monosyllabic stems; and apart from a very few adjectival exceptions, like *youngster*, *oldster*, *lewdster*, these stems are nominal. In many cases there is a synonym in -*er*, whose stem is verbal: *jobber/jobster*, *rhymer/rhymester* and so on; but this does not seem to have shaken the affinity of the suffix for noun stems, and the feeling of native speakers, where the stem could be nominal or verbal, that it is in fact nominal. This preference is modern: in Old and Middle English times, -*ster* was attached to verbal stems, as in *lærestre*, 'female teacher', *chattestere*, 'gossip', *brewster* (1308, = 'brewer') and *deemster* (1300, = 'judge'). In these words the suffix functions exactly like the agentive -*er*. As the OED observes (s.v. -*ster*), 'It is probable that -*ster* was often preferred to -*er* as more unambiguously referring to the holder of a professional function as distinguished from the doer of an occasional act.' This is true today; in spite of all its other developments, the suffix can still be used as it was in Middle English.[8] Witness twentieth-century *pollster* (c 1940), 'one whose occupation is conducting opinion polls', cf 'This is the latest verdict from Opinion Research Centre – the only pollsters who got the winning right in the June General Election' [*Evening Standard* 3 December 1970, 17/2].

I have not examined the various connective relations between stem and suffix. As Lubbers points out, -*ster* words can be classified on this basis, for example, 'one *who is* adjective' (*youngster*, *lewdster*); 'one *who sells, makes, furnishes* noun' (*tipster*, *songster*, *punster*), and so on. Undoubtedly, an analysis of this sort is necessary in establishing exactly how a suffix behaves; but here I am concerned with tendencies and trends which cut across this kind of classification. Other examples in this chapter give support to the view that the word-class of the stem and its paraphrasable relation to the affix are perhaps less important factors in determining the way a group develops than those of sound and meaning.

13.3.3 -EER

The third suffix to be considered, -*eer*, has depreciative uses similar to the first two, especially *-ster*. Compare for instance the three seventeenth-century terms for 'preacher': *pulpiteer* (1642), *pulpitarian* (1654) and *tubster* (1681), *cf* 'Mechanique Pulpiteers and Tub preachers' [OED, s.v. *pulpiteer*, 1681]. Like *-arian*, *-eer* prefers a stem of, usually, two syllables ending in *t* or *n*. Besides the *pulpit-* pair, we have *parliamenteer*, *parliamentarian; chariteer*, *charitarian; packeteer*, *packetarian*.

The earliest notable group of *-eer* words concerns military matters; in some, the stem is the name of a weapon, as in *cannoneer* (1562), *musketeer* (1590), *pistoleer* and *rocketeer* (1832), and recently, *weaponeer* (= 'one who activates an atomic bomb into readiness for release upon a target'). Also in this area are *buccaneer* (1690 in the sense of 'piratical rover'), *privateer* (1646, = 'private man of war'; 1664, = 'an armed vessel privately owned', later extended to the crew of such a vessel), *volunteer*, originally (1600) of military application only, and, much later, the verb *commandeer*, from an Afrikaans word, *kommanderen*, which happened to suggest an *-eer* word fitting into the 'military' group.

One apparently odd formation is *waistcoateer* (1616, = 'low-class prostitute'). This word is comparable in both composition and meaning with its contemporary *smockster* (from *smock*, = 'woman's undergarment'), though its relation to other *-eer* formations is not clear: possibly it was formed on the analogy of a 'military' word like *targeteer* (1586-8, = 'a foot-soldier armed with a target'). It does not seem to fit into the group of depreciative words in *-eer* that arose in the seventeenth century. This group is similar to the *penster-rhymester-wordster* group; its members denote inferior or false practitioners of something, in most cases speaking or writing. Examples are *pulpiteer*, possibly *pamphleteer* (1642, = 'a writer of pamphlets'), though the disparaging uses of this word are probably due more to (temporary) political, than aesthetic considerations. (Marchand (1969, 269) suggests that these two words are the result of an extension of the idea of 'battle' to the fields of speaking and writing.) *Sonneteer* (1665) belongs here, *cf* 'I have heard many a little Sonneteer called a fine Genius' [OED, s.v. *sonneteer sb.*, 1711]; and *garreteer* (1720, = 'literary hack'). *Gazetteer* in the eighteenth century meant 'journalist' (1611) or 'newspaper' (1730) or, its present meaning, 'geographical index' (1704). Dr Johnson gives evidence in his dictionary (1755) that in the first of these senses the word could be used depreciatively: 'it was lately a term of the utmost infamy, being usually applied to wretches who were hired to vindicate the court.' This group gained some new members in the twentieth century with *jargoneer* (1913), *fictioneer* (1923), *cf* 'sentimental fictioneering' [OEDS, s.v. *fictioneer*] and *sloganeer* (1922), *cf* 'In other colleges, he had had evidence that young people today were irreverent towards sloganeering ... and now, even this audience of over a thousand couldn't keep him contentedly bombasting for more than 20 minutes' [Sinclair Lewis, *Gideon Planish*, 1943, 417–18]. Two words in this 'false' group which are not connected with speaking or writing are *patrioteer*, stated by Mencken (1936, 180) to be 'at least as early as 1913', *cf* 'Patriotism too often means patrioteering. It means concealing a world of error and wrong judgment beneath the flag' [Lyndon B. Johnson, quoted in *Observer* 4 September 1967, 10/6–7]; and *coquetteering*: 'One of the two girls at that table was already coquetteering with Leontiev in an exaggerated and ostentatious manner; but he knew that she was of the type who considered this kind of display as part of the ritual of visiting a nightclub' [Arthur Koestler, *The Age of Longing*, 1951, 327].

Another group of uncomplimentary formations refers to generally dishonest pursuits. The noun *profiteer* (1797 according to the SOED) is the first of these, but both noun and verb have chiefly been used in the twentieth century, during and since the first world war; *cf* 'The tricks of the armament profiteers are fresh in the public mind' [OEDS, s.v. *profiteer sb.*, 1914]. The OED gives a nineteenth-century example of a word in this group, *moskeneer, v.* (1874, = 'to pawn (an article) for more than it is worth'), but all the others appeared in the twentieth century. One of the most widely used is *racketeer* (1928), which preceded a number of more or less transient formations, of which the best-known is *black marketeer* (*c* 1942). Others are *blacketeer* (= 'black marketeer'), *stockateer* (= 'a broker dealing in fraudulent securities'), *banketeer* (= 'a bank racketeer') and *speaketeer* (= 'a speakeasy racketeer'). A formation which seems to have been influenced by these is *Municheer*: 'Today they are the assistants of Hitler and the Municheers in Britain' [*New Statesman* 3 January 1942, 9/1].

As with *-ster* words, many *-eer* words, such as *auctioneer*, *mountaineer*, *puppeteer*, have remained free of any group affiliations; but there are a number which are less obviously, or only sometimes, pejorative, for instance the 'political' words, like *electioneer, v.* (1789), *cf* 'One who intrigued and bargained for the office, and openly electioneered for himself' [OEDS, s.v. *electioneer v.*, 1817]. Other words of this kind are *parliamenteering* (1711, = 'engagement in parliamentary affairs'), *factioneer* (*c* 1710, = 'a member of a faction'), *revolutioneering* (= 'the carrying out of revolutions') and *crotcheteer* (1815, = 'a person with a crotchet; especially one who pushes his crotchets in politics'). (A *crotchet* = 'a peculiar notion on some point', *cf* OED, s.v. *crotchet sb.*[1] 9.) A recent 'political' coinage is *motioneering*: 'We believe that the recent epidemic of motioneering has tended to obscure the Government's achievements. . . . we intend to make it felt that there are other views among the new intake [*ie* into Parliament] than those of nature's naggers and snarlers' [*Evening Standard* 5 July 1966, 32/3].

This 'political' group perhaps has something of the sense of the verb *engineer*, in the sense of 'to contrive'. The noun *engineer* seems to be the earliest of the depreciative *-eer* words, dating from the fifteenth century, and the OED's quotations make it clear that the meaning was uncomplimentary, *cf* 'The deuil's enginers', 'That great engineer, Satan' [OED, s.v. *engineer sb.*, 1611, 1635]. This sense did not interfere with the contemporary 'military' sense (= 'a constructor of military engines'), and according to the OED, became obsolete after the seventeenth century. Both noun and verb are now current in general contexts, and political ones, *cf* Webster (1961)'s illustrations of the noun: 'a political engineer of some note'; 'a skilled engineer of the economy of the nation'; and the quotations for the verb in the OEDS: 'The lobbying or engineering a bill through the Legislature' (1864); 'When he undertakes to engineer a resolution through this House for the expulsion of a brother member' (1865).

13.3.4 -NIK

This is a suffix most of whose activity in English is very recent. It is from the Russian suffix *-nik*, denoting 'a person engaged in or connected with something specified'. It first became widely known to speakers of British English after the launching of the first Russian space satellite, the Sputnik, in October 1957. A second Russian satellite containing a dog (and christened *Muttnik* by the Americans) was sent up a month later, and the American press at once began to coin *-nik* words. As *Time* magazine remarked, under the heading 'Dog Story':

> Man sights Dog: Headlines yelped such barbaric new words as pupnik and poochnik, sputpup and woofnik. Cartoonists filled outer space with gloomy GOPniks and gleeful Demo-niks . . . Readers reported mysterious flying objects that the Fort Worth *Star-Telegram* promptly dubbed whatniks . . . Even Manhattan's usually longfaced Communist *Daily Worker* bayed in a headline: EVERY DOGNIK HAS ITS DAYNIK.
>
> [*Time* 18 November 1957, 56–7]

The failure of an American satellite (unofficially *Yanknik*) in December of that year inspired *flopnik*, *kaputnik*, *goofnik*, *sputternik* and other words like them.

This fashion was a short-lived one, and produced only very transient formations. -*nik*, however, was already familiar to Americans in such words as *nudnik* (= 'a person who is a bore; a nuisance'), a Yiddish word from Russia, in which the -*nik* is depreciative. Other words of Yiddish inspiration are *nogoodnik*,[9] *cf* 'Nerts to these Average Guys, Harry, they're just a set of peanut-circuit nogoodniks' [Len Deighton, *Horse Under Water*, 1963, Penguin 1965, 77]; *allrightnik*, *cf* 'Only Allrightniks eat with the Captain – so you don't appreciate all that high society? Well, excuse me, no kikes wanted, hein?' [Katherine Anne Porter, *Ship of Fools*, 1945, Secker & Warburg 1962, 254]; and *holdupnik:* '"Telephone the police," cried Karp. "The car is parked across the street." "What car?" "The holdupniks." ' [Bernard Malamud, *The Assistant*, 1957, Penguin 1967, 26]. In all of these examples the speakers are Jewish. *Shakespearenik* was used [New York *Herald Tribune* 12 August 1960, 15/6] in an article on the Yiddish theatre, with no uncomplimentary implication.

At about the time that the Sputnik appeared, another word, destined to become even more well-known, made its appearance: *beatnik*. It is not certain which sense of *beat* furnished its first element: Webster (1961) suggests that it was 'exhausted', 'beaten'. The -*nik* is presumably the depreciative one of *nudnik*, but may have been in part suggested by the contemporary popularity of *sputnik*. A number of recent coinages have overtones which suggest *beatnik* rather than *nudnik* as their inspiration. In *beatnik*, for which a precise definition is difficult to frame, we have the notions of 'rejection of conventional standards', and therefore sometimes 'political rebel', 'intellectual' and 'youth'. The first notion is supported by coinages such as *far-outnik*, *way-outnik*, and the example given in 11.1, *straightnik* (= 'a conventional person trying to be unconventional'). The second notion has prompted names for those opposed to the war in Vietnam, such as *peacenik*. Of the following uses, the first is disparaging and the second is not: 'According to Mr Heren, [President Johnson's opinion of Mr Wilson] is low, with Mr Wilson regarded as a "peacenik in striped trousers" ' [*Evening Standard* 23 February 1968, 6/2]; 'Probably at no stage for many years have the ideas and attitudes of peaceniks been given a more sympathetic hearing' [*Peace News* 4 February 1966, 4/3]. Other examples in the 'peacenik' group are *draftnik* (= 'draft-dodger') and *Vietnik*, *cf* 'The crowded headquarters of the young draftniks and Vietniks pulse with an almost religious fervor' [*Newsweek* 1 November 1965, 31/3]; *protestnik*, and *limpnik* (the last in reference to the tactic used by demonstrators of going limp in the hands of the police).

The 'intellectual' component of *beatnik* is supported by *monknik:* '"We have 3000 people here some days," says Father Brocard Sewell, one of the 20 Carmelite Friars, a jovial man known in monastic circles as a "monk-nik" because of his interest in literature' [*Evening Standard* 22 April 1965, 10/1], and *poetnik*: '. . . Mr Allen Ginsberg and other Beat poets . . . I need not now stop to illustrate these linguistic features in the work of Ginsberg and other poetniks' [Randolph Quirk, *The Study of the Mother Tongue*, 1961, 20].

Another small group of -*nik* formations has to do with popular music and is perhaps the result of the 'youth' component of *beatnik* combined with the understanding of *beat* in its musical sense. One member of it is *folknik* (*cf* 11.1); *popnik*, *rocknik* and *discothequenik* have also appeared. -*nik* here also has the sense of 'enthusiast', and in the following examples it seems to have chiefly this meaning: *boatnik*: 'What is the mysterious force that makes fervent boatmen? . . . "Out there," says one boatnik huskily, "a man's a boy and a boy's a man . . ." ' [*Time*, Atlantic edn, 18 May 1959, 58/3]; *greasenik*: 'For ten years now, each March has brought from 30,000 to 50,000 greaseniks of the sports car persuasion here for the 12-hour orgy of noise and grime called the Sebring International Grand Prix of Endurance' [New York *Herald Tribune* 28 March 1960, 31/1–2].

It might also be noted in passing that a number of -*nik* words have been used by American advertisers as names for clothes; here presumably homonymy with *knick*- is sometimes relevant, and the associations of such -*nik* formations as I have already mentioned are not. *Cf* 'Beachniks at sea by Jantzen. Surfing pants' (1960, see Harder 1966).

It seems clear that the rapid development of -*nik* during the nineteen sixties[10] is the result of three factors: (1) the prior existence of the Yiddish borrowing *nudnik*, containing elements of depreciatory significance – as we have seen, such elements are peculiarly likely to be productive; (2) an event – the launching of the Sputnik – which caught the public imagina-tion, and (3) the emergence of beatniks, a subject of much social interest and comment.

13.4 Native compound-elements

13.4.1 -IN

The particle -*in* appears in a number of compounds of the *break-down* type (see 8.2.1 above), that is, compounds made up of a noun derived by zero suffix from a verb, and the particle which is associated with the verb. This -*in* group has developed even more quickly than the (*beat*)*nik* one, and most of its members are probably just as ephemeral; but again the interest lies not so much in the items themselves as in what happens to them as a group. *Sit-in* is the earliest of those we are concerned with here: Harder (1968, 58) notes that this word appeared in 1947, but it was not until 1960 that it became the pattern for analogous forms. At this time, in the southern states of America, there were a great many demonstrations against racial segregation; these took the form of gatherings – sitting in – holding sit-ins – in places frequented by the public, such as lunch-counters. There were also *wade-ins* at segregated beaches, *cf* 'Into the already-roiled waters of the South, Negroes will wade this summer in a campaign to break down segregation at public beaches – a wade-in counterpart to the widespread lunch-counter sit-ins of recent weeks' [*Newsweek* 16 May 1960, 34/1]; *read-ins* at city libraries, and many more. Other -*in* words denoted demonstrations aimed at obstructing movement in public places, *cf* 'As the reported demonstration plans grew – for an auto *stall-in* on access roads to the fair to sit-ins, *lie-ins* and alike on other major highways, bridges and in tunnels throughout the city – reverberations sounded in Congress' [American newspaper, quoted in *American Speech* 39, 1964, 219]. Inevitably the pattern spread to names for other kinds of protest, and became widely used in England as well, *cf: pray-in;* first used in America for a demonstration by the Congress of Racial Equality about 1963, it appeared in another context later: 'when Fr McCabe is dismissed, it is the despised progressives in the Newman Association, the Catholic graduates, who plan a pray-in in Westminster Cathedral' [*Observer* 5 March 1967, 21/5].

Teach-in became one of the best-known examples of these -*in* compounds, and by the time it appeared, the nominalization+ -*in* pattern was no longer dependent on the existence of an underlying verb–particle collocation of the same form. Harder (1968, 60), however, notes that *teach-in* was coined by a university professor as a verb in contrast with *to teach out* (= 'to address people outside the university on the subject of the Vietnam war'). A meeting within the university, attended by its members, was then a *teach-in*.[11] The definition of this word in the Addenda (1971) to Webster (1961) is: 'an extended meeting usu. held on a college campus for lectures, debates, and discussions on critical topics (as U.S. foreign policy)'.[12] There followed such words as *be-in*, *cf* 'I am, therefore I protest. The latest style in protesting inaction, superseding sit-ins and Oxfam's flop-ins, comes from New York and is simply styled a be-in. All you need to make your rebellion felt is for several friends of like mind to turn up, and a spot for them to turn up in' [*Guardian* 4 April 1967, 10/6].

An example containing an adjectival first element is *fat-in*, the name for a demonstration held in New York in June 1967 on the principle that 'If everyone was fat there'd be no war. No one would pass the physical' [quoted in *Observer* 11 June 1967, 10/7].

All the examples mentioned so far show that the *-in* element implies a protest of some kind. Since an *-in* occasion is often one in which large numbers of people participate on equal terms, the *-in* has acquired a component of 'audience participation'. During the latter half of the nine-teen-sixties, numerous words were coined in which the 'protest' ingredient is less prominent or altogether absent. Some uses of *be-in* are not concerned with protest (see Harder 1968, 61–2). Further examples are *think-in, cf: World Design Science Decade Think-In*, and *Design In*, both names for events held in the summer of 1967. *Audience-in* was used [*Evening Standard* 10 March 1969, 10/4] to describe a theatrical occasion on which actors and audience collaborated in working out the conclusion of a play. *Death-in* does not denote a meeting: the *-in* signifies merely 'large number' or perhaps 'widespread': 'Perhaps it's still hard for some Euro-peans to realize the degree of death-in that we're feeling here: from the ghetto and Vietnam to the campus, across the hall or in the laundry, up-stairs or after lunch or on the way home' [*New Statesman* 7 August 1970, 158/1].

In *Enoch-in:* 'The Royal Court Theatre . . . is planning to stage a "serious, sophisticated, satirical and funny" attack on Mr Enoch Powell' [*Evening Standard* 13 February 1969, 160/2], the 'protest' element seems to have become one of 'attack'. Clearly, *-in* has been used in such a wide variety of contexts that it has become altogether more versatile and less precise in meaning. As a final example, notice the polysemy of *fly-in*, first used analogously with *drive-in* (= 'a place of business equipped so as to allow its patrons to be served or accommodated while remaining in their automobiles'): 'With space for 25 planes, Brown's "fly-in" pro-vides jeeps to tow its winged clientele to a ramp facing the screen and has loudspeakers to pipe the sound track into closed cockpits' [*Newsweek* 19 July 1947, 82/3]. Later, it joins the 'protest/participation' group; in the following example it denotes 'political discussion': 'My chief reason in going to Washington was to take part in a TV "fly-in" with Dean Rusk' [*New Statesman* 10 February 1967, 182/1]; and later still it is used to denote simply an event, attended by large numbers of people and planes: 'The Helicopter Club of Great Britain is having a "fly-in" at Woburn on Saturday, May 17. Come and join the excitement . . .' [*Evening Standard* 15 May 1969, 17/5–6, advertisement].

13.4.2 -HAPPY

Among adjective compound-elements that have become productive may be mentioned -*happy*. This element seems to have enjoyed a period of productivity from about 1940 onwards,[13] beginning with *slap-happy*, a synonym of *punch-drunk* (= 'dizzy'). A study of -*happy* formations shows that this element may take various additions to its basic meaning: the latter seems to be present to a greater or lesser extent in all the coinages mentioned. Among these additional components are 'frightened', as in *battle-happy*, 'bored', as in *queue-happy*, or 'obsessed' as in *gadget-happy*. It seems difficult to delimit the meaning of -*happy* precisely in any one example, but Webster (1961) distinguishes three groups, which can be exemplified by (1) *slap-happy*, *ie* 'dazed, irresponsible', *cf: demob happy:* 'I joined two marines who were taking cover behind a bank. One . . . was reading a paperback. His white comrade was keeping his head down and laughing. They had two more days left in Vietnam and were demob happy' [*New Statesman* 3 March 1967, 1/2]; *travel-happy:* '. . . an American tourist, apparently so travel-happy that he did not know which country he was in . . .' [*Evening Standard* 26 October 1971, 12/6]; (2) *trigger-happy*, *ie* 'nervously quick to use something', *cf: scissor-happy:* 'the length of his hair would leave little work for a scissor-happy prison barber' [*Sunday Times* 8 August 1971, 3/6]; and (3) *gadget-happy*, *ie* 'enthusiastic to the point of obsession'.

13.4.3 -PROOF

-*proof*, as in *sound-proof*, *burglar-proof* has been productive for several centuries. The earliest nonce formation with -*proof* listed by the OED is *claret-proof*: 'clarret proofe *i.e.* a good wine-bibber' [OED, s.v. *proof a. (adv.)*, 1602]. But in spite of a wide range of first elements, abstract as well as concrete, -*proof* has not developed any meaning other than 'affording protection against what is denoted by the first element'. Contrasting examples appear in the following sentence, quoted by the OED: 'If the heavy mackintosh overalls were expletive-proof as well as snow-proof it would not be a bad thing' (1901).

13.5 Neo-classical compound elements

13.5.1 -CRACY, -CRAT

These elements have been in the language from the time of the Renaissance, in words meaning either 'ruling group', 'elite', or 'state governed by a certain elite'. *Autocracy* (1655), *aristocracy* (1561) and *democracy* (1576) gave rise to such formations as *mobocracy* (1754, = 'the rule of the mob': Greek -κρατία, -*kratia*, means 'rule'); *cottonocracy* (1845, = 'cotton lords as a class'), *beerocracy* (1881, = 'the brewing and beer-selling interest') and *technocracy* (1932, = 'government by technical experts'). Aside from various American coinages analogous to *Democrat* (= 'member of the Democratic party'), such as *Dixiecrat* (1948) and *Eisencrat* (1952), -*cracy* and -*crat* have continued to be productive, with such forma-tions as *meritocracy* (1958): 'not an aristocracy of birth, not a plutocracy of wealth, but a true meritocracy of talent' [Michael Young, *The Rise of the Meritocracy*, 1958, Penguin 1961, 21]. A similar coinage is *brightocracy* in the following: 'Because their superior intelligence makes normal school work easy, bright children easily develop the "butterfly mind" ... [the Brentwood experiment] ... could provide the answer to the problem of the junior brightocracy' [*Evening Standard* 17 May 1966, 7/6]. Here, -*cracy* seems no longer to denote 'a ruling group' but simply 'a (superior) group'.

Bureaucrat (1850) has possibly inspired *Eurocrat* (c 1960, = 'a member of the staff of European organizations such as the European Economic Community'), *cf* 'In the weeks before the fatal meeting French officials had been gratifyingly cooperative with the "Eurocrats" who run the European Economic Commission' [*Observer* 11 July 1965, 9/1]; and *minicrat*: 'These records ... are also going to be available to any Jack-in-office working for the Minister of Health, the Registrar General, and the Director of Public Prosecutions. Once again, the fact that these minicrats will have to get permission from their boss before they snoop affords no protection' [*New Statesman* 26 April 1968, 543/1].

13.5.2 -DROME

Hippodrome, (from Greek ἱππόδρομος, ἵππος, 'horse' and δρόμος, 'race', 'course'), the earliest word containing -*drome* to appear in English (1585), meant in classical times a race course for horses and chariots, and modern establishments of a similar kind are *autodrome* (= 'a driving or racing course for automobiles'), *motordrome* (already noticed as a blend, 12.2), *sportsdrome*, and *velodrome* (1902, = 'a building in which exhibitions of cycle-riding, cycle or motor races, etc, are held'). An *aquadrome* is a stretch of water for boating or swimming.

Hippodrome came to be used as the name for a place of non-sporting entertainment, in particular a music hall, and there followed *picture-drome* (1914, = 'picture palace') and the more colloquial *flickerdrome*. A recent formation is *pleasuredrome*, *cf* 'Mr Patrick Guinness frequented such pleasure-dromes as the Palace Hotel, St Moritz' [*Evening Standard* 6 October 1965, 6/2], in which *-drome* signifies merely 'a place of relaxation'.

ἀεροδρόμος, *aerodromos*, in Greek, means 'running through or traversing the air'; the English word *aerodrome* was used for 'aeroplane' in the eighteen-nineties, but at the beginning of the twentieth century it acquired its present sense, perhaps by analogy with *hippodrome* in its meaning of 'an open space for vehicles'. Words in the 'aerodrome' group are *tankodrome* (1918, = 'a park for a military tank'), *seadrome* (1923, = 'a floating construction moored in the sea for the landing of aeroplanes'); *helidrome* (*c* 1950, = 'an aerodrome for helicopters'), *cosmodrome* (*c* 1960, = 'an aerodrome for space ships'), and *weatherdrome* (= 'a floating weather station which looks like an aerodrome'), in which only resemblance to an aerodrome is indicated.

13.5.3 -NAUT

This element first appeared in English in *Argonaut* (1596), a sailor (*nautes*) in the legendary Argo, which went in quest of the Golden Fleece. When, in the middle of the nineteenth century, it was used to denote a traveller to California in search of gold, the 'sailing' component was not in evidence. But earlier, in the eighteenth century, *-naut* words were used for sailors in the air, balloonists, since *argonaut* conveys the idea of 'exploring unknown regions'. *Aeronaut* (a borrowing from French) appeared in 1784, and Walpole's word *airgonaut* (1784) is a kind of blend of the two *-naut* words. *Astronaut* inevitably followed. This word has of course had most use since the beginning of space travel, but it appeared as the name of a vessel in a nineteenth-century work of science fiction: 'In shape my Astronaut somewhat resembled the form of an antique Dutch East-Indiaman' [P. Greg, *Across the Zodiac*, 1880, Vol I, 27]. The nineteen-sixties brought more *-naut* words: *cosmonaut*, *lunarnaut*, *chimponaut* (in reference to a chimpanzee sent up in a rocket in 1961, *cf muttnik*, 13.3.4); and *plastinaut* (1961, = 'plastic dummy astronaut', 12.3). Undersea exploration provided another little group: *aquanaut*, *bathynaut* (= 'sailor in a bathyscaphe'), *hydronaut*, *oceanaut* (12.6). *-naut* words mainly denote passengers in some vessel, but *aluminaut* (1964) and *telenaut* (1968) are names for underwater craft, the latter for one equipped with television cameras.

In all these examples, the (extended) ideas of 'sailor' and 'explorer' are prominent. *Hovernaut* (= 'sailor in a hovercraft') contains only the former notion. A *-naut* word not connected with travel is *cybernaut*, which has appeared in science-fictional contexts, but in the following quotation seems to exploit the 'explorer' component metaphorically: 'Under the delicate guidance of some cybernaut in California, a computer there has already produced a split-second Mona Lisa' [*Guardian* 8 December 1966, 28/5]. The first element of the word is from *cybernetics* (= 'the comparative study of complex calculating machines and the human nervous system'). *Broker-naut* uses the 'space-explorer' notion metaphorically: 'Incorporated Broker-nauts. There are 4000 earthbound Incorporated Insurance Brokers operating from more than 1300 launching pads in the United Kingdom ready and able to get you off the ground with your insurances' [*Evening Standard* 21 July 1969, 3/5-6, advertisement]. *Responaut*, the title of a periodical for people living by breathing apparatus, perhaps contains an allusion to the conditions under which astronauts and aquanauts travel. The first element is a splinter of *respiratory* or *respiration*. At any rate, it is clear that *-naut* at present has favourable associations, and that it has become rather generalized in meaning.

13.5.4 -SCOPE

There are numerous compounds containing the element *-scope*, from Greek σκοπεῖν, *scopein*, 'to look at, examine', as in *laryngoscope*. Formations with *-scope*, especially the less technical ones, may fall into various groups, according to what kind of instrument is denoted. The idea of 'microscope' is perhaps behind the formation of *comparoscope* (= 'an apparatus used for simultaneous microscope study of two objects'), *diamondscope* (= 'an instrument for the examination of diamonds'), and *biographoscope*: 'Certainly the indefatigable man of letters . . . brings some extra special equipment to the task of examining the President of the United States under his biographoscope' [*New York Times Book Review* 5 June 1938, 1/1]. In the 'telescope' group are *stratoscope:* 'Photographs of stars and planets three times more detailed than any obtained before should result from this week's flight of Stratoscope II, America's giant balloon-borne telescope' [*Observer* 22 January 1964, 3/5]; *spotting scope* (= 'a telescope for locating the strike of a bullet on a target') and the punning *choruscope:* 'Choruscope . . . they are always on the look-out for works which provide scope for their celebrated chorus' [*Observer* 2 May 1965, 23/1]. A 'periscope', 'optical instrument' group contains *trenchscope* (1915, = 'a periscope designed for use in the trenches') and *sniperscope* (= 'a device based on the principle of the periscope, attached to a rifle'). *Cinemascope* appeared in the nineteen-fifties as a trade name for a technique of wide screen cinema photography; *cf: Biblescope*, formed after it: 'If it weren't for the fact that audiences filing in to see the newest length of Biblescope tend reverentially to leave their minds at home, then George Stevens's *The Greatest Story Ever Told* ... ought surely to prove the biggest setback to Christianity since the invention of printing' [*New Statesman* 16 April 1965, 621/3].

13.5.5 –TOPIA

The element *-topia*, first seen in *Utopia*, has appeared in a number of words recently. *Utopia* was formed by Sir Thomas More in 1516, from Greek οὐ, *ou*, 'not' and τόπος, *topos*, 'place', = 'no place', as a name for an imaginary island with a perfect social, legal and political system. The following year *eutopia* was coined, from Greek εὐ-, *eu-*, 'good', meaning 'a region of ideal happiness or good order'. Modern *-topia* words include the antonymous *dystopia*, from Greek δυσ-, *dys-*, 'bad': 'a mad dystopia is created, whose citizens are exclusively involved in horrible crimes and complex litigation' [*New Statesman* 26 January 1968, 117/1]. Probably the best known *-topia* word is *subtopia*, of which the first element is usually interpreted as that of *suburban*. It appeared in 1955: 'By the end of the century Great Britain will consist of isolated cases of preserved monuments in a desert of wire, concrete roads, cosy plots and bungalows. ... Upon this new Britain the REVIEW bestows a name in the hope that it will stick – SUBTOPIA' [*Architectural Review* June 1955, 365]. Winston Churchill had previously coined *queuetopia* (1950); others are *newtopia*, *semitopia*, the first element of which is from *semi-detached*: 'Semitopia: Middlesex and Hertfordshire' [*Punch* 25 August 1965, 262] and *pornotopia*: 'Pornography can be studied and generalized about, and its characteristic features defined: an ideal, problem-free setting, which Marcus has happily called Pornotopia . . .' [*New Statesman* 16 December 1966, 913/1].

13.5.6 –GENIC

An adjectival neo-classical element that has undergone some change in meaning is *-genic*, productive in scientific contexts, where it usually corresponds to a noun ending in *-gen* or *-geny*, for example *allergenic* (= 'inducing allergy'). *Photogenic*, similarly, may mean 'producing or generating light' (*photo-* is from Greek φῶς, φωτ-, *phos, phot-*, 'light'), but it has also acquired the sense 'eminently suitable for being photographed'. This sense probably dates from the nineteen-thirties; there followed *phonogenic, radiogenic, telegenic* and *videogenic* in the next decade, all meaning 'attractive when seen or heard by means of the instrument denoted by the first element'. J. D. Salinger has *billboard-genic*: 'I drew ruddy billboard-genic children, beside themselves with delight and good health' [*For Esmé with Love and Squalor*, 1953, Ace Books 1959, 130]. *Leg-o-genic* appeared (1954) in an American textiles advertisement: here *-genic* means no more than 'attractive'; and recently *biogenic*, in an advertisement describing a cosmetic preparation, takes advantage of both the 'scientific' and 'aesthetic' associations of this element.

13.6 Splinters

It will be apparent by now that the distinction between affixes, compound-elements and splinters is not always clear-cut, and that we cannot easily disentangle blending from other processes of word-formation and treat it on its own. Among the suffixes, *-nik* words in particular partake more or less of the nature of blends, and so do several of the neo-classical words that have been discussed in the preceding section. It is difficult to decide whether *-scope*, for instance, in some of the examples of 13.5.4 is simply a compound-element, meaning 'instrument for viewing', or whether it stands for a particular *-scope* word, like *microscope*, and can be regarded as a splinter. Possibly *biographoscope* is more of a blend than *diamondscope* from this point of view; *laryngoscope* we would presumably not think of calling a blend. Some of the elements which I have here called splinters, such as *para-* (13.6.6) or *tele-* (13.6.7) might have been put with the compound-elements. The justification for placing them in this section is that in the examples discussed, they definitely stand for a particular source word, *parachute, television, telephone*. The same goes for *-cast, -dozer, -legger*, also in this section; in form, these are 'native' compound-elements, but here they are actually representative of *broadcast, bulldozer, bootlegger*, and therefore, by the definition in 11.2 above, splinters.

13.6.1 -CADE

This splinter is from *cavalcade;* the suffix of this word, historically, is *-ade*, a French ending ultimately from the Latin participial *-ata*. Words in English formed with *-ade* are various: they include *arcade, blockade, cannonade, lemonade*, in which the ending has no identifiable meaning for us. However, we do find *processionade*, a nonce word of 1745, defined by the OED as 'an epic of a procession', 'a ceremonial procession', formed perhaps with words like *cavalcade, masquerade, parade* in mind. Other words, like *fanfaronade* (1652, = 'boisterous or arrogant language'; 1812, = 'fanfare'), and *rodomontade* (1612, = 'a vainglorious brag or boast'), have the element of 'show' in common. But since we have the words *cavalier, cavalry*, it is natural to see *-cade* as an element of *cavalcade* rather than *-ade*. *Motorcade* (1924) is the best-known formation containing *-cade*, but *camelcade* (= 'a train of people on camels') appeared in 1886. It re-appeared some eighty years later, after a number of other *-cade* words had been coined: 'Down Britain jeers as Queen watches a mighty camelcade' [*Evening Standard* 10 February 1965, 15/1–2]. Another nineteenth-century example of a *-cade* word was given by the French linguist Michel Bréal in 1892. He noted that the organizers of a Nice festival 'outre les cavalcades annoncent au public des analcades' – that is, 'cavalcades d'ânes'. Maurice Bloomfield (1895, 410), commenting on this, thought the splinter would probably 'never extend beyond this single new word, and perish with the breezy doings which begot it'; but today, in spite of prescriptive condemnation – Partridge (1958, 842) says *motorcade* is a 'monstrosity' and Hogben (1969, 146) calls it an example of 'counterfeit coinage' – there are a number of words containing *-cade*, all meaning a show or procession of some kind. After *motorcade*, there appeared *autocade, aerocade, Hoovercade*: 'President Hoover's motorcade . . . entered the news . . . when a big bus cut in behind the President's car near Fairfax. Three of the four Hoovercade cars finally got around it' [*Time* 20 July 1931, 15/2]. *Aquacade* (= 'a water spectacle with music') appeared in 1937, *shouldercade* in 1952, and *Beatlecade* in the nineteen-sixties: 'Paul and George arrived in their blue Bentley at the head of the "Beatlecade"' [*Evening Standard* 13 March 1965, 10/5].

13.6.2 -CAST

The second element of *broadcast*, noun and verb, has appeared in a number of words since 1921, when *broadcast* first appeared. Examples are *radiocast* (1928), *newscast, sportscast* and *telecast* (1940), *colourcast*, noun, (1950, = 'a television broadcast in colour'), *beercasting* (= 'broadcasting (on television) by brewers'): 'They charged that brewers have taken over TV with their "beercasting" because "they need a new crop of drinkers to replace chronic alcoholics"' [*Time* 16 June 1952, 39/3]; *simulcast*, verb, (= 'to broadcast simultaneously over radio and television'), and various others. *-cast* in these words has clearly undergone no changes of meaning at all: in all of them it means simply 'broadcast'.

13.6.3 -DOZER

A small and perhaps rather unexpected group of blends is that stemming from *bulldozer* (1930 in the sense of 'tractor'). The OED gives a date of 1876 for the noun *bull-dose* or *-doze*, 'a severe flogging' or 'dose fit for a bull', hence *bull-dozer* (1878, = 'one who bull-dozes'). (To this explanation the OED adds cautiously 'According to U.S. newspapers'.) After 1930 we find a number of *-dozer* words: *angledozer* (1942, = 'a tractor-driven pusher and scraper with the blade at an angle'), *tankdozer* (1944, = 'a tank with a bulldozer blade attached'), *treedozer* (1948, = 'a bull-dozer adapted for felling trees') and *calfdozer* (1949, = 'a small bulldozer').

Hopperdozer (1904) contains the *-dozer* of *bulldozer* in its nineteenth-century sense, and denotes a device for 'dosing' insects with a poisonous substance. The first element may mean 'container', or it may be a shortened form of *grasshopper*, generalized to mean 'insect'. *Aphidozer*, according to Webster (1961), is a blend of *aphid* (a kind of insect) and *hopperdozer;* it is defined as 'a device consisting of a *hopper* (= "container") and revolving brushes used to brush off and collect aphids'. The derivation of *hopperdozer* in Webster (1934) suggests an additional sense of *-dozer:* 'grass*hopper* + *doze* or *dose;* because conceived as putting insects to sleep or dosing them with poison'. Since both aphidozers and hopperdozers are moving and mechanical devices, it is tempting to understand them as kinds of 'bulldozers' in the 'tractor' sense.

13.6.4 HELI-, -COPTER

Helicopter (1872) is made up of two elements, *helico-* and *-pter*. *Helico-* is from Greek ἕλιξ, *helix*, 'spiral', as in *helicogyre* (1929, the name of a helicopter design), *helicoplane* (1908, = 'an aircraft combining the characteristics of the helicopter and the aeroplane'); *-pter* is from Greek πτερόν, *pteron*, 'wing', as in *ornithopter* (1910, = 'a flying machine propelled by flapping wings'). The medial *-i-*, however, was naturally taken to be the combining vowel, so that the word was understood as *heli-* + *-copter*. There have been a number of formations with both of these elements. The nineteen-forties and fifties produced words in *heli-*, such as *helibus*, *helidrome*, *heliport*, *helistop*. *-copter* had become productive earlier with *gyrocopter* (1915). More recent *-copter* formations include *seacopter* (1958, = 'an amphibious helicopter'), *ambucopter* (1959, = 'a helicopter used as an ambulance'), and *turbocopter* (1959, = 'a turbine-powered helicopter').

13.6.5 -LEGGER, -LEGGING

From the nineteen-twenties onwards, the elements *-legger*, *-legging* have enjoyed some productivity. *Bootlegger* (1889, = 'one who unlawfully makes or sells liquor') is from *bootleg*, noun and verb, coined in reference to the carrying of a flask in the leg of a boot. The word was applied to illicit trading in other commodities, and various coinages resulted. The first was probably *booklegger* (*c* 1925, = 'a person who deals in forbidden books'). There followed in the nineteen-thirties *beerlegger* (1931), *gaslegging* (1931, = 'gasoline bootlegging'), *coallegger* (1937). During the second world war appeared *foodlegger*: 'Foodleggers. One sinister development that aggravated the food situation was the rise in wartime Britain of a new kind of criminal: the food racketeer' [*Time* 2 June 1941, 30/1]; *meatlegger* (1943), and others. The pattern continued into the nineteen-fifties with *butterlegger* (1950), in reference to attempts to pass off margarine as butter, and *carlegging* (1955), for illegal methods of selling cars. In all these examples the first element denotes a commodity, and the second refers to the illegal selling of it, or some illegal practice connected with selling.

13.6.6 PARA-

This element in words like *parasol, parapet*, is ultimately from the imperative of the Latin verb *parare*, 'to defend (from)'. Thus *para-sol* means 'sunshade'. *Parachute*, coined in French from this *para-* and *chute* (= 'fall'), first appeared in English in 1785, but the device was not widely used until the second world war. *Para-* words which appeared at this time are *parabomb* (= 'a bomb dropped by parachute'), *paradoctor, paraspy*: 'Paraspies dropped in Germany. Agents for the Allies are being dropped by parachute in Germany, said Berlin Radio last night' [*Daily Express* 10 September 1943, 1/5–6]; *paratroop*, and very many others in which the second element denotes that which is dropped by parachute. *Para-* words in which the second element has a different relationship with the first are *parabrake*, an Instrumental formation: 'a parachute used to assist braking an aeroplane'; *para-kite*, perhaps a coordinative formation, 'parachute-kite', *cf* 'Helicopter saves Para-Kite Man from Channel. Army lieutenant Gerald Gooderham ... was rescued today after attempting to kite-parachute across the channel' [*Evening Standard* 6 August 1964, 15/1–2]; and *paratent* (= 'a tent made of parachute material').

13.6.7 TELE-

Tele-, from Greek τῆλε, *tele*, 'afar, far off', appears in a great many nineteenth- and twentieth-century scientific and technical terms, such as *telegraph, telecommunications*. Recently, numerous words in which it stands for *television* have appeared, a few of which are *telecast* (13.6.2), *telegenic* (13.5.6), *telegogue* (12.3), *telethon* (= 'television marathon', 'a television programme lasting for several hours'), *televersity*: 'Televersity. ...

Michigan will start weekly Sunday afternoon telecasts . . . next fall, hopes to interest 1,000,000 stay-at-home students in the Detroit area' [*Time* 21 August 1950, 28/2].

Perhaps confusingly, *tele-* in some recent words represents *telephone*. One example is *tele-lecture* (= 'a lecture delivered by means of a loudspeaker connected to a telephone line'): 'The Stephens College programme of tele-lectures is the most extensive yet tried but the other colleges . . . are using the telephone in their regular classrooms' [*Times Educational Supplement* 9 October 1964, 579].

13.6.8 –TRON, –TRONIC, –ONICS, –TRONICS

The suffix of *electron* (*-on*), first appeared in the words *anion, cation, ion*, names given by Faraday in 1834 to charged elementary particles. (*Ion* is from Greek ἰόν, *ion*, neuter present participle of ἰέναι, *ienai*, 'to go'.) *Electr-* is from Greek ἤλεκτρον, *electron*, Latin *electrum*, 'amber': electricity was first observed as a result of rubbing amber. The suffix *-on* occurs in *photon* (= 'a quantum of radiant energy'), *meson* (the name of a particle). But with support from *positron* (= 'positive electron'), *negatron* (= 'negative electron') and *neutron* (= 'uncharged elementary particle'), the suffix *-tron* was established. Webster (1961) identifies this suffix with the Greek instrumental suffix *-tron*, as in Greek *arotron*, 'plough', but in the very numerous modern *-tron* coinages such as *betatron, biotron, cyclotron*, it is undoubtedly to be identified with the ending of *electron*. In the field of electronics, *-tron* has been very productive.[14] Besides words with neoclassical stems, we have coinages like *perhapsatron, phantastron, swindletron* and *spinatron*: 'We started (I think) with *cyclotron;* this led, among others, to *phytotron* (a building where plants are grown under controlled environmental conditions); now I have seen at Wageningen the only *spinatron* in the world – a charming word meaning a phytotron devoted to spinach' [*Times Literary Supplement* 29 July 1965, 664/4].

Webster (1961) defines the suffix *-on* as '**1**: elementary particle **2**: unit: quantum'[15]; but without scientific knowledge, the exact meaning of *-tron* in all its contexts is not readily apparent. It has however become familiar to the layman, to whom it appears in trade names, *cf: Discatron:* '. . . you can hear a spate of pop music, issuing crystal-clear, from the "Discatron"' [*Evening Standard* 3 August 1966, 10/3, advertisement]; and *Detektron:* '. . . the "Detektron Centre" – a brand-new word created out of a rough soldering together with "detection" and "electronics" to describe a new approach to diagnosis of what really ails your car, and why' [*Evening Standard* 13 February 1967, 10/4, advertisement]. In these words, -*tron* is used to convey the idea 'impressively scientific'; the following passage from a recent novel contains an apposite comment on -*tron*:

'Don't forget that the best thing you can have is still a good suffix,' he said. 'And of all the suffixes going, my friend, the best bar none is *tron*. Cyclotron, betatron, positron, – you see what I mean? Really packs a punch. Get one well-placed *tron*, and you'll scoop up millions of grants ... Say you invent a robot to work in the kitchen – a really revolutionary, fantastic, faultless discovery. No one will offer you anything to develop it. But present it as a magitron – from *mageiros*, you know, the Greek for kitchen – and you'll find yourself showered with gold. All very simple. You just have to know how to serve up your *tron*.'   [Robert Escarpit, *Le Littératron*, 1964, translated as *The Novel Computer* by Peter Green, 1966, 34]

Among words containing the -*tronic* of *electronic* are *animatronic:* 'Some 45,000 people a day are seated in Ford's latest convertibles, which take off on a ... ride ... past ... life-size moving "audio-animatronic" animals' [*Observer* 24 May 1964, 36/5]; *autotronic* (= 'pertaining to elevators controlled by an automatic electronic system'); *Computronic* (a trade name) and *technetronic* (= 'of or being a society shaped by the impact of computers and communications', see the Addenda (1971) to Webster (1961)).

From the ending of *electronics* we have *astronics*, or *astrionics* (= 'electronics applied to aerospace flight'); *avionics* (= 'aviation electronics'); *bionics:* 'an infant science born of biology and electronics has made its appearance. Its name: bionics. Its aim: to study living creatures in hope of gaining knowledge to improve man-made mechanisms' [*Time* 3 October 1960, 51/1–2]; *fluidonics* (= 'fluid electronics', 'the technology of fluidic devices'); *Inforonics* (the name of a company concerned with recording information by computer) and *radionics* (= 'radio electronics').

Finally, various words in -*tronics* have appeared: *intellectronics* (= 'the science of electronic computers'), *molectronics* (= 'molecular electronics'), *sculptronics* (= 'sculpture with the aid of an electronic machine'), all recorded by *The Britannica Book of the Year*, 1961; and *olfactronics:* 'Olfactronics is a term referring to detection and measurement by analytical instruments of vapors and particles emitted from surfaces of various source substances' [*Science News* 11 June 1966, 463/3].

This miscellany of examples illustrates one small way in which the vocabulary of science has spilled over into the general vocabulary.[16] The principles of electronics and related subjects may not be quickly or easily grasped by the layman, but this has not prevented these splinters from becoming productive in non-scientific as well as scientific words.

13.7 General comments

On the evidence of the examples in this chapter, we may make a few generalizations about the behaviour of productive elements and how they become productive. We have seen that, in many cases, one particular word, such as *racketeer*, *teach-in*, *beatnik*, appears to be more influential than others in its group: by the frequency of its use it helps to make the productive element it contains more familiar and hence more likely to appear in new contexts. If a word happens to have a referent which excites popular interest, or a meaning which is depreciatory, it is the more likely to provide the focus for a group. On the other hand, a word which proves later to contain a group-forming element is not necessarily one which is frequently used or particularly in vogue at any time: the elements of *bulldozer*, *cavalcade*, *utopia* do not at first glance look likely to appear in new coinages. Elements which become productive may be familiar, like *-in* or *-cast*, or unfamiliar, like *-nik* or *-tron*. The foreignness of *-nik* and the esoteric nature of the meaning of *-tron* have not prevented their becoming productive in the general vocabulary.

Connected with a given element, there may be various 'components' of meaning: in *-nik* words for instance, we noticed components of 'protest', 'intellectual' and so on; *-naut* words may carry the notions of 'pioneer' or 'traveller' or both. These different components do not necessarily interfere with one another in different words. It seems likely that *tele-* (='telephone') and *tele-* (='television') existing side by side will prove inconvenient, and that the former of these meanings will not be much used, but in most cases of groups containing subgroups, the situation seems quite manageable and acceptable. The component of 'depreciation' seems to be rather unpredictable. We noticed in particular with *-ster*, *-eer* and *-nik* that many words carried no nuance of disapproval; some seemed to hover on the borderline between favourable and unfavourable interpretations, like the 'political' *-eer* words; and that a word like *songster*, otherwise entirely neutral or favourable in its evaluative meaning, could temporarily show the influence of a group of depreciatory words.

The rapidity with which semantic developments in productive elements can take place is noticeable in the cases of *-in* and *-nik*, both of which have undergone various changes in the space of a decade. These changes were connected with bursts of productivity. On the other hand, developments may take place in spite of small productivity, as with *-genic*, and persist over quite long periods, as with the 'communicative' component of *-acious*, or the 'bad art' implication of *-eer*.

Some productive elements have not changed in meaning at all, but there seems no general reason why they should not have done so. *Para-* (= 'parachute') is clearly too specific and concrete to be a likely candidate for semantic change, and *-topia* perhaps not productive enough to give scope for it. But, just as *-drome* in *pleasuredrome* has become 'a place of entertainment' rather than, as previously, 'a place of sporting or theatrical entertainment', *-topia* might well become generalized from 'ideal political state' to 'state', or perhaps it might come to signify, through the influence of *dys-*, *queue-*, *porno-*, *sub-*, 'undesirable state'.

Notes

1 For a discussion of this phenomenon, and numerous examples of it, see Wimsatt (1954).

2 'Prefixoid' is Malkiel's term (1966, 322–3), which he introduces analogously with his term 'suffixoid' for an element which is not productive as a suffix, though it may be homophonous with a suffix, but which may in some sense take part in, or influence, a productive process.

3 Historically of course, this set of elements is derived from the Latin prefix *de-*. Greenbaum (1970, 74) comments on it in a discussion of verbs co-occurring with *utterly*.

4 See Wentworth (1941) for a great many examples.

5 In what follows, I give the date of the earliest *-arian* word, whether it happens to be a noun, an adjective, or a nominalization in *-ism*. Definitions are usually of the noun in *-arian*.

6 See Chapin (1970) and references given there. Also, see Malkiel (1966, 343–6) for a short discussion, mainly in the context of Romance word-formation. Among his English examples is the nominal suffix *-ry*, for which he demonstrates a preference for stems ending in *t*, such as *rocketry*, which follows a pattern established by such words as *pleasantry*, *gallantry*. It might be added that this preference appears to have been strong enough to 'generate' a *t* in *deviltry* (1819), though this may be, partially at least, phonetic in origin.

7 See Lubbers (1965) who cites and discusses a great many examples of *-ster* words.

8 I have not touched on the controversy about whether *-ster* was used in Old English with exclusively feminine reference, and only later formed nouns referring to men. Jespersen (1933a) argues, against other authorities, including the OED, that nouns formed with *-ster* were applicable from the beginning to both sexes.

9 Folk-etymology may have played a part in the coining of this word, since there is a Russian word негодник, *negodnik*, meaning 'worthless person', 'good-for-nothing'. I am indebted for this point to Dr Robert Ilson.

10 See especially Harder (1966) for numerous examples.

11 Potter (1969), however, gives a date of 1962 for *teach-in*.

12 By permission. From Webster's Third New International Dictionary ©1971 by G. & C. Merriam Co, Publishers of the Merriam-Webster Dictionaries.

13 See *American Speech* 19, 1944, 60–1 and 22, 1947, 266–31.

14 S. Handel, author of the Penguin *Dictionary of Electronics* (1962), writes in his Preface: 'as a keen collector of names ending in '-tron', the author was amazed to find in a recent issue of *British Communications and Electronics* a list of 561 members of the TRON family which included dozens of names he had never heard of.'

15 See note 12 above.

16 It is interesting to note that this kind of thing was happening before the beginning of the twentieth century. Bloomfield (1895, 411) writes: 'Chemists, manufacturers of quack medicines, inventors of new explosives etc, supported by the freemasonry of their respective classes and the acquiescent public, float their *-ites* and *-ates*, *-ides* and *-ades*, with dire intent: *terrorite* and *americanite* have been invented recently to match *dynamite*, and one feels like drawing the curtain over the indecently profuse offspring of *vaseline* – the *rosalines*, the *bloomines*, the *fragelines* and the *nosulines*.' Of these new words, only *americanite* is to be found in Webster (1961).

Chapter 14

Word-formation and rules

14.1 Productivity

In the preceding chapters, we have looked at a variety of complex words, and I have now and then used the epithet 'productive' to describe a pattern, meaning that when occasion demands, the pattern may be used as a model for new items. It appears that there are not many patterns which we can call 'fully productive' – that is, on which we may coin whatever new words we please without the risk of producing words that we cannot use. The derivational adjective–noun-*ed* compound type exemplified by *bright-eyed* is possibly such a pattern; and, as examples like *capacity-filled, hardware-detected, pattern-sensitive* show, probably we may make almost any collocation consisting of adjective/participle+ preposition+ noun into an adjective compound, should we find it convenient to do so. Among noun compounds, the syntactically unambiguous adjective–noun kind, for instance *blank cheque*, in which neither element is a derived one, may be freely employed (although the conditions dictating the accentual patterns of such compounds appear to be idiosyncratic); and the Instrumental *battering-ram* pattern also seems adaptable to all the circumstances for which we may wish to use it. But here we are on shaky ground since, as we saw in 5.1, a rather surprising nonce example, *escalator-napping*, was formed on a pattern which is illustrated by only half a dozen institutionalized examples (see 5.2, VIC1); it proved unexpectedly difficult to think of more. It may be, in some cases, that ease in forming nonce examples correlates with a dearth of established examples; the body of adjective compounds as a whole suggests this, as do the groups of suffixed noun+ particle compounds exemplified by *diner-out, dressing-down* (8.2.1, VA and VB). On the other hand, both established and nonce compounds of the *break-down* type (VC), corresponding to verb–particle collocations, are extremely numerous.

The zero-suffixed examples of Chapter 4 are not nearly so freely formed – with the possible exception of Instrumental verbs of the *to axe, to bomb* kind (4.3, ID). It seems hard to think of 'instrument' nouns from which we cannot coin corresponding zero-suffixed verbs, so long as some other corresponding verb does not already exist. We do not say, for instance, *he rubbered the writing*, since we are used to either *rub out* or *erase* in this context. The fact that we can say *they stoned him* but not *they tomatoed him* may indicate the need for further subclassification of Instrumental derived verbs: possibly *to stone* belongs not with the *to axe* examples, but in a smaller, more restricted, subgroup which we might label 'to affect (someone or something) by throwing what the noun denotes at him/it'. Or the oddness of *they tomatoed him* may be due to the fact that throwing fruit as a sign of disagreement or ridicule is less well-established as an institution than throwing stones as a form of punishment. It is however notoriously difficult to judge of the acceptability of words; as we noticed in Chapter 1, a word, unlike a sentence, is an addition to an inventory, and the more used to it we become, the more disposed we are to accept it. Moreover, we may observe that words not usable in everyday language will very easily be found acceptable in specialized spheres. Thus in the terminology of computer science, for instance, we may speak of *an interrupt, a logical multiply*, and we may use the verbs *to dimension, to subset*.

In discussions of these matters, terms like 'fully productive', 'semi-productive', or 'mildly productive', and 'non-productive' are often used. It is difficult to know how we should understand 'semi-' and 'non-productive'. All we can do in the case of most patterns is to list the observed examples, and comment that one list is longer than another. Or, again as we noticed in Chapter 1, we can describe rules for the formation of words, while pointing out that these rules may not necessarily be allowed to operate. The label 'non-productive' is used in cases where we can analyse a word, like *warmth* (adjective stem + nominalizing suffix), but where we cannot use our analysis to construct similar examples. However, as we saw particularly in Chapters 11 and 12, the most unexpected things – from the point of view of the 'rules' – may happen, and we may wonder whether all patterns, even those with very short lists of representative examples, should not be described as potentially productive. *Dampth* after all breaks no rule except one of linguistic convention, and it is moreover perfectly understandable. As far as negative attitudes to words are concerned, we should perhaps in most cases refer not to 'unacceptability', but to 'resistance to use'.

14.2 Factors interfering with regularities

Various characteristics of the vocabulary have a part in our difficulties with rules of word-formation. There are for instance anomalies arising from historical development. We noticed, especially in Chapter 7, that some nominalizations have been borrowed from Latin without their corresponding verbs, so that the normal 'verb → noun + suffix' process has had to be reversed (and this reversal is felt in a sense as abnormal); so we get backformed verbs like *intuit*, *negate*, *orate*. The English habit of borrowing has left us with some synonymous suffixes, like the Teutonic *-ness* and the Romance *-ity*, both of which nominalize adjectives. The latter suffix is reserved for stems of Romance origin – with the exception of *oddity*, coined in the eighteenth century and perhaps influenced by *curiosity*, *cf* '. . . their Beauty, Colour, Oddity, Curiosity' [OED, s.v. *oddity*, 1750]. *-ness*, on the other hand, may be attached to stems of any origin. Only our previous acquaintance with the words tells us that the nominalizations of *brutal* and *fatal* are *brutality* and *fatality* rather than *brutalness* or *fatalness*; that *diversity* and *diverseness* are both in use; and that we do not use either *justness* or *justity* (more accurately, the former is sometimes possible, as in *the justness of his decision*, and the latter is not at all possible), but *justice*, borrowed as a whole from French.

Formal features may interfere in odd ways: in Chapter 7 we saw that the appearance of a word-element can cause it to be 'mistaken' for a different element, and that this has happened with the endings of *beggar* and *grovelling*. In Chapter 12 we noticed a tendency for blends to assume a neo-classical shape – two 'stem' syllables sandwiching a medial vowel; and in Chapter 13 we saw that suffixes may develop 'preferences' for stems of a certain form.

Other difficulties in the way of a neat arrangement of patterns have been noticed, particularly in Chapter 5, where we saw that compounds could be interpreted in more than one way, for example *scrubbing brush*, *witch doctor*, and that they may be learned as wholes, like *banana republic*, making irrelevant any recipe for constructing them that we may concoct. It also seems that the outward form of a compound, like *killer shark* (verb stem + -*er* + noun) is likely to be as much involved in the use of the pattern as a model for new formations as its inward structure, in this case subject–verb, but in the case of *marker buoy*, verb–'instrument'. In the adjective–noun groups, in particular the denominal adjective + noun group (IXE), it was clear that the form: noun stem + adjective-suffix + noun concealed a variety of syntactic relations. And finally, in Chapter

13, there was ample evidence that the elements within a word may have a semantic influence on one another, causing series of new formations to take idiosyncratic courses.

We noticed in 1.1 above that new words may arouse antipathy for various cultural and linguistic reasons. But one of the more puzzling aspects of word-formation is the way in which apparently unexceptionable words may be stubbornly and silently resisted. A striking example of this is the nominalization of the verb *to despise*. Until the middle of the seventeenth century, the noun *despite* filled this role; subsequently *despite* appears in poetic contexts only in the OED. The noun *despise* was used a few times in the fifteenth and sixteenth centuries, and *despisement* is also recorded by the OED, as obsolete, occurring once in 1603: 'Contempt and despisement of worldly wealth.' In the OEDS, however, we find 'Delete † Obs. and add' two late nineteenth-century quotations. In a training college examination paper of 1969, this word turns up again: 'Paul Morel's love of the common people has become in Gerald . . . a despisement of the working-class for their lack of culture.' The expression this candidate would have used, had he not been pressed for time, is of course *contempt for*, and it might be argued that *despisement* (or some other nominalization of this stem) has not become generally accepted because the synonyms *contempt, scorn, disdain* are available and there is therefore no need for it. The OED also has *despiciency* (last attested in 1672) and *despisal* (occurring as late as 1887). Webster (1961), which excludes 'in general words that had become obsolete before 1755' (Preface 6a), includes *despiciency, despisal, despisement* and *despite* – the last with a quotation from the *Yale Review*. And I have heard people use *despisery, despision* and *despise* (each one said of course in such a way as to suggest inverted commas, or followed by a deprecatory laugh). Informants whom I have consulted condemn every one of these nominalizations as 'unacceptable'. But the persistence of attempts to nominalize the verb *despise* seems to indicate a continuing need to fill this gap in the vocabulary. Synonyms are a normal feature of language; and for a language as richly endowed with them as English, the 'no need' argument is a particularly weak one.

14.3 Nature and art

Related to the question of productivity is the slippery issue of 'deliberateness' versus 'unconsciousness' in the coining of words. Jespersen (1933b) has pointed out that in language the notions of 'natural' and 'artificial' are by no means distinct; but we can perhaps, at least in theory, distinguish three levels of 'awareness' (cf Bolinger 1971, 173ff). It would be a hopeless task to try to place the products of word-formation in a cline of 'conscious' to 'unconscious' creation, though it is safe to say that compound-blends, particularly those of the punning type like *fakesimile*, exemplified in Chapter 12, together with acronyms and clippings, are undoubtedly the results of conscious efforts to produce new formations. Below this level of deliberateness, things are much less clear-cut. Perhaps compound verbs like *to window-shop*, and other backformations, are produced by speakers with a more definite sense of creatively manipulating the resources at their disposal than are new adjective compounds like *machine-independent*, or new noun compounds like *meter-feeding*. The noun and adjective compound examples just mentioned represent patterns which are more productive (or have longer representative lists) than the pattern of backformation. New noun–particle compounds like *bounce-back*, *pull-out*, *split-up* are coined with little or no sense of creating new items, and in this respect the pattern they represent is like a sentence-pattern. They rarely involve the ambiguity which clings to other kinds of compound: context – it need hardly be said – is enough to distinguish between the three uses of *break-down* in *I did a break-down of the figures*, *we had a break-down on the motorway* and *she suffered a break-down*.

It has been often remarked that a process as freely employable as the one illustrated here, as adaptable, and as productive of easily understandable compounds, is a useful asset to the vocabulary; and it has been observed by some of those who have advocated planned languages (as distinct from 'natural' or 'ethnic' ones) that all processes of word-formation ought to be like this. In the following section I shall look briefly at some of these planned languages – those which appeared in the last quarter of the nineteenth century and the early years of the twentieth. The aim of the language planners is of course to construct a 'regular' language, which, with the minimum difficulty in learning, could become a successful medium of international communication. During the period I have mentioned, the advocates of planned languages tended to pay much less attention to syntax than to word-formation: they saw the creation of a regular system of word-formation as one of their most important concerns, and it is interesting therefore to look briefly at their work, and to see if we can discover how nearly they approached their ideal as regards word-formation, and how realistic that ideal was.

14.4 'Ideal word-formation'

Sapir (1949, 110–21) comments on the unsystematicness of English word-formation, describing it (114) as 'a perfect hornet's nest of bizarre and arbitrary usages'. He adds however: 'behind the vagaries of idiomatic usage there are perfectly clear-cut logical relations which are only weakly brought out in the overt form of English' (115). These remarks occur in a paper advocating the use of a constructed language, which would be 'simple, regular, and logical, but also rich and creative' (117), and in which, of course, the accidents produced by historical development, and the irrational resistance to the use of regularly-formed words like *wideness*, *beautifulness*, *despisement*, would have no place. Among the best-known international auxiliary languages – or IALs as we may conveniently call them – are Esperanto, Ido (a modified form of Esperanto), Occidental and Novial. These languages have much in common, but they vary in the concessions which they make to the features of ethnic languages that Europeans are accustomed to. Occidental, for instance, defines its suffixes less precisely than the other languages mentioned: its creator, Edgar de Wahl, attached some importance to giving it the aspect of a natural language. Jacob (1947, 121) classifies IALs as 'autonomistic' (for example Esperanto and Ido) and 'naturalistic' (for example Occidental). Novial, Jespersen's invention, is in some respects a compromise between these two types. I shall comment here only on some features of Esperanto, Ido and Novial.

An important autonomistic principle is that all elements, roots and affixes, should have only one meaning each; and the meaning of an element must remain the same in all its combinations. This means that word-formation can be seen as always strictly an additive process, semantically as well as formally. But it was clearly recognized that a genuinely one-element : one-meaning language would be impractical, and that to disallow a certain amount of polysemy, and to disregard the value of context in our understanding of words in sentences would be folly. Following from this necessarily imperfectly-adhered-to principle of 'monosignificance', as it was called, is the principle of 'reversibility'; that is, for every rule by which we build up a combination, we should be able to formulate a rule which is its exact reverse, to analyse and dissect that combination. These principles were emphasized particularly by the advocates of Ido.

All three languages build up words from the starting-point of roots, which are classified as nominal, adjectival or verbal. All 'lexical' words consist of a root and an ending. In the case of Esperanto and Ido, the class of the ending, and hence of the word, is indicated by the form of that ending. This class division is necessarily arbitrary in many cases, and leads to difficulties. In Esperanto, for instance, we meet the kind of inconsistency which we noticed in Chapter 4: some nouns are derived from verbs when we might have expected a reverse process, and vice versa. Thus, *arm-*, *komb-* and *ŝovel-* are classified as verbal roots; the distinctive verbal ending is *-i*, so we have the verbs *armi*, *kombi*, *ŝoveli*, = 'to arm', 'to comb', 'to shovel' respectively. The suffix denoting 'instrument' is *-il-*; accordingly, we derive the nouns *arm-il-o*, *kombilo*, *ŝovelilo*, = 'a weapon', 'a comb', 'a shovel'. (*-o* is the distinctive nominal ending.) There is greater clarity and explicitness here than we find with English derived Instrumental nouns (see 4.6, ID above): the 'instrument' nouns of Esperanto contain within themselves a sign of their instrumental, and derived, nature. However, *bros-* and *martel-* are classified as nominal roots; thus we have *broso*, *martelo*, = 'a brush', 'a hammer'. The instrumental suffix *-il-* is not here used, since the notions of 'brush' and 'hammer' already imply that of 'instrument' (*cf* Wells 1969, 8). 'An act of hammering' is *martel-ad-o*: the 'action' suffix *-ad-* must be present since *martel-* is a nominal root; but 'an act of shovelling' is *ŝovelo:* only the nominal *-o* is required, since *ŝovel-* is a verbal root and therefore already implies 'action'.[1] Clearly, the class membership of a root may not be at all intuitively obvious, and we need to know it before we can embark on derivational processes.

Derivation by the simple addition of an ending appropriate to one class attached to a root of another class, illustrated above by *ŝovelo*, is called 'direct' or 'immediate' derivation. It may be regarded as equivalent to our zero derivation. The direct derivation of nouns from verbal roots is permitted in all three languages only if the abstract, 'action' meaning of the resulting nominalization is adhered to. Jespersen, however, realizes that some inconsistency in this matter is hard to avoid. Novial permits *dona satisfaktione*, = 'give satisfaction', a concession to international usage, since 'it would not be natural to say *dona satisfakto*, for give the act of satisfying has no proper sense' (Jespersen 1928, 132). Novial differs from the other languages in that it has a special *-o* ending indicating 'action' nominalization; thus *sonja*, = 'to dream', *sonjo*, = 'dreaming'; *brose*, = 'a brush', *broso*, = 'brushing'. It thus avoids the asymmetry we noticed above in Esperanto, exemplified by *martelado*, = 'hammering', but *ŝovelo*, = 'shovelling'. But on the other hand, Novial does not preserve the principle of consistently indicating class membership of words by distinctive endings.

As far as the direct derivation of verbs from nouns is concerned, Esperanto allows patterns very similar to the English ones of 4.3 above, with the rational improvement that there are no idiosyncratic restrictions such as prevent English-speakers from using certain possible verbs, like *to violin.* Some Esperanto noun-to-verb examples are *ekzempli*, = 'to be an *ekzemplo* ('example') of', *repliki*, = 'to make a *repliko* ('retort')', *vernisi*, = 'to put on *verniso* ('varnish')', *violoni*, = 'to play the *violono* ('violin')'. Novial allows direct noun-to-verb derivation, but only 'where there cannot be the slightest doubt as to the meaning of the verb thus created' (Jespersen 1928, 128). Denominal verbs, aside from 'meteorological' ones like *niva*, = 'to snow', from *nive*, = 'snow', may be formed on two patterns: (1) 'to use an instrument', for example *brosa*, = 'to use a brush', and (2) 'to secrete', for example *sudora*, 'to emit *sudore* ('sweat')'. Jespersen points out that a verb meaning 'to provide with (the noun)' may be ambiguous, so *arma*, = 'to arm' is not permitted, since it could be interpreted instrumentally, like *brosa*, to mean 'to use weapons against'. Accordingly, the notion 'to provide with' in Novial is expressed by a suffix. We have already noticed (4.3, ID 1 and 2) how difficult it is to distinguish clearly between 'instrumental' and 'provide with' zero-derived verbs in English.

Ido is far more rigorous than either Esperanto or Novial as far as noun-to-verb direct derivation is concerned. This process is hardly allowed at all because of the large variety of patterns to which it gives rise. Instead, Ido employs a number of rather carefully defined suffixes. *-ag-* is used for 'to act with an instrument': *martelagar*, = 'to hammer'; *-if-* for 'to generate, produce, secrete': *sudorifar*, = 'to perspire', *elektrifar*, = 'to electrify'. (An 'illogicality' is detectable here incidentally: should it be *elektragar*?) *-ig-* is used for 'to make, render, transform into': *petrigar*, = 'to petrify'; *-iz-* for 'to cover with, provide with': *armizar*, = 'to arm', *kronizar*, = 'to crown', *salizar*, = 'to salt'. It is interesting, though perhaps not surprising, to find that the use of such suffixes has proved difficult, even for experienced Idists. Jespersen comments: 'In writing Ido one is constantly confronted with the problem: am I here logically justified in using the immediate [direct] formation, or should I use a suffix, and which?... *grupar, grupifar, grupigar, grupizar*...; [*ie* 'to group'] which is it to be?' (1928, 129–30) Perhaps the definitions of the suffixes are at fault; but it seems likely that the very 'indefiniteness' that the Idists were trying to eliminate plays a necessary part in our ability to derive words. Sweet, indeed, in his discussion of compounds, says as much (see his remarks quoted at the end of Chapter 5 above).

The IALs have in fact allowed compounds, with all their inbuilt inexplicitness; *cf* Esperanto *feria aŭtobuso* (or *feriaŭtobuso*), = 'holiday coach' (*feri-o* = 'holiday'; *-a* is the adjective ending). While we do not find idiosyncrasies of form, such as English *pitchfork*, not *pitching fork*, or *carving* *knife*, not *carve knife*, the problem of ambiguity remains. The stricter Ido has fewer compounds, and correspondingly a greater number of simple roots, but some compounds are admitted, for example *post-marko* (or *postmarko* or *postala marko*), = 'postage stamp', a combination which is hardly reconcilable with a viable principle of 'reversibility'.

There have been differences of opinion about how versatile an IAL can be, or ought to be. Sapir emphasizes that it should be able to cope with 'every type of expression of the human spirit' (1949, 111). Jespersen, on the other hand, says 'It must necessarily remain an intellectual language, a language for the brain, not for the heart. ... There will always be something dry and prosaic about it and it is a mistake to try to translate very deep poetry into it, for it will be capable of rendering only those elements of poetry which might as well have been expressed through a paraphrase in native prose' (1928, 27). It was this 'dry and prosaic' effect of a planned language that George Orwell found appropriate for, and sought to exaggerate in, his totalitarian language Newspeak, described at the end of *Nineteen Eighty Four* (1949). We may note Orwell's use of the 'regular' infinitive forms replacing the 'archaic' *speech* and *thought* in words like *newspeak, crimethink*; the strictly neutral affixes, such as *plus-, un-, -ful, -wise;* the additive *ungood* instead of *bad, doubleplusungood* instead of *very bad indeed*, or *horrible* (*cf* Esperanto *bona*, = 'good', *malbona*, = 'bad').

But a glance at some examples given earlier in this book, particularly in Chapter 13, may suggest that Jespersen's 'brain' and 'heart' distinction is oversimplified – in fact invalid, and that it is not only in poetry that linguistic expression is beyond the control of planning. Jespersen's contrast, we notice, is between planned and poetic language; Orwell's more perceptive one is between planned and everyday language. Everyday language involves a great deal of 'poetic' activity in its use of the associations which cling to words and elements, its subtle shifts of meaning, its constant employment of familiar items in slightly different new senses. Words like *coquetteering, death-in, peacenik*, to take some very obvious examples, are 'poetic' in their compression and allusiveness, in the extent to which they refer back to, and rely on, half-remembered words with similar shapes and associations. Esperanto has one 'derogatory' suffix, *-aĉ-*, as in *domaĉo*, = 'a hovel', *skribaĉo*, = 'a scrawl', *virinaĉo*, = 'a hag'. (*-aĉ-a* may be used as an independent adjective, meaning 'wretched', 'no good'.) Of the various English derogatory suffixes which exist, we have looked at two in detail, *-ster* and *-eer*. These are closely comparable in certain cases – *smockster : waistcoateer, rhymester : sonneteer, gangster : racketeer* – but they nevertheless retain strongly individual flavours. Jespersen, in his account of Novial, suggests two suffixes for deriving verbs: *-(i)sa* and *-(i)fika* (corresponding to our *-ize* and *-ify*); and he decrees that Novialists are free to choose either suffix as they wish. Novial suffixed verbs would thus be unlikely to acquire nuances like that noticeable in *argufy, countrified, pigmify, speechify*. But he suggests making a distinction between *elektrisa*, = 'to charge with electricity', hence figuratively 'to thrill', and *elektrifika*, = 'to electrify (a railway etc)' (1928, 137), and this division of labour immediately points to a way in which the two suffixes might diverge, were Novial to become a medium of everyday communication.

The few illustrations that I have given in this section seem to indicate at least the possibility that the IAL mechanisms for word-formation could satisfy Sapir's demand for 'every type of expression' only at the cost of such 'logicality' as distinguishes them from the ethnic languages. Among the factors working against 'logicality' are, as we have seen, the necessity for word-class distinctions, and the failure so far to discover a rational basis for these; the apparent need for some imprecision in affix-definitions, and for some inexplicitness in the relations between compound-elements; and the difficulty of controlling the activity of suffixes, which tend to be 'influenced' by features of the stems they are attached to. But certain areas of experience permit – indeed require – a measure of the logicality for which the Interlinguists were striving. These areas are of course scientific ones. We have a fleeting glimpse of order in the literature of electricity, with its two forms of nominalization, in *-ance* and *-ivity; examples are conductance : conductivity, elastance : elasticity, reluctance : reluctivity, resistance: resistivity*.[2] Here we have nominalizations taking forms not dictated by tradition, or by shape of stem, or by provenance of stem, but which bear some relation to the reality behind the words. These terms, and others like them, are largely definable with reference to one another, and some knowledge of the principles of electricity is necessary to understand them fully. To explain *capacitance*, for instance, as formed from *capaci*ty + reac*tance* (*cf* Marchand 1969, 445) is an oversimplification amounting to untruth. In the next section, I shall look at a more extensive case of regularity and planning in scientific vocabulary, and comment on the kind of real-life situation which makes such planning practicable.

14.5 A case of 'ideal' word-formation

The vocabulary of organic chemistry is of some interest to the student of word-formation. It is hardly possible here to give an adequate account of the principles behind this science's nomenclature, since the chemical knowledge required to understand it is too great, but I shall attempt a brief indication of some of its features. We need to know first that organic chemistry is the study of the element carbon, and of the ways in which carbon atoms combine with those of other elements (hydrogen, oxygen, sulphur) and the halogens (chlorine, bromine and iodine). Organic chemistry thus concerns an enormous number of combinations made up of fairly few ingredients; and the name of a compound substance must give an indication, not only of the composition of that substance, but of its chemical structure – the ways in which the chemical elements are combined in it. Chemical names may be 'trivial' for everyday purposes, or 'systematic' for technical use. 'Systematic' describes 'a name composed wholly of specially coined or selected syllables'; a 'trivial' name is 'a name no part of which is used in a systematic sense' (see *Handbook for Chemical Society Authors*, 1961, 48). Unavoidably, some trivial names have been retained in systematic nomenclature because of the way chemical knowledge has developed.[3] *Methane*, for example, has a trivial stem and a systematic suffix: *meth-* is understood to mean 'one carbon atom', while *-ane* occurs in a series of words, and identifies a series of similar substances. *Pentane* is another member of this series; *pent-* denotes 'five carbon atoms'. This name is wholly systematic.

Methane is the simplest compound of carbon and hydrogen; it has the formula CH_4, and may be diagrammed

$$
\begin{array}{c}
\text{H} \\
| \\
\text{H}-\text{C}-\text{H} \\
| \\
\text{H}
\end{array}
$$

(Each letter represents an atom.)

Names of chemical structures are formed with reference to the substitution for a hydrogen atom of an atom of another element. Thus, benzene consists of a 'ring' of carbon atoms, each of which has a hydrogen atom attached to it (diagram *a* below).

If one hydrogen atom is replaced by a chlorine atom (diagram *b*), a substance called *monochlorobenzene* is formed. If two hydrogen atoms are replaced by chlorine atoms, we have *dichlorobenzene*. In the latter case we need to know the relative positions on the benzene ring of these replaced atoms. The substance resulting from a situation in which hydrogen atoms at positions 1 and 2 are replaced is called *orthodichlorobenzene;* if those at 1 and 4 are substituted, we have *paradichlorobenzene*. Or we may use the

[a]   [b]

numbers themselves as prefixes and write *1:2-dichlorobenzene* and *1:4-dichlorobenzene*.

We can see from this simple, and simplified, example that here we have 'logic' in the language planners' sense. The principle of reversibility is strictly adhered to: we may take apart a (linguistic) compound by putting into reverse the process by which we build it up; and using the information given by a linguistic compound, we can construct a diagram showing the composition and structure of the chemical compound it denotes. Necessarily, each of the linguistic elements used in chemistry has a strictly defined meaning which does not encroach on the meaning of any other element. The linguistic elements of chemistry are obviously free from the tendency to gather associations and to become allusive that characterizes the elements of everyday language, and so the logicality of the system can be maintained.

Chemical names are, as we have seen, basically neo-classical in form. There are 'stems': *benz-*, *chlor-*; 'prefixes': *di-*, *para-*; and 'suffixes': *-ene*, *-ine*. We noticed in 1.5 above that in ordinary language prefixes and suffixes are typically less specific in meaning than stems. This semantic difference between the 'lexical' and the 'grammatical' elements is much less marked in the language of organic chemistry, since all elements have specific meanings. The word *propanol*, for instance, indicates to the chemist that three carbon atoms are linked in a 'chain' (*propan-*), and that one of the hydrogen atoms attached to one of the carbon atoms has been replaced by a 'hydroxy' group: (*-ol*). Since there is no real difference, except as regards typical form – a legacy of the neo-classical tradition – between prefix, suffix and stem, the three kinds of constituent are versatile in their behaviour. Words composed of prefix+suffix occur, such as *biose*, from *bi-*, = 'two' and *-ose*, the suffix indicating the name of a sugar; and even words composed of suffix+suffix, such as *osone*, from *-ose* and *-one*. Infixes are used: *-id-* is inserted, for example, into *cyanine*, to produce the name of a related substance, *cyanidine*. Chemical names may be very long, containing a number of prefixes, stems and suffixes; the limitations obtaining in normal language on the number of affixes, especially prefixes that may appear in a word do not operate. Any resulting difficulties in the analysis of very long complex words may be solved by the use of brackets, as in *2-(dichloroacetylamino)-3-hydroxy-3-(paranitrophenyl)-propanol*, – for everyday purposes necessarily known by a shorter, trivial name, *chloramphenicol* (from *chlor*+ *amide*+ *phenyl*+ *nitro*+ gly*col*). There are rules for deciding when to hyphenate words and when to write two words separately, or solidly; rules for the italicization of certain elements, and rules of ordering for prefixes and suffixes. Some of these orthographic rules, like the one which directs that under certain conditions prefixes shall occur in alphabetical order, are devised to ensure consistency among chemists, but others, like those for the joining of compound-elements, are related to chemical theory.

The beginnings of this 'logical' system are found in the work of the eighteenth-century French chemist Lavoisier, and his associates. By the last quarter of the eighteenth century it was clear that chemistry was advancing so fast as to be hindered by the use of the old picturesque names, such as *Fuming Liquor of Libavius, Vitriol of Venus*, and so on. Lavoisier, in a speech of 1787 outlining the new principles of naming, makes some interesting observations on language. He compares natural language with algebra, pointing out that algebraic operations may be translated into common speech. 'Languages are not only intended, as is commonly supposed, to express ideas and images by signs, but also are real analytical systems by means of which we advance from the known to the unknown, and to a certain extent in the manner of mathematicians . . . If languages really are instruments fashioned by men to make thinking easier, they should be of the best possible kind; and to strive to perfect them is indeed to work for the advancement of science.' Sapir in his essay on 'The Function of an International Auxiliary Language' from which I quoted in the previous section, makes some observations of a similar kind. He says: 'The modern mind tends to be more and more critical and analytical in spirit, hence it must devise for itself an engine of expression which is logically defensible at every point and which tends to correspond to the rigorous spirit of modern science' (1949, 112). Science, however, is in a sense simpler than day-to-day living; to continue quoting Lavoisier:

we shall have three things to distinguish in every physical science; the series of facts that constitute the science; the ideas that call the facts to mind; and the words that express them. The words should give birth to the idea; the idea should depict the fact; ... The perfecting of the nomenclature of chemistry ... consists in conveying the ideas and facts in their strict verity, without suppressing anything that they present, and above all without adding anything to them; it should be nothing less than a faithful mirror; for we can never too often repeat that it is not Nature, nor the facts that Nature presents, but our own reasoning that deceives us'

(quoted in Douglas McKie, *Antoine Lavoisier*, 1952, Chapter 22).[4]

Chemical nomenclature has a morphology which is more complex than that of everyday English, but unlike everyday English it is comparatively regular and entirely unambiguous, and since concrete nouns only are involved, complexities arising from interaction with syntax are absent. Problems arise only when multiple chemical relations lead to conflicting, synonymous, names; the organic chemist must then consult manuals of naming to make sure that his names are correct. We have here examined a fragment of a special situation: organic chemistry concerns the combination of chemical elements in certain limited ways, and word-formation concerns the combination of linguistic elements. The linguistic situation and the chemical one are therefore well suited to one another, and the linguistic resources of neo-classical word-formation – a little augmented – have proved adequate, in this field, as a 'faithful mirror' of nature.

14.6 Word-formation, syntax and sense-development

We have glanced at two important principles of the language planners, those of 'monosignificance' and 'reversibility', and we have seen that these principles are to some extent embodied in a certain kind of word-formation rather far removed from the language of every day. I shall now return to some characteristics of the kind of word-formation with which this book has been concerned. It is clear that the planners were placing too much reliance on the regularity of outward forms, that they gave too little thought to the implications of the fact that all natural languages contain apparent 'illogicalities', and that they underestimated the complexity and difficulty of the task they had set themselves. The examples I have discussed in the earlier chapters of this book have been grouped according to formal features. We have looked at the formation of different kinds of compounds, and at the use of various affixes; and some important, non-formal, likenesses have thereby been pushed into the background.

The reader may have noticed, for example, how often I have had to refer to the notion of 'resemblance'. In 4.3, IC there were several groups of denominal verbs with the meaning 'to be, or act like what the base noun denotes', for instance *to wolf* means 'to eat like a wolf'; *to chicken* (out of) means 'to act from fear' – the idea of 'fear' being conveyed by a reference to the chicken, and hence to its characteristic 'fearful' behaviour; *to sponge* (on someone) means 'to soak up someone's money, etc as a sponge soaks up water'. In Chapter 5, we distinguished a class of Resemblance compounds (VII), for example *sponge cake* (= 'cake resembling a sponge in appearance and texture'), *umbrella tree* (= 'tree shaped like an umbrella'); and in Chapter 6 there were some Resemblance adjective compounds (X), like *chicken-hearted*, *eagle-eyed*, *wasp-waisted*. Chapter 13 gave ample evidence of the part played by resemblances in the spread of word-elements to new coinages: *monknik* is like *beatnik* in its implication of 'intellectual'; *think-in* shares with *teach-in* the notion 'participation on equal terms by a large number of people'. Notice that the same secondary use of the concept 'chicken' has given us the zero-derived verb, the compound adjective, and a phrase containing the noun, *to turn chicken* (= 'to become frightened'). The following example indicates that in some cases of sense-development we may regard a process of word-formation as a catalyst: 'the Prime Minister kept silent about how severe a butcher he will be and when he will act' [*Evening Standard* 15 October 1971, 1/1–2]. This passage refers to the Prime Minister's decision to *axe* (in the metaphorical sense) some ministers. We noticed in Chapter 4 (note 2) how verbs derived from nouns characteristically have a wider field of reference than those nouns. Thus, *to butcher* means 'to act like a butcher, and not only with respect to meat'. In the quotation I have just given, we have a noun, *butcher*, meaning not 'slaughterer and/or dresser and seller of meat', but 'one who acts like a butcher' in a way made clear by the context. Possibly, then, we can regard this sense of *butcher* as rederived from the zero-derived verb rather than simply as a metaphorical extension of the noun in its basic meaning.

The diagram below shows what we have done, semantically, syntactically and word-formationally, with the concrete concept 'sponge'.

We can see from this diagram that three characteristics of the 'marine animal' are important: its appearance and texture, its 'squeezableness', and its capacity to absorb liquid. It is apparent also how often the notion of 'resemblance' has been responsible for a new use of the word *sponge*,[5] and how each new use selects one, or two, or all three of these characteristics. The noun *sponge* (4b) in the sense of 'a source of profit' is no longer a

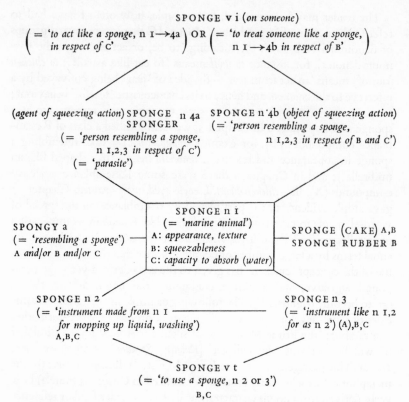

(The numbers attached to the nouns are not intended to indicate a historical progression.)

regular sense of the word, but it shows interestingly that the notion of 'sponge' in its 'absorption' aspect allows meanings which contrast in a reciprocal way (4a and 4b), since a sponge may be in a saturated (unsqueezed) or dry (squeezed) state. Shakespeare exploits this fact in the following passage:

ROSENCRANTZ: Take you me for a sponge, my lord?
      HAMLET: Ay sir; that soaks up the king's countenance, his re-
              wards, his authorities. But ... when he needs what
              you have gleaned, it is but squeezing you, and, sponge,
              you shall be dry again.   [*Hamlet* IV ii]

For sense 4b alone, *cf* 'Ireland has been made all along a sponge for sinecurists, a field for jobbers' [OED, s.v. *sponge*, sb.[1] 9d, 1821]. In everyday speech we may very easily use the noun *sponge* in senses not quite like any of those illustrated in the diagram; we may compare a person to a sponge without any implication that he is either a parasite or the victim of a parasite, *cf: he's very eager to learn – he soaks up knowledge like a sponge.*

For the adjective *spongy*, Webster (1961) gives among its illustrations: 'spongy earth', 'spongy cheese', 'spongy roots', 'spongy action of a steering gear'. And as far as the verbal use of *sponge* is concerned, we find in the OED, as well as the senses given above, quotations illustrating the sense 'rub out', 'efface' (with a sponge); and the OED points out under *expunge* (from Latin *expungere* (*pungere*='to prick'), = 'to mark for deletion (a name on a list) by points . . .') that this verb has probably been influenced in its use by the 'rub out' sense of the verb *to sponge*.

This example of *sponge* serves to emphasize how closely involved with one another are the three territories which have been traditionally separated by the labels 'syntax', 'word-formation' and 'sense-development'. The apparatus of word-formation is sometimes present to signal a shift in meaning or use, but often it is not, and we are not aware of any lack. McCawley (1968, 130) points out that *this coat is warm* is ambiguous between *this coat has a relatively high temperature* and *this coat makes the wearer feel warm*. We might express the latter, more usual, meaning by using a zero-derived verb: *this coat warms the wearer*, or even, if custom and convention were not against it, by a suffixed verb: *this coat warmifies the wearer*. We can say *I had a marvellous weekend*, meaning *I had a marvellous time during the weekend*, in which we are using the noun *weekend* (= 'period of time') temporarily to mean 'what I did during that period of time'. This covert shift emerges in the zero-derived verb *to weekend*, = 'to pass, spend the period of time called the "weekend"'. We have already (14.4 above) noticed the allusive, 'poetic' nature of some complex words used in 'prosaic' contexts; it is clear that this kind of figurative language use is not only manifested in word-formation. As the examples in this section show, we may employ what in literary terms are called 'figures of speech' – metaphor and metonymy – so unobtrusively that we may not be aware of what we are doing. From these 'figures' arise new complex words, new senses of words, and new ways of using words.

There are various processes concerned with the senses and uses of words which are not usually considered to be part of the subject called word-formation. Examples are the abstract→concrete development of nouns and nominalizations, noted in 2.7 above, such as *offering*, = 'act of offering'→'gift'; the concrete result→object process, such as *contact*, = 'instance, sensation of contact'→'person with whom one makes contact'; changes in nouns from 'mass' to 'count' meanings, such as *food→a food*; and vice versa, such as *a stone→stone*. As far as verbs are concerned, there are changes in transitivity, from intransitive to transitive, as in *he walked : he walked the dog;* and vice versa, as in *Mary washed the clothes : the clothes washed well*. With all of these processes, intuition, which may not always be reliable, as we saw in 4.2 above sometimes tells us which sense may be considered primary and which secondary; and sometimes it does not. But we can see from the *sponge* diagram that here at least we cannot easily discuss a transitive→intransitive process (or the other way round), since the two senses of the verb *to sponge* are derived from different senses of the noun, and have only an indirect relationship with one another.

But word-derivation and transitivity are matters relevant to one another: transitivity is a particularly embarrassing topic for the linguist who wishes to keep word-formation distinct from syntax. Lyons (1969, 360) points out that *he warms the milk* (with zero-derived verb) is related to *the milk is warm* just as *he moves the stone* is related to *the stone moves*. We should perhaps really consider both pairs as involving a case of zero derivation. And Jespersen points out (MEG III, 16.5) that verbs derived from adjectives or nouns tend to be 'double-faced' as regards transitivity; for example *to cool,* = 'to make (something) cool' or 'to become cool'; *to benefit,* = 'to give benefit' or 'to receive benefit'; *to colour* = 'to apply colour' or 'to become coloured'. In Old English, some corresponding transitive and intransitive verbs had distinct forms: thus, *celan,* = 'to make cool', *colian,* = 'to become cool'. If this situation had been general, and had formed the basis for a productive pattern, we should doubtless be in the habit of treating changes in transitivity under the heading of 'word-formation'.

It has been pointed out, for instance by Givón (1967b) that 'derived' items of all kinds may be considered more complex semantically than 'basic' ones. Thus, *to stone,* = 'to throw stones at (someone)', *to declare* (in cricket), = 'to declare an innings closed', *a sponge* (in a specialized sense), = 'a sponge cake', *an engine* (in a specialized sense), = 'a steam engine'. In word-formation this complexity may be given formal expression by compounding and affixation; but shifts in sense are not necessarily signalled by changes in form. We have seen how new formations, changes in meaning and changes in syntactic behaviour may all be connected with one another and with certain aspects of the 'figurative' use of language. Perhaps, then, there is little justification for the study of word-formation as a self-contained topic. I have dealt in this book primarily with forms, and

I have pointed out over and over again that form and meaning interfere with each other in words. But I shall conclude with the suggestion that it is with semantics and syntax that we should really begin if our study is to have results more interesting than lists of patterns, although I believe that our knowledge of how language works is at present not far enough advanced to make an attempt at such an approach practicable, at any rate in a book of this kind.[6]

As a final note, it is interesting to observe that the conjectures of the late nineteenth- and early twentieth-century language planners about the principles underlying the use of language were after all not so very dissimilar to the speculations of linguists today. In an essay concerning the application of logic to language, the French philosopher Louis Couturat, whose name is prominently associated with Ido, wrote of his belief that an ideal language should 'conform to that indwelling and instinctive logic which, in spite of all sorts of irregularities and exceptions, animates our languages' (Couturat *et al*, 1910, 51). Linguists are still looking for that 'logic' (though they do not call it that), with the difference that they now realize that it is far more inaccessible to superficial observation than Couturat and his associates dreamed.

Notes

1 In practice, however, an Esperanto-speaker is most likely to use the form *šovelado*, in order to avoid any risk of misunderstanding. I am indebted for this information to Dr J. C. Wells.

2 The electrical *-ance* termination is the subject of a protest from Fowler, who condemns *impedance*: 'if these combinations are made they should be made correctly; the word should have been *impedience* (*cf: expedient*). ... By all means let the electricians have their *impedance*, but in the interests of both electricity and English let it be confined to the former' (1965, 254). In this case it seems likely that Fowler's hopes will be naturally fulfilled.

3 It should perhaps be pointed out that there is still a great deal that is unsystematic in the nomenclature of organic chemistry. R. S. Cahn in *An Introduction to Chemical Nomenclature* (1964) begins his section on Organic Chemistry as follows:

> Organic chemical literature is an infuriating subject. Since some three-quarters of a million organic compounds are known and it is a century since Couper and Kekulé explained the fundamental principles of structure, we might expect chemists to define the constitutions and interrelations in an orderly way. Instead, systems of nomenclature predating Kekulé survive; Heilbron's *Dictionary* and Beilstein's *Handbuch* show trivial names in profusion to benumb memory . . . (32)

4 Lavoisier's ideas on language are also discussed in Hogben (1969, 28*ff*).

5 Under *fungus* the OED notes that the Latin word *fungus* is 'commonly believed to

be cognate with or ad. Gr. σφόγγος, σπόγγος SPONGE'. It is not clear, however, which object was named first and which was named on the basis of its resemblance to the other.

6 Some interesting suggestions for the treatment of, among other phenomena, adjective-to-verb derivation, are to be found in Weinreich (1966, 395–477, especially 461ff). A sentence such as *he trues the rumour* is arrived at in a way which accounts for both our ability to interpret it and our sense of what is 'odd' or 'new' about it. Weinreich's account is within the framework of the theory of syntax proposed by Chomsky (1965); the technical details would obviously be inappropriate here.

References and abbreviations

Arnold, G. F. [1957] 'Stress in English Words', *Lingua* 6, 221–67 and 397–441.

Bergström, G. A. [1906] *On Blendings of Synonymous or Cognate Expressions in English*. Lund.

Berman, J. M. [1961] 'Contribution on Blending', *Zeitschrift für Anglistik und Amerikanistik* 9, 278–81.

Berrey, L. V. and Van Den Bark, M. [1943] *The American Thesaurus of Slang*. London.

Biese, Y. M. [1941] *Origin and Development of Conversions in English*, Annales Academiae Scientiarum Fennicae, B 45, 2. Helsinki.

Bladin, V. [1911] *Studies on Denominative Verbs in English*. Uppsala.

Bloomfield, L. [1933] *Language*. New York.

Bloomfield, M. [1895] 'On Assimilation and Adaptation in Congeneric Classes of Words', *American Journal of Philology* 16, 409–34.

Bolinger, D. L. [1940] 'Word Affinities', *American Speech* 15, 62–73.

Bolinger, D. L. [1948] 'On Defining the Morpheme', *Word* 4, 18–23.

Bolinger, D. L. [1961a] 'Ambiguities in Pitch Accent', *Word* 17, 309–17.

Bolinger, D. L. [1961b] 'Verbal Evocation', *Lingua* 10, 113–27.

Bolinger, D. L. [1967] 'Adjectives in English: Attribution and Predication', *Lingua* 18, 1–34.

Bolinger, D. L. [1971] *The Phrasal Verb in English*. Cambridge, Mass.

Chapin, P. G. [1970] 'On Affixation in English', in *Progress in Linguistics*, edited by M. Bierwisch and K. E. Heidolph. The Hague (*pp* 51–63).

Chomsky, N. [1957] *Syntactic Structures*. The Hague.

Chomsky, N. [1965] *Aspects of the Theory of Syntax*. Cambridge, Mass.

Coates, J. [1971] 'Denominal Adjectives: a Study in Syntactic Relationships between Modifier and Head', *Lingua* 27, 160–9.

Couturat, L. *et al* [1910] *International Language and Science*, translated by F. G. Donnan (*Weltsprache und Wissenschaft*). London.

Curme, G. O. [1931] *A Grammar of the English Language*, **3**, *Syntax*. Boston, Mass.

DAE. *A Dictionary of American English*, edited by Sir W. A. Craigie, 1938–44. Chicago and London.

de Saussure, F. [1916] *Course in General Linguistics*, edited by C. Bally and A. Sechehaye in collaboration with A. Reidlinger, translated by W. Baskin (*Cours de linguistique générale*). London, 1960.

EDD. *The English Dialect Dictionary*, edited by J. Wright, 1898–1905. London.

EETS. Early English Text Society.

Fairclough, N. L. [1965] *Studies in the Collocation of Lexical Items with Prepositions and Adverbs in a Corpus of Spoken and Written Present-Day English*. Unpublished M.A. dissertation, University of London.

Firth, J. R. [1930] *Speech*. London.

Firth, J. R. [1951] 'Modes of Meaning', *Essays and Studies* (the English Association), New Series **4**, 118–49; also in J. R. Firth, *Papers in Linguistics 1934–1951*. London, 1957 (*pp* 190–228).

Flood, W. E. [1960] *Scientific Words, their Structure and Meaning*. London.

Fowler, H. W. [1965] *Modern English Usage*, 1926, second edition revised by Sir E. Gowers. Oxford.

Fraser, B. [1970] 'Some Remarks on the Action Nominalization in English', in *Readings in English Transformational Grammar*, edited by R. A. Jacobs and P. S. Rosenbaum. Waltham, Mass. (*pp* 83–98).

Fries, C. C. [1952] *The Structure of English*. New York.

Gimson, A. C. [1970] *An Introduction to the Pronunciation of English*, second edition. London.

Givón, T. [1967a] *Some Noun-to-Noun Derivational Affixes*. System Development Corporation, SP 2893, 20 July. Santa Monica, Cal.

Givón, T. [1967b] *Transformations of Ellipsis, Sense Development and Rules of Lexical Derivation*. System Development Corporation, SP 2896, 22 July. Santa Monica, Cal.

Gove, P. B. [1964] ' "Noun often Attributive" and "Adjective" ', *American Speech* **39**, 136–75.

Greenbaum, S. [1970] *Verb-Intensifier Collocations in English*. The Hague.

Groom, B. [1937] *The Formation and Use of Compound Epithets in English Poetry from 1579*. Society for Pure English, Tract 49.

Harder, K. B. [1966] 'More Instances of "-nik" ', *American Speech* **41**, 150–4.

Harder, K. B. [1968] 'Coinages of the Type of "Sit-In" ', *American Speech* **43**, 58–64.

Harris, Z. S. [1951] *Structural Linguistics*. Chicago.

Hatcher, A. G. [1951] *Modern English Word-Formation and Neo-Latin*. Baltimore.

Hirtle, W. H. [1970] '-Ed Adjectives like "verandahed" and "blue-eyed" ', *Journal of Linguistics* **6**, 19–36.

Hogben, L. T. [1969] *The Vocabulary of Science*. London.

Huddleston, R. D. [1971] *The Sentence in Written English*. Cambridge.

Jacob, H. [1947] *A Planned Auxiliary Language*. London.

Jespersen, O. (MEG) *A Modern English Grammar on Historical Principles*, Volumes I–VII. London and Copenhagen, 1909–1949.

Jespersen, O. [1905] *Growth and Structure of the English Language*, ninth edition. Oxford 1954.

Jespersen, O. [1918] *Chapters on English*, in *Selected Writings of Otto Jespersen*. London, 1962 (*pp* 153–345). (Reprinted from *Progress in Language*. London, 1894.)

Jespersen, O. [1922] *Language: its Nature, Development and Origin*. London.

Jespersen, O. [1924] *The Philosophy of Grammar*. London.

Jespersen, O. [1928] *An International Language*. London.

Jespersen, O. [1933a] 'A Supposed Feminine Ending', in *Selected Writings of Otto Jespersen*. London, 1962 (*pp* 371–80); also in O. Jespersen, *Linguistica*. Copenhagen, 1933 (*pp* 420–29).

Jespersen, O. [1933b] 'Nature and Art in Language', in *Selected Writings of Otto Jespersen*. London, 1962 (*pp* 135–45); also in O. Jespersen, *Linguistica*, Copenhagen, 1933 (*pp* 434–53).

Jespersen, O. [1935] 'A Few Back-Formations', in *Selected Writings of Otto Jespersen*. London, 1962 (*pp* 473–8); also in *Englische Studien* **70**, 1935, 117–22.

Johnson, E. L. [1931] *Latin Words of Common English*. Boston, Mass.

Kingdon, R. [1958] *The Groundwork of English Stress*. London.

Kruisinga, E. [1932] *A Handbook of Present-Day English*, Part II, *English Accidence and Syntax* **3**, fifth edition. Groningen.

Kuryłowicz, J. [1936] 'Dérivation lexicale et dérivation syntaxique', *Bulletin de la Société de Linguistique de Paris* **37**, 79–92.

Lakoff, G. [1970] *Irregularity in Syntax*. New York.

Leech, G. N. [1966] *English in Advertising*. London.

Leech, G. N. [1969] *A Linguistic Guide to English Poetry*. London.

Lees, R. B. [1960] *The Grammar of English Nominalizations*. The Hague.

Lees, R. B. [1970] 'Problems in the Grammatical Analysis of English Nominal Compounds', in *Progress in Linguistics*, edited by M. Bierwisch and K. E. Heidolph. The Hague (*pp* 174–86).

Lindelöf, U. [1937] *English Verb–Adverb Groups Converted into Nouns.* Societas Scientiarum Fennica, Commentationes Humanarum Litterarum **9**, No 5. Helsinki.

Litz, A. W. [1964] *The Art of James Joyce.* New York.

Lubbers, K. [1965] 'The Development of "-ster" in Modern British and American English', *English Studies* **46**, 449–70.

Lyons, J. [1969] *Introduction to Theoretical Linguistics.* Cambridge.

McCawley, J. D. [1968] 'The Role of Semantics in a Grammar', in *Universals in Linguistic Theory*, edited by E. Bach and R. T. Harms. New York (*pp* 125–69).

McIntosh, A. [1961] 'Patterns and Ranges', *Language* **37**, 325–37.

Malkiel, Y. [1959] 'Studies in Irreversible Binomials' *Lingua* **8**, 113–60.

Malkiel, Y. [1966] 'Genetic Analysis of Word Formation', in *Current Trends in Linguistics* III, *Theoretical Foundations*, edited by T. A. Sebeok. The Hague (*pp* 305–64).

Marchand, H. [1963] 'On a Question of Contrary Analysis with Derivationally Connected but Morphologically Uncharacterized Words', *English Studies* **44**, 176–87.

Marchand, H. [1964] 'A Set of Criteria for the Establishing of Derivational Relationship between Words Unmarked by Derivational Morphemes', *Indogermanische Forschungen* **69**, 10–19.

Marchand, H. [1969] *The Categories and Types of Present-Day English Word-Formation*, second edition. Munich.

Mencken, A. L. [1936] *The American Language*, fourth edition. New York.

Mitchell, T. F. [1966] 'Some English Phrasal Types', in *In Memory of J. R. Firth*, edited by C. E. Bazell, J. C. Catford, M. A. K. Halliday and R. H. Robins. London (*pp* 335–58).

OED. *The Oxford English Dictionary*, Oxford 1933.

OEDS. Supplement to *The Oxford English Dictionary.*

Olsson, Y. [1964] 'Implications and Complications of the Stressed Suffix -el', in *English Studies presented to R. W. Zandvoort on the occasion of his Seventieth Birthday*: Supplement to *English Studies* **45**, 1964 (*pp* 40–3).

Osselton, N. E. and Osselton-Bleeker, C. J. [1962] 'The Plural Attributive in Contemporary English', *English Studies* **43**, 476–84.

Partridge, E. [1958] *Origins.* London.

Paul, H. [1886] *Principles of the History of Language*, translated from the second edition by H. A. Strong (*Prinzipien der Sprachgeschichte*). London, 1891.

Pennanen, E. V. [1966] *Contributions to the Study of Back-Formation in English*. Acta Academiae Socialis A, **4**. Tampere.

Pennanen, E. V. [1972] 'Current Views of Word-Formation', *in Studies Presented to Tauno F. Mustanoja on the Occasion of his Sixtieth Birthday*. *Neuphilologische Mitteilungen* **73**, 292–308.

Potter, S. [1969] *Changing English*. London.

Pound, L. [1914] *Blends. Their Relation to English Word Formation*. Anglistische Forschungen **42**. Heidelberg.

Pound, L. [1951] 'Trade-Name Irradiations', *American Speech* **26**, 166–9.

Poutsma, H. [1914] *A Grammar of Late Modern English*, Part II, *The Parts of Speech* I A. Groningen.

Praninskas, J. [1968] *Trade Name Creation: Processes and Patterns*. The Hague.

Quirk, R. [1968] *The Use of English*, second edition. London.

Quirk, R. and Mulholland, J. [1964] 'Complex Prepositions and Related Sequences', in *English Studies presented to R. W. Zandvoort on the occasion of his Seventieth Birthday:* Supplement to *English Studies* **45**, 1964 (*pp* 64–73).

Rensky, M. [1964] 'English Verbo-Nominal Phrases', *Travaux Linguistiques de Prague* **1**, 289–99.

Reuter, O. [1934] *On the Development of English Verbs from Latin and French Past Participles*. Societas Scientiarum Fennica, Commentationes Humanarum Litterarum **6**, No 6. Helsinki.

Robins, R. H. [1959] 'In Defence of WP', *Transactions of the Philological Society*, 116–44.

Robins, R. H. [1964] *General Linguistics: An Introductory Survey*. London.

Robins, R. H. [1967] *A Short History of Linguistics*. London.

Sapir, E. [1921] *Language*. New York. Harvest Books edition.

Sapir, E. [1949] *Selected Writings of Edward Sapir in Language, Culture and Personality*, edited by D. G. Mandelbaum. Berkeley and Los Angeles, Cal.

Sledd, J. [1959] *A Short Introduction to English Grammar*. Chicago.

SOED. *The Shorter Oxford English Dictionary*, third edition 1944, reprinted 1959. Oxford.

Svartvik, J. [1966] *On Voice in the English Verb*. The Hague.

Sweet, H. [1875–6] 'Words, Logic and Grammar', *Transactions of the Philological Society*, 470–503.

Sweet, H. [1891] *A New English Grammar*, Part I. Oxford.

Ullmann, S. [1962] *Semantics*. Oxford.

Vechtman-Veth, A. C. E. [1962] *A Syntax of Living English*. Groningen.

Webster [1934] *Webster's New International Dictionary of the English Language*, second edition. Editor in Chief, W. A. Neilson. London and Cambridge, Mass.

Webster [1961] *Webster's Third New International Dictionary*. Editor in Chief, P. B. Gove. London and Springfield, Mass.

Weinreich, U. [1966] 'Explorations in Semantic Theory', in *Current Trends in Linguistics* III, *Theoretical Foundations*, edited by T. A. Sebeok. The Hague (*pp* 395–477).

Wells, J. C. [1969] *The E.U.P. Concise Esperanto and English Dictionary*. London.

Wells, R. S. [1956] 'Acronymy', in *For Roman Jakobson*, compiled by M. Halle, H. G. Lunt, H. McLean and C. H. van Schooneveld. The Hague (*pp* 662–7).

Wentworth, H. [1941] 'The Allegedly Dead Suffix -dom in Modern English', *Publications of the Modern Language Association* **56**, 280–306.

Wentworth, H. and Flexner, S. B. [1960] *Dictionary of American Slang*. London.

Wheeler, B. I. [1887] *Analogy and the Scope of its Application in Language*. Cornell University Studies in Classical Philology **2**. Ithaca, N.Y.

Wimsatt, W. K. [1954] 'One Relation of Rhyme to Reason', in *The Verbal Icon*. Lexington, Kentucky. Noonday Paperback edition 1964 (*pp* 153–66).

Zandvoort, R. W. [1957] *Wartime English. Materials for a Linguistic History of World War II*. Groningen Studies in English **6**. Groningen.

Zandvoort, R. W. [1969] *A Handbook of English Grammar*, fifth edition. London.

Zimmer, K. E. [1964] 'Affixal Negation in English and Other Languages', *Word* **20**, No 2, Supplement. Monograph No 5.

Index

DATE DUE

DEC 2 0 1980		
AUG 8 1986		

DEMCO 38-297